American Legal Institutions
Recent Scholarship

Edited by Eric Rise

A Series from LFB Scholarly

Right-to-Die Policies in the American States
Judicial and Legislative Innovation

J. Donald Smith

LFB Scholarly Publishing LLC
New York 2002

Copyright © 2002 by LFB Scholarly Publishing LLC

All rights reserved.

Library of Congress Cataloging-in-Publication Data

Smith, J. Donald, 1969-
  Right-to-die policies in the American states : judicial and legislative innovation / J. Donald Smith.
     p. cm. -- (American legal institutions)
  Includes bibliographical references and index.
  ISBN 1-931202-40-0 (alk. paper)
  1. Right to die--United States--States. 2. Right to die--Government policy--United States--States. I. Title. II. Series.
  KF3827.E87 S635 2002
  344.73'04197--dc21
                                                    2002010425

ISBN 1-931202-40-0

Printed on acid-free 250-year-life paper.

Manufactured in the United States of America.

To
David and Sharon Smith,
exemplars of hard work, responsibility, and the celebration of life

Table of Contents

Preface   ix

Chapter 1   Medical Decision-Making and the Terminally Ill   1
     Introduction   1
     Three Case Vignettes   2
     End-of-Life Medical Decision-Making Policies   13
     Research Question   18
     Plan of the Book   21

Chapter 2   A Theory of Policy Adoption and Reinvention   23
     Research on Innovation   23
     A Typology of Legislative Policy Innovations   30
     Permissive Policies and Legislative Innovation   33
     Permissive Policies: Judicial Innovation   44
     Judicial and Legislative Innovation   52

Chapter 3   Research Design and Methods   57
     Introduction   57
     Legislative Innovation and Reinvention   57
     Judicial Innovation and Renovation   64
     Integrated Models   69

Chapter 4   Legislative Innovation and Reinvention   75
     The Advent of Legislative Policy-Making   75
     Living Will Laws   78
     Health Care Proxy Statutes   100
     Surrogate Decision-Making Laws   114
     Conclusion   128

Chapter 5 Judicial Innovation and Reinvention 133
   The Rise of Litigation and Judicial Policy-Making 133
   The Adoption and Diffusion of Surrogate Decision-Making Policies 137
   Judicial Reinvention 150
   Reinvention and Renovation: Six States, Six Policies 164

Chapter 6 Judicial and Legislative Interaction 183
   The Complex Web of Relationships 183
   Legislative and Judicial Innovation Contrasted 188
   Adoption and Reinvention: Integrated Models 195
   Innovation and Renovation in Six States 208
   General Observations and Conclusions 236

Chapter 7 Conclusion 239
   Taking Stock 239
   Legislative Innovation and Reinvention 240
   Judicial Innovation and Reinvention 244
   Judicial-Legislative Interaction in the Policy Process 246

Appendix A   Listing of Right-to-Die Statutes 249
Appendix B   Measurement Operations and Data Sources 257
Appendix C   Facility Score Construction 263
Appendix D   Listing of Right-to-Die Cases 279

Notes 283
References 291
Index 303

Preface

This book attempts to tell the story of the adoption and creation of right-to-die policies in the American states. The focus of this work is not physician assisted suicide or any other type of widely publicized active euthanasia, but on passive euthanasia and policies regulating the refusal of unwanted, life-prolonging medical treatment for persons with terminal illnesses.

Like many analyses in the social sciences, my study utilizes a policy innovation framework, but there are several features which distinguish my approach from much of the scholarship found in the extant literature. First, I argue that the diffusion of policy innovations is a dynamic process through which states (and other adopting entities) continuously revise and update their policy creations. Accordingly, instead of simply focusing on the date of adoption of a single policy, the most common type of effort in innovation research, I explicitly model the interaction of time-serial and cross-sectional changes in policy content throughout the study period. In addition, I develop a theory of policy adoption which attempts to show how the enactment of one policy type (a "core" innovation) may set in motion a series of delayed and extended diffusion cycles during which states adopt new policy instruments ("tangential" innovations) to address the same social problem or policy objectives. Finally, most political science research has focused on the adoption of legislative policies in the American states. While state assembles are important sources of policy production, it is important to realize that "innovative" elected lawmakers are often "forced in to action" by the decisions of actors in other branches of government, particularly state judiciaries. In addition to estimating models of legislative policy adoption and renovation, this study also presents and tests a theory of judicial policy innovation. The empirical analysis concludes with an examination of the interaction between these two branches of government.

I first became interested in this substantive policy area while a political science graduate student at The Florida State University. I had the good fortune of being assigned as a research assistant to Professors Henry Glick and Marie Cowart in the Claude Pepper Institute on Aging and Public Policy. Under their tutelage, I learned a great deal about health care policy and was made a junior author in a series of conference papers and journal articles. Henry Glick continued to mentor me throughout the course of my studies, and he suggested that I write my dissertation on a topic on which he had made a seminal contribution. The present book is an extension of my doctoral dissertation, and I am grateful to my committee members. William Berry, Paul Brace, Melissa Hardy, Evan Ringquist, and (especially) Henry Glick made helpful comments and offered advice on how to improve the analyses. I am also indebted to Professor Eric Rise of the University of Delaware for his careful review of the manuscript and to Leo Balk for his advice and guidance.

One of the major challenges of this work was the content analysis of hundreds of statutes and court cases. The policy facility scores used in the legislative and judicial innovation models took over a year to calculate, and my confidence in these measures is increased by the efforts of those friends and colleagues who assisted with establishing intercoder reliability. Dr. Steven Lewis and Professor Randy Stevenson, both of Rice University, endured many hours of statute coding, and Jennifer Potter and Mickey Hampton, my research assistants at Cornell College, did a conscientious job of replicating my work and catching several errors.

I wish to extend my thanks to all of those persons who read and commented on various drafts of this manuscript; I am particularly grateful to my political science colleagues at the University of North Texas who offered advice and encouragement. While many offered assistance in this endeavor, I alone am responsible for any errors or shortcomings.

This book is dedicated to my parents, Sharon and David Smith – both retired after years of hard work and now enjoying the wide range of pleasures life has to offer.

CHAPTER 1
Medical Decision-Making and the Terminally Ill

INTRODUCTION

The United States has a rich tradition, rooted in constitutional and common law doctrines extending back to the infancy of the republic, of individual liberty and self-determination. Freedom of religion, speech, assembly and association are widely regarded as hallmarks of, and prerequisites to, democratic governance. The past century has been host to a number of important milestones and gains in civil rights and liberties. The successful campaign for women's suffrage and the civil rights movement that destroyed Jim-Crowism have been followed by continuing advances towards gender and racial equality. Individuals now possess greater freedoms in the workplace, at school, and in their neighborhoods and other public places than at any other time in our nation's history.

In recent years, the quest for individual liberties and personal freedom has extended into the health care arena. Expanded health care access, accessibility to health insurance, and, most recently, the movement for a "Patients' Bill of Rights" are all examples of attempts to counter medical paternalism and to increase individual autonomy and choices in the clinical setting. Perhaps the most controversial aspect of the patients' rights movement concerns the push for self-determination at the end of life. Advances in medical technology, while largely welcomed and beneficial to society as a whole, have also enabled physicians to increasingly protract and prolong the dying process. It has become clear that many individuals do not wish to avail themselves to the "medical miracles" that are capable of postponing a natural death. Consider the cases in the following section.

THREE CASE VIGNETTES

Two Tragic Accidents in Maine[1]

<u>The Gardner Case.</u>
On May 11, 1985, just a few weeks before his twenty-third birthday, Joseph V. Gardner, an active and independent native of central Maine, fell from the back of a moving pick-up truck and sustained numerous injuries. Despite heroic efforts by emergency response technicians and surgical personnel, Joseph's prognosis for return to a conscious and productive life was bleak at best. Neurologists concluded that he was in a persistent vegetative state, a medical condition in which the brain stem functions to maintain circulation, respiration, blood pressure and other vital processes, but the rest of the brain is damaged, usually beyond repair, and the patient is unable to regain consciousness or otherwise respond to stimuli. Although successfully weaned from a respirator and able to breathe on his own, Joseph was kept alive through the use of a surgically implanted feeding tube. All of the many medical experts who examined him reached the same conclusion: there was no reasonable possibility that he would ever regain consciousness or be able to interact, even nominally, with his environment. As long as he continued to receive artificial nutrition and hydration, Joseph's doctors predicted that he could stay alive for an indefinite number of years, possibly even decades.

Joseph's mother, who was appointed his guardian by a probate court, consulted with family members, the family minister, and her son's friends; she concluded that Joseph would not wish to be kept alive if there was no possibility that he could return to a cognitive state. Several individuals recalled instances when Joseph, reacting to visits with patients in the nursing home where his girlfriend had once worked or to events in the news, articulated his desire not to be kept alive in a vegetative state nor to receive artificial nutrition and hydration should there be no chance of a recovery to a meaningful state of life. Mrs. Gardner requested that her son's feeding tube be disconnected so that he be permitted a natural death.

This decision was supported by both Joseph's court-appointed guardian *ad litem* and by a case worker from the Maine Department of Human Services. While his physicians also appeared supportive of this decision to discontinue artificial feedings, the hospital, perhaps out of fear of liability, sought court approval of the nontreatment decision.

A lower court judge ruled in favor of Mrs. Gardner's request, but the decision was appealed by the District Attorney, who argued that withdrawal of life-supports was tantamount to homicide. The case was appealed to the Supreme Judicial Court of Maine, and Joseph Gardner was sustained in his persistent vegetative state, pending the outcome of the deliberations. On December 3, 1987, over two years after the accident, the high court ruled in favor of the request to discontinue treatment. The justices found that, by virtue of the common law doctrine of informed consent, whereby a competent patient is free to approve or to refuse any type of medical treatment, the feedings could be discontinued because clear evidence existed that the patient would not wish to be kept alive in his debilitated and hopeless condition. Shortly after this opinion was handed down, hospital officials disconnected the nasogastric tube, and Joseph Gardner died eight days later (Choice in Dying 1997).

For the Gardner family, the Supreme Court decision undoubtedly brought some sense of closure to a sad chapter in their lives by granting Joseph's wish for a natural death. For the citizens of Maine, the broader policy implications of the high court's ruling were a bit more unclear. The opinion was extremely limited, as the majority justices confined the scope of their holding to the very narrow facts of the case: artificial nutrition could be discontinued when an adult was in a persistent vegetative state, provided that clear and convincing evidence of her or his preference to decline this type of treatment existed. The legality of discontinuing other types of life supports, particularly for incompetent patients who had not left incontrovertible evidence of their end-of-life care preferences, was left essentially "up in the air." Moreover, the seven member court was divided, with three justices producing dissenting opinions. A future change in the court's composition, many observers (and providers) undoubtedly speculated, could result in a very different public policy outcome.

The Swan Case.
Only a few years after the *Gardner* case had captured state-wide attention in Maine, history essentially repeated itself. At age seventeen, Chad Eric Swan, a popular senior at a public high school in the central part of the state, was seriously injured in an automobile accident on January 20, 1989. Chad was taken to the same hospital that had treated Joseph Gardner only a few years earlier, and, just like Joseph, Chad was diagnosed as being in a persistent vegetative state with no possibility of recovery. A feeding tube was surgically implanted into Chad's abdomen, and he was sustained through the administration of artificial hydration and nutrients. When the insertion point of the tube became infected, doctors warned that surgery to correct the problem posed tremendous medical risks, and Chad's parents requested that he be permitted to die.

The hospital and physicians agreed to the family's nontreatment decision, and a court order was sought to obtain permission to remove the feeding tube. The lower court approved the request, but once again the District Attorney's office appealed the decision to the Supreme Judicial Court of Maine. In a unanimous decision, the justices reiterated their previous holding in *Gardner*. They held that, because Chad had previously indicated to his mother and brother, in a discussion ironically precipitated by television coverage of Joseph Gardner's predicament, that he would not wish to be kept alive by artificial means should he ever be rendered vegetative or permanently unconscious, clear and convincing evidence of the patient's wishes existed to support the decision to discontinue feedings. The court was not swayed by the argument that Chad's pre-accident statement was unacceptable because he was under eighteen years of age when he made his declaration; the court held that its evidentiary standard applied to adults and mature minors alike. The unified court's reaffirmation of the *Gardner* policy seemed to put to rest fears that a reversal of the judicial policy was likely in the foreseeable future. Chad Eric Swan died a natural death shortly after the tube was disconnected.

Implications.
The above cases are significant because they illustrate two concepts central to public policy making at the state-level: judicial innovation and

judicial renovation. In 1987 Maine had no formal policy governing refusal of treatment on behalf of incompetent patients; the *Gardner* ruling articulated a series of guidelines to be followed by practitioners in future situations. This decision was a judicial innovation – a policy new to the state of Maine approved by an appellate court. The high court's decision in *Swan*, in which the policy was extended to cover mature minors, is an example of judicial reinvention – an extant judicial innovation was modified and revised to cover new situations and contingencies.

It is important to stress the limited scope of the *Gardner* and *Swan* decisions. Because the court did not address the legality of withdrawing or withholding treatment from incompetent patients who had not documented or otherwise left clear instructions regarding medical care preferences in the event of a future condition such as permanent unconsciousness, a large group of persons was essentially left uncovered by these decisions. Courts often exercise considerable judicial restraint, and the Maine justices confined their holdings to the narrow and specific facts of the two cases. A more comprehensive policy (i.e., one covering all incompetent persons, regardless of whether or not they had articulated specific instructions in the event of medical tragedy) would eventually require legislative action.

In 1991, less than one year after the *Swan* ruling, Maine legislators enacted a statute, the Maine Uniform Health Care Decisions Act, that allowed an incompetent patient's next of kin to direct the discontinuation of life-prolonging treatment when that family member believed that such a course of action would be in the patient's best interest. In so doing, the Maine General Assembly engaged in both policy reinvention and innovation. The former term denotes a process whereby decision makers in a state expand or alter an existing policy to better accommodate diverse societal needs, as the Maine legislature effectively adapted their state's judicial policy to cover more citizens and potential future situations. The 1991 statute is also a legislative innovation – a statutory policy that had not previously been adopted in the state. The timing of this 1991 legislative policy was not coincidental; lawmakers were clearly responding to the limited judicial policy which had received so much media attention in the months leading up to the start of the legislative session. This type of legislative-judicial interaction was not unique to Maine nor is it limited to policy making on the right to die. Risk averse lawmakers are often catalyzed into action by prior judicial innovations; similarly, courts, reactive political actors by their very nature, frequently adopt judicial policies only after a legislative policy is challenged in court. The interplay between these two branches of government must be taken into account if we are to work toward a complete understanding of how policies are made and revised at the state-level.

Confusion and Concern in a California Hospital[2]

A sixty-five year old resident of Orange County, California, "Mrs T." was a vivacious widow who enjoyed playing cards, golfing, and being involved in a number of community groups and social activities. In a routine physical examination, her doctor discovered a carotid bruit, a common vascular defect that, if left untreated, could induce a disabling stroke. Corrective surgery was recommended, and Mrs. T. was admitted as an inpatient to an area hospital in the Spring of 1982. At the time of admission, Mrs. T provided the admitting nurse with a copy of an advance directive she had completed several years earlier.

The document she produced was a living will, a formal declaration of health care treatment preferences designed to instruct caregivers in the event of future incompetence arising from terminal or irreversible illness. The living will was drafted in accordance with the provisions of the California Natural Death Act, a law approved by the state General Assembly in 1976. This statute, the first of its kind in the nation, allowed citizens to request in writing that certain types of life-sustaining procedures be withheld or discontinued in the event of a hopeless diagnosis. Mrs. T.'s living will contained the following language:

> If a situation should arise in which there is no reasonable expectation of my recovery from physical or mental disability, I request that I be allowed to die and not be kept alive by artificial means or heroic measures. (2055)

In accordance with her instructions, the living will was entered in Mrs. T.'s medical record.

By all accounts, the surgery was routine and uneventful; surgeons successfully lanced the bruit, and a full recovery was expected. However, while in recovery, Mrs. T. suffered a stroke, and emergency surgery was necessary to remove an extensive clot formation from her carotid artery. Following the surgery, Mrs. T. was unable to regain consciousness, and her physicians feared she had a profound neurological deficit, with the preliminary diagnosis indicating that it was unlikely that she would ever return to a cognitive state. A ventilator was used to assist her breathing, and she was fed intravenously. After two days, Mrs. T. developed pneumonia, and her physicians recommended that a tracheostomy (surgical implantation of a ventilator tube) be performed and that a feeding tube be surgically implanted.

At this point, several staff members questioned the viability of performing these surgeries. Pointing to the language in her living will, one specialist expressed grave doubts about further administration of life-prolonging procedures:

> Why are we doing this to this lady? Wasn't her living will specific in spelling out what she didn't want to happen? As a previously vigorous woman, this is exactly what she did not want. (2056)

The attending neurologists countered by cautioning that it could take several months before they would be able to assess exactly how much brain damage had been caused, and that acute care would have to be continued until such time as the diagnosis indicated with certainty that she was irreversibly vegetative. The surgeries were performed, and Mrs. T.'s condition was stabilized. When he was informed of the events that had transpired, the patient's brother, referring to previous statements his sister had made about wishing to avoid living in a medically futile condition, asked doctors to discontinue artificial ventilation and remove the feeding tube. When hospital administrators refused to honor the brother's request, he indicated that he might begin litigation if Mrs. T.'s life was unduly prolonged.

A meeting of the hospital's newly-formed medical ethics committee was convened; a group comprised of neurologists, palliative care specialists, psychiatrists and social workers reviewed the patient's medical records and ultimately made a recommendation. After much deliberation, the committee adopted the position that life-supports should be continued, as there might be a possibility that the patient's consciousness could eventually be restored. The team also noted that the California Natural Death Act contained a very restrictive provision requiring that life-sustaining treatment be provided to a patient, regardless of the instructions contained in a living will, unless death was "imminent with or without" the provision of such treatment. Mrs. T., they opined, was ineligible for removal from life-supports, because she could continue to live if her treatment was continued. Reluctantly, Mrs. T.'s brother assented to the committee's decision, and no lawsuit was filed. Ventilation and artificial feedings were continued.

Less than one month after her stroke, Mrs. T.'s condition improved dramatically, and she regained consciousness and gradually regained speech and motor skills. Her attending physicians were pleasantly surprised by her rapid recovery. She was eventually discharged to a nursing home, and when she was later asked if she felt that her physicians had made the right decision by refusing to discontinue treatment, she responded in the affirmative saying that her diagnosis did not warrant the invocation of her living will and that she only wanted to be allowed to die should she ever be rendered a "permanent vegetable" (2056).

Implications.
Mrs. T.'s case had a happy ending, but her swift recovery was a rarity, and there are all too many instances in which patients who have executed a living will or similar document see their wishes ignored or disregarded by litigation-averse health care providers. The California Natural Death Act, the legislative innovation that made it possible for Mrs. T. to execute her document, was very restrictive and narrowly defined the conditions under which treatment could be withheld to essentially exclude almost all patients in the state who were at risk of being suspended in vegetative limbo.

This example is also illustrative of the fact that, even when patients have taken the time to record their wishes in the form of an advance directive for health care, these documents often contain simple and vague language, making it difficult for medical personnel in the clinical setting to implement a patient's requests. Recall that Mrs. T.'s living will instructed physicians to discontinue "artificial means and heroic measures" in the event there was "no reasonable expectation of recovery." These terms were never explicitly explained in the living will. Who would define, for example, what "recovery" meant? Did it mean that she expected to be returned to an ambulatory condition enabling her to resume her weekly golf games, or did it mean having cognition restored even if she would be confined to a wheelchair or nursing home bed? Similar definitional problems plague the terms "reasonable expectation" and "artificial means and heroic measures." Documents that lack specificity and precise definitions induce confusion and disagreement on the part of caregivers, meaning these directives can be "more help than hindrance" (2054).

As a postscript to this case, it should be noted that the California General Assembly modified the living will statute twice in the 1990s – a process called reinvention through renovation – in order to ease many of the implementation restrictions and to allow patients to specify the exact types of treatments they wished to decline and to record the specific types of conditions under which these withdrawals were to be made. In addition, in 1984, state legislators also adopted another type of innovation, the durable power of attorney for health care, a document allowing an individual to designate a person to make difficult treatment decisions on their behalf should the draftee be rendered incompetent.

While the General Assembly engaged in a good deal of policy reinvention in order to make its right-to-die laws more accessible to citizens and practitioners, the state's statutory law did not address the legality of withdrawing treatment from an incompetent patient who had not executed a written directive. A comprehensive refusal of treatment policy would eventually have to be approved by state appellate courts. From 1983 to 1993, California courts addressed the legality of decision making by family members on behalf of incompetent loved ones. By 1993, California had one of the most permissive judicial surrogate policies in the nation, covering individuals who had not availed themselves to the provisions of the state's advance directive laws.

Policy making in California and in Maine is demonstrative of the fact that legislative and judicial innovation are inextricably linked. In the latter state, judicial innovation preceded legislative innovation on surrogate decision-making, with the Maine General Assembly eventually expanding and revising the judicial policy. In California, the reverse pattern held true: the state legislature took a series of "baby steps," which were followed by "judicial leaps and bounds."

"Shopping" for the Right-to-Die: Disparate State Laws in Maryland and Florida[3]

Ronald W. Mack had just graduated from a Maryland public high school when he married his high school sweetheart, Deanna, in 1980. The couple had a happy marriage, and Deanna Mack gave birth to two children during the first two years of their union. Ronald enlisted in the U.S. Army in November of 1982. After successfully completing basic training, he was assigned to a base in California, and the young family left their Maryland home to begin a new life on the West Coast.

In June of 1983, Ronald was involved in an automobile accident, and he sustained numerous and massive cerebral injuries. Despite excellent medical care and the application of numerous therapies by accomplished neurologists, Ronald Mack never regained consciousness after the accident. All of the physicians who examined him agreed that Ronald Mack was in a persistent vegetative state with little-to-no expectation of recovery. He was successfully weaned from a respirator and able to breathe on his own, but Ronald had to be fed through a surgically implanted gastrostomy tube; he was also catheterized, and a tracheostomy tube was inserted into his lungs to suction excess secretions.

In September of 1983, Deanna Mack moved her children back to Maryland, and her husband was transferred to a Baltimore County veterans' hospital. In may of 1984, Deanna was appointed guardian of Ronald's person. Mrs. Mack asked hospital physicians if it would be possible to remove the feeding tube, in order to allow nature to take its course and to allow Ronald a peaceful and dignified death. Hospital administrators were adamant in their refusal to comply with this request, stating that such a course of action was not sanctioned by Maryland law. Deanna did not "push" the issue, and, in September of 1984, she remarried and moved to Florida. At the request of the U.S. Veteran's Administration,

Deanna petitioned a Florida probate court for guardianship of Ronald, and this request was granted. Ronald remained in the hospital in Maryland for the next six years, and Deanna visited him every three to four months. She continued to ask hospital staff to remove the feeding tube, but to no avail. In May of 1991, Deanna learned through conversation with a registered nurse that, under Florida law, she could request to have Ronald's feeding tube removed if he were transferred to a Florida hospital. Deanna retained a lawyer, who advised her to arrange the transfer. It was at this point that Ronald E. Mack and Karen Mack Carson, the patient's father and sister, respectively, objected to Deanna's decision to make the transfer to Florida in order to allow a natural death. A hearing was held in a Baltimore county court, and the judge ruled that the Florida court erred in granting Deanna guardianship and that treatment could not be withheld from Ronald unless there was clear and convincing evidence of Ronald's intent to refuse such treatment. The court also transferred guardianship to Ronald's father.

Deanna appealed the decision to the Court of Appeals of Maryland (court of last resort). After reviewing the record of the case, the high court, in a lengthy opinion, affirmed most of the holdings of the lower court. The justices concluded that Florida did not have jurisdiction over Ronald's person and that full faith and credit could not be extended in this case. In addition, the court majority agreed that, absent a living will or durable power of attorney, life-supports could only be withheld from a patient when clear and convincing evidence of her or his wishes existed. Because Ronald had never discussed his preferences regarding treatment should he be rendered vegetative, health care providers had to be guided by the presumption in favor of continued life. Although they made clear that treatment could not be discontinued for Ronald nor could he be moved to a hospital in Florida, the justices did order that guardianship be transferred back to Deanna. As of December 1998, Ronald W. Mack still remained in a persistent vegetative state in the Baltimore hospital (Choice in Dying 1998).

Implications.

This case illustrates a number of important points. First, the decision by the Maryland Court of Appeals, while it denied the request for relief at bar, still constitutes a judicial policy innovation. The high court articulated a series of procedures to be followed in future instances involving requests for withdrawal of treatment made by family members on behalf on incompetent patients. In addition, the court identified an evidentiary standard, subject to verification by a probate court, that had to be satisfied in order for cessation of life-supports to be granted. A policy mechanism was now in place in Maryland to guide families and practitioners in the clinical setting.

The *Mack* case is also important because it was clearly the catalyst for legislative innovation. (Indeed, the justices made clear the fact their policy was only to serve as controlling authority until such time as the legislature addressed the issue.) Just thirteen weeks after the court rendered its decision, the General Assembly of Maryland adopted a surrogate decision making policy. Lawmakers abandoned the high court's reliance on a clear and convincing evidentiary standard, instead opting for a "best interests of the patient" standard; in addition, legislators directed that when all of a patient's family members are in agreement as to the propriety of a nontreatment decision, no prior court approval is required. The Court of Appeals produced a limited innovation, and the General Assembly, which had previously avoided the surrogate decision making issue, responded by liberalizing the previous policy (i.e., the statute made it easier for treatment to be discontinued). Judicial innovation led legislative innovation in Maryland.

Finally, this case underscores the fact that right to die policies vary across states. The state of Florida had a comprehensive surrogate decision making policy (created through a mixture of judicial and legislative innovation), while policy makers in Maryland had been disinclined to take up the issue throughout most of the 1980s, a period during which many states enacted policies. As right to die laws diffused throughout the nation, states were influenced by one another. The 1993 Maryland law, for example, was clearly modeled after statutes in Florida and West Virginia; however, Maryland lawmakers reinvented those states' policies to include

Medical Decision-Making and the Terminally Ill 13

additional provisions designed to expedite decision-making at the end of life.

Even though Deanna attempted to move Ronald to Florida in order to discontinue his artificial feedings, it is unlikely that states with permissive right-to-die policies are in danger of becoming "euthanasia magnets." However, given the high rate of residential mobility in the United States, it should be noted that many terminally ill patients are routinely moved from nursing homes and rehabilitation centers in one state to another, often to be closer to family members who have relocated. Documents such as living wills, which have been executed in one state, may not necessarily be entitled to recognition in another. Portability of advance directives can be a major problem, and (as discussed in Chapter 5) there has been no shortage of these types of lawsuits. Controversial cases invite publicity and increase public awareness of policy status at the intrastate level, often forcing legislators (and sometimes judges) to reconsider the viability of existing policies in their jurisdictions.

As policies diffuse through the federal system, cross-pollination of ideas is inevitable. Policy formation does not take place in fifty, contained intrastate vacuums; rather, states learn from, and are influenced by, early innovators and neighboring states.

This manuscript examines the ways in which different types of right to die policies make their way through courts and legislatures in the American states. A complete theory of this process is specified in the next chapter, but first it is necessary to identify the different types of refusal of treatment policies to which states have availed themselves.

END-OF-LIFE MEDICAL DECISION-MAKING POLICIES[4]

A Brief History of the Right-to-Die Movement in the Unites States

The past several decades have witnessed major advances in medical knowledge and health care technology, including new techniques for extending life and prolonging the dying process. It is now standard practice for terminally ill patients to receive treatments such as artificial respiration, intubated feeding, renal dialysis, and cardiopulmonary resuscitation. However, these treatments are often unwanted, as many patients (and their families) argue that such practices are invasive and only serve to protract suffering at the end of life.

Although of concern to experts and elites for years, the right to die issue did not reach the mass agenda until the 1970s when Karen Ann Quinlan's situation captured the attention of the nation (*In Re Quinlan*, 355 A.2d 647, 1976). *Quinlan* called attention to the problem of vegetative and comatose patients receiving intrusive and expensive treatment to which, given the choice, these individuals might not have consented. In 1976 California became the first state to give patients the right to specify, in a living will, the kind of treatment they wanted or would refuse in the case of a terminal illness. California's lead stimulated a surge of innovation in several other western states in 1977, and nearly every state legislature soon had one or more right-to-die proposals before it (Glick 1992; Urofsky 2000).

The innovation diffused throughout the states, and the issue first reached the United States Supreme Court in the landmark 1990 case of Nancy Cruzan (*Cruzan* v. *Director, Missouri Department of Health*, 497 U.S. 160). In *Cruzan*, the Court ruled that in order to refuse potentially lifesaving treatment, a patient must make her or his wishes clearly known, and it endorsed written documents such as living wills. However, the Court did not produce a uniform national policy; rather, the justices left the right-to-die issue in the hands of state legislators, noting that formulation of laws regulating treatment at the end of life is a responsibility reserved to the individual states. Refusal of treatment has proven a controversial topic, and a number of different approaches have been developed to address it.

Legislative Policies

States legislatures have adopted three main types of mechanisms by which the rights of dying patients are protected. As already mentioned, the living will was the first such tool. Living wills or "natural death" laws provide a means by which people may specify, in writing, their wishes about the use of life-sustaining treatment. One potential problem with living wills, as illustrated by the case of Mrs. T., is the inability of those who execute them to foresee and cover all possible treatment contingencies

(Eisendrath and Jonsen 1983; Peters 1987; Weir 1989). Another concern is that there is tremendous variation across states in the types of treatment which patients can specify (Beebe 1992; Lieberson 1992; Meisel 1992). In order to remedy some of the problems with the living will, a second type of policy emerged: the "durable power of attorney" or "health care agent/proxy" law. These laws enable individuals to appoint someone to make decisions about artificial life-prolonging treatment for them, if they should become incapacitated. While most states have adopted health care agent statutes, many observers have argued that these laws suffer from some of the same weaknesses that plague the living will laws (Sabatino 1992; Tillman 1992).

Perhaps the greatest shortcoming of both of the above policies is the fact that very few persons avail themselves opportunity to execute advance directives (Glick et al. 1995; Solomon et al. 1993). A third type of policy, "surrogate/family decisionmaking" laws, specify the persons who are empowered to make decisions on behalf of an incompetent patient who has not executed an advance directive. While some argue that these laws have the greatest potential to ensure freedom from unwanted treatment (Hamann 1993), only about half of the states have adopted surrogate policies, and many of these states have adopted extremely restrictive policies (Busby-Mott 1993; Roach 1991; Tillman 1992).

Judicial Policies

There are two primary types of right to die cases that have made their way before state appellate courts. The first, and less common type, involves a request for discontinuance of medical treatment made by a competent, mentally-sound patient. Almost without exception, courts, relying upon common law doctrines of informed consent and self-determination, have approved such requests (Meisel 1992).

Far more controversial are cases like those brought by the relatives of Chad Swan, Joseph Gardner, and Ronald Mack, in which family members request that treatment be withdrawn from a loved one who cannot speak on her or his behalf due to unconsciousness or incompetency. When courts have approved such requests (and sometimes even when they have not), they have usually done so in detailed opinions spelling out the requirements that must be satisfied before an incompetent patient's life-prolonging treatment can be discontinued. These procedural prescriptions furnish the basis of states' "judicial surrogate policies." It is these policies, as opposed to their relatively noncontroversial cousin cases involving competent patients, that are of primary interest in this book.

Areas of Contention and Policy Terms[5]

There are a number of aspects of the right to die that have proven particularly controversial in every state to consider adopting a policy. Whether approved by a legislative body or an appellate court, three types of considerations have divided lawmakers: the appropriate range of triggering conditions, the permissibility of discontinuing artificial nutrition and hydration, and the specification of surrogate evidentiary standards.

<u>Triggering Conditions</u>.
This term is used to denote the particular medical conditions under which a request for discontinuance of treatment can be considered by caregivers. Some states have strictly limited the diagnostic requirements for ending treatment, while others have allowed withdrawal under a wider range of circumstances. Almost all states now recognize medical conditions such as brain death, end-stage cancer, and vital organ failure as conditions under which treatment can be ended; these are conditions that will ultimately produce death, regardless of whether or not life-sustaining procedures are administered. Far more controversial, however, is the recognition of irreversible comas and persistent vegetative states (PVS). A patient in PVS is "wakeful without awareness;" it is not uncommon for persons in such a condition to make sporadic movements, spontaneously blink their eyes, appear to sleep and awaken, or to exhibit reflex reactions to painful stimuli. A vegetative patient's cerebral hemispheres are so damaged that she or he is incapable of cognition; however, the individual's brain stem is usually left intact, and vital biological functions such as respiration, digestion, and circulation are usually maintained without the use of artificial therapies (Lynn and Childress 1983, 17-18).

In order to continue to live, persons in PVS require the administration of artificial nutrition and hydration.

Delivery of Sustenance.
Almost all courts and legislatures have come to recognize the legality, under certain circumstances, of discontinuing "standard" therapies such as assisted ventilation, renal dialysis, and chemotherapy. However, many states "draw the line" at withholding artificially administered food and hydration. Many statutes contain explicit restrictions on discontinuing this type of treatment. In addition, other state legislatures have approved laws which are ambiguous on the sustenance question, requiring, for example, the administration of food and water when necessary for "comfort care" or "palliative therapy."

For a typical patient recovering from major surgery, nutrition is delivered by way of an intravenous line (commonly called an "IV drip"). However, after a period of a few weeks, blood vessels typically collapse and it usually becomes necessary to surgically implant a feeding tube through a patient's nostrils down into her stomach (a nasogastric implantation) or to "cut" a direct path for the tube through his abdomen (a gastrostomy) (Hastings Center 1987). When a feeding tube is disconnected, it usually takes between seven to ten days for the patient to die, and when that happens, the biological cause of death is starvation or dehydration (Cantor 1987, 112).

Supporters of ending artificial sustenance maintain that the death-producing agent is the underlying disease which prohibits a patient from being able to chew or swallow; opponents counter that withdrawing a feeding tube is an active measure, tantamount to "sentencing an individual to death by starvation." A certain symbolism attaches to the act of ending the delivery of sustenance, and this issue has been hotly contested in the halls of state legislatures and in judicial chambers.

Evidentiary Standards for Surrogate Decision-Making.
There is tremendous interstate variation when it comes to allowing family members or other surrogates to direct the withdrawal of treatment from an incompetent patient. At one end of the continuum are policies which allow discontinuation only if the surrogate can present "clear and convincing

evidence" that the patient previously articulated her or his desire to discontinue the particular type of treatment under consideration; this is by far the strictest evidentiary standard, and judicial approval is usually required to satisfy it. A more flexible policy is the "substituted judgment" standard, under which a surrogate attempts to "stand in the shoes" of the patient and reach the decision that she or he would most likely have made. The most permissive standard is the "best interests of the patient standard;" when such a criterion is operative, a decision maker need only determine that a particular course of action is best for the patient; in this case, judicial approval is rarely required.

RESEARCH QUESTIONS

Students of public policy have devoted considerable effort to the study of the diffusion of policy innovations in the American states. I hope to contribute to this body of knowledge by exploring a topic that has not been studied extensively in the literature: policy reinvention during the diffusion process. A general theory of the reinvention process will be presented, and the theory will be illustrated with an analysis of state adoptions of end-of-life medical decision-making statutes and judicial policies.

Most innovation research focuses on the correlates of the date of adoption of a single policy; implicit in these studies is the assumption that all states adopt a uniform policy. However, reinvention theory suggests that this assumption is often unjustified. Later adopters may enact innovations that differ markedly from those of early innovators. In addition, states continually amend and revise their original innovations over time. Because there are numerous ways in which states innovate and reinvent, it is necessary to consider both interstate and intrastate production of policy.

In order to distinguish between the various ways in which states adopt innovations, I have developed a typology of innovations. Allowing for both time-serial and cross-sectional innovation, this organization scheme identifies a number of ways that existing policies lead to new policies. Central to the typology is the distinction between "first" policies and "tangential" ones; the latter term denotes a new policy instrument adopted

Medical Decision-Making and the Terminally Ill

in order to achieve the same general means being sought through the existing "first" policy. This typology applies to all types of innovations. However, the scope of this book is confined to one specific class of policies: permissive policies. The right-to-die statutes being considered in this book fit neatly into the categorization scheme. Living will laws are the first policy, and durable power of attorney and surrogate decision-making laws are both treated as examples of tangential policies.

Determinants of Legislative Innovation

For each of the above legislative policies, the theory focuses on two issues. First, the theory attempts to explain why some states adopt permissive innovations when they do, and why some states are innovators while others remain nonadopters. Using event history analysis, three testable models are estimated. I hypothesize that propensity to innovate is influenced by a number of state-level institutional, political and environmental factors. In contrast to most previous research, socioeconomic variables are not believed to play an important role in the diffusion process. Instead, a number of new explanations are considered. Specifically, the content of first innovations is expected to influence the likelihood of adoption of tangential innovations.

The second question this theory addresses is likelihood of legislative renovation. Renovation occurs when a state legislature amends an existing policy in order to "update" it or to tailor it to changing needs and demands. Some state legislatures renovate their policies numerous times over the course of a decade, while assemblies in other states appear averse to ever revisiting a controversial policy area like refusal of treatment law. I hypothesize that the propensity to renovate is a function of the same variables that caused a state to adopt an innovation in the first place; however, I also test, using logistic regression analysis, the proposition that states renovate in response to horizontal influences, particularly policy liberalization in other states.

The final legislative question concerns variation in the content of innovations. Why do some states adopt very comprehensive or "permissive" policies while others enact limited and restrictive laws? For each policy, facility scores are calculated and regressed on date of original adoption, reflecting the belief that early adopters, in order to neutralize opposition to a policy, approve fairly limited and restrictive laws; later adopters, on the other hand, are able to adopt more permissive laws, owing partly to the fact that early innovators successfully "broke the ice." In order to allow for renovation over time, for each policy, states are scored on both their original and most recent innovations; by estimating each model twice, it is possible to further explore the concept of reinvention through renovation.

Determinants of Judicial Innovation

Few efforts have been made to examine the diffusion of judicial doctrines and policies. In order to help remedy this paucity of empirical studies, I offer a theory of judicial adoption and renovation that focuses on a number of environmental, structural and political variables. Policies are hypothesized to diffuse differently across state courts than they do across state legislatures. Horizontal variables are not expected to be nearly as important in the former as in the latter. In addition to estimating an event history analysis of the likelihood of judicial surrogate adoptions, I also report the results from a model that attempts to account for the timing of judicial renovations, and I compare the content of first and last judicial adoptions.

Linking Judicial and Legislative Innovation

As the California, Maine and Maryland examples introduced earlier in the chapter indicate, judicial and legislative innovation are linked. Courts are often forced to address a policy question when legislatures refuse to face the issue. Similarly, legislators have been known to alter statutes in response to judicial rulings they believe to run counter to the public interest or to legislative intent. A theory of judicial and legislative interaction is offered, and each of the legislative and judicial policy adoption and renovation models discussed above are re-estimated to account for policy actions taken in the "other" branch of government.

PLAN OF THE BOOK

In the second chapter, a theory of policy adoption and reinvention is presented; definitions of central concepts are offered, and testable hypotheses are accompanied by theoretical rationale. In the third chapter, I discuss model specification and estimation, and all of the measurement operations and data sources are detailed. Chapter 4 examines the results from the legislative adoption and renovation models, and variation in interstate policy content is emphasized. Chapter 5 repeats this process for the judicial models; this effort is supplemented by six case studies of judicial policy renovation. In the sixth chapter, attention shifts to the interplay between courts and legislatures. The results of the "integrated" policy models are discussed, and case studies are presented in order to compare and contrast patterns of legislative-judicial interplay in six states. The book concludes with a recapitulation of the major finding and their implications for future research on policy renovation in the American states.

CHAPTER 2
A Theory of Policy Adoption and Reinvention

RESEARCH ON INNOVATION

The diffusion of innovations is not a modern social phenomenon, but has been observed since antiquity (Musmann and Kennedy 1989, v). Because of its interdisciplinary nature, the subject has been studied by scholars from many different disciplines, especially anthropology (Bose and Saxena 1965; Scott-Stevens 1987), sociology (Allison 1978; Lauer 1971; Pankhurst 1982; Smith 1979; Yecaris 1970), history (Brittain 1974; Kenwood and Lougheed 1982; Saxonhouse 1974), and agriculture (Feder 1982; Griliches 1957). Research on innovation has achieved prominence and credibility in the social sciences, including political science, and a good deal of the credit for this goes to Everett Rogers's (1966) painstaking accumulation and fusion of hundreds of previous diffusion studies.

Within political science, interest in policy diffusion surfaced in the same subfield as did comparative public policy analysis: politics in the American states. The seminal work in this literature is Walker's (1969) examination of the adoption of 88 different innovations by state governments. This work precipitated a series of pioneering articles by Gray (1973), Grupp and Richards (1975) and Eyestone (1977). While innovation was the subject of considerable research in the 1970s, the 1980s was a period of "greatly diminished activity" in the field (Berry and Berry 1992, 716). However, with the adoption of new theory and methodological techniques, the 1990s marks a period of renewed interest in the topic (e.g., Berry and Berry 1990; 1992; Glick and Hays 1991; Glick 1992; Hays 1995; Mintrom 1997; Mintrom and Vergari 1998; Mooney and Lee 1995; Nice 1994), and this enthusiasm appears to have carried over into the new millenium (Haider-Markel 2001; Mooney 2001).

Research on innovation in the American states has usually followed one of three approaches (Glick 1992). The first body of work examines the correlates of the timing of the adoption of innovations, while the second corpus of literature focuses on how extensively adopted innovations are used. A final, seemingly nascent, vein of research explores the dynamics of policy reinvention. Before discussing each of these avenues of research, it is necessary to offer a precise definition of innovation.

The Concept of Innovation

The most widely accepted definition of innovation is "a program or policy which is new to the state adopting it, no matter how old the program may be or how many other states have adopted it" (Walker 1969, 881). Consider the following hypothetical situation. State A is the first to adopt a new regulatory program (thereby making state A the "initial adopter") and, over the next fifteen years, 48 other states enact identical programs. State Z (a "laggard") is the last to consider the program, and adopts it a full twenty years after State A originally introduced the policy. Each state, "A through Z," regardless of how soon or late it addresses the issue, is said to innovate at the time when it adopts the regulatory program, and once the diffusion process is complete, all fifty states are said to have adopted the innovation. For purposes of this study, an innovation is any policy, program or law that is new to a potential adopter. This definition is consistent with the predominant conceptualization in the literature (Eyestone 1977; Gray 1973; Rogers 1962; 1983; Savage 1985).

It is important to differentiate between innovation and "marginal" or "incremental" adjustments. March and Simon (1958, 174-75) suggest that innovation is present when "change requires the devising and evaluation of new performance programs that have not previously been part of the organization's repertory and cannot be introduced by a simple application

A Theory of Policy Adoption and Reinvention

of programmed switching roles." Nice (1994, 5) suggests that to be classified as an innovation, a policy must involve "the introduction of new decision rules, new technology, new approaches to organizing, or new goals." For purposes of the present study, the criteria offered by March and Simon and by Nice are accepted. An innovation is characterized by a legislative, executive, or legal utilization of new means to achieve a policy end.

For example, suppose a state approves a ten percent increase in an agency's operating budget; does this constitute an innovation? It is necessary to distinguish between policy instruments and policy means. The former term denotes actual legislation or laws, whereas the latter refers to the ways in which policies are implemented or funded. New laws or policies are innovations, while the money and resources necessary for their execution are the policy means; the latter do not qualify as innovations.

Having made this clarification, it is clear that a ten percent increase in an agency's operating budget does not constitute an innovation. However, if this increase were allocated in order to extend the scope of an agency's authority to include previously unregulated groups or industries or to provide for the enforcement of a new class of regulations, then the new (or amended) policy should be considered an innovation. Similarly, when a state adopts a sales tax for the first time, it adopts an innovation. However, if the state approves a one cent increase in the existing sales tax, the increase does not qualify as an innovation. But, if a state broadens the scope of the existing sales tax to include a previously exempt class of goods (e.g., food staples) then the state is said to adopt an innovation. The criteria as to what constitutes an innovation will prove critical when the concept of policy reinvention is considered. (Indeed both the extension of a sales tax to cover groceries and the promulgation of a new class of regulations are examples of reinvented policies.) The largest body of existing research, however, focuses only on the initial date of adoption of a general type of innovation (e.g., sales tax, income tax, sodomy laws, "lemon" laws, etc.) and does not allow for variation in program scope or policy content.

The Correlates and Timing of the Adoption of Innovations

In political science, most studies of innovation attempt to identify those state-level social and political factors which cause a state to innovate. This avenue of research has been termed the "internal determinants" model (Berry and Berry 1990). In his seminal analysis, Walker (1969) analyzed the propensity of state legislatures to adopt a wide variety of policy innovations, and he constructed an "index of innovation" for each state based on the year of adoption for 88 different policies. A few states emerged as innovation "leaders," and a number of economic and political variables were positively correlated with the innovation scores. Specifically, he found that larger, wealthier and more industrialized states were more likely to be early innovators than were smaller, less developed states. Political factors, such as legislative turnover and malapportionment were also associated with a state's willingness to innovate. Gray (1973) argued for a new approach to the analysis of innovations. Criticizing Walker's macro-level analysis, she argued for a narrower, policy-focused technique. Concentrating on individual policies, Gray found that the relative influence of political and economic variables on the propensity to innovate varied by policy area.

The debate between Gray and Walker fueled a number of subsequent internal determinants studies (Canon and Baum 1981; Glick 1981; Nice 1984; 1986; Regens 1980; Sigelman, Roeder, and Sigelman 1981). The findings of these studies suggest a tension between a "general-trait" perspective and an "issue-specific" perspective (Nice 1994, 8-9):

> The first body of work [general trait perspective] addresses the questions Are some states (or other units) generally faster to adopt or more inclined to adopt new policies than others? If so, which states? The second body [issue-specific perspective] addresses the questions Are some states (or other units) faster or more inclined to adopt new initiatives in the field of civil rights or law enforcement or whatever in other states? If so, which states?

Findings from research on American state politics demonstrate that when the rate at which state governments have adopted an aggregate of a wide

A Theory of Policy Adoption and Reinvention

variety of policies is studied, some states are clearly more likely to be early adopters than are others. However, when the speed of adoptions is disaggregated by policy area, the types of states that are leaders in one area do not necessarily exhibit the same leadership roles in other policy areas.

In addition to identifying important correlates of adoption, researchers have also examined the role of "interaction" in the diffusion process. Both interstate and national communications have been found to play important roles. Studies based on factor analysis (Canon and Baum 1981; Walker 1969) and surveys of state leaders and officials (Grupp and Richards 1975; Mendel and Feller 1977) suggest that later adopters take cues from a small number of policy leaders/early adopters. The "regional diffusion model" (Berry and Berry 1990) suggests that the diffusion process has a remarkably regional flavor; states emulate and borrow from their neighbors. Much of the evidence suggests that regional leaders play the preponderant role in the diffusion process (Freeman 1985; Grupp and Richards 1975; Light 1978; Lutz 1986; Menzel and Feller 1977; Walker 1969).

Berry and Berry (1990; 1992) make a major leap by testing the internal determinants and regional diffusion explanations in the same model. Using event history analysis, they find support for both classes of explanations in the areas of lottery adoptions and tax policies, respectively. A similar approach is employed by Glick and Hays (1995) to account for adoption of living will laws by state legislatures, but the analysis suggests that the effect of region is insignificant. While more tests of these two explanations are needed, the limited evidence indicates that the strength of regional influences on innovation varies by policy area.

The Extent of Innovation

Another, but considerably smaller corpus of literature, examines the magnitude of adoption of a particular innovation. These studies focus on how extensively a given innovation is used by different adopters. For example, there is a tendency for legislatures to grant facile concessions to latent interests by enacting "symbolic" or "token" innovations on such a small scale that no risk is involved, thereby ensuring that the policy produces no appreciable departure from the status quo (Edelman 1964; Downs and Mohr 1980; Mohr 1969). Downs (1976, 39) argues that the extent approach allows the analyst to differentiate between such "deep" and "superficial" adoptions; rather than simply scoring a governmental unit on when and/or whether it adopts an innovation, studies of the extent of adoption reveal an adopter's commitment to a policy.

Scholars have examined the pervasiveness of innovations in the areas of criminal justice reforms (Gray and Williams 1980), the degree of centralization in state court management (Glick 1981), and in numerous other policy areas (Bingham 1976; Downs 1976).

Policy Reinvention

A related, and even smaller, body of research deals with "reinvention" of an innovation by adopting units during the diffusion process. It is necessary to distinguish between extent of adoption and reinvention. Rogers (1983) defines reinvention as an alteration of an original innovation by a later adopter; extent, on the other hand, refers to the degree of adoption of a constant innovation (173). A hypothetical example may prove illustrative. State A is the first to establish an equal employment opportunity commission. Over the course of the next ten years, the remaining 49 states all adopt similar bureaus. A study of the extent of innovation might examine interstate variation in the proportion of discrimination claims processed. An analysis of reinvention, by contrast, might reveal that state A's original policy prioritized only the reduction of racial discrimination and granted the agency very limited powers of enforcement, while state X established an agency with broad power to investigate and try cases of racial, gender, and age discrimination. By modifying state A's core innovation, state X is said to have reinvented the policy. Reinvention studies have explored variation in the size of city urban renewal programs (T. Clark, 1968), state commitment to local government resource equalization through redistributive revenue sharing programs (J. Clark and French 1984), and differences in the stringency of state lobby regulations (J. Clark 1985).

A Theory of Policy Adoption and Reinvention

Glick (1992) notes that reinvention not only occurs as new adopters produce varied policies during the diffusion process, but also takes place when early adopters amend their original legislation. In the agency example, it is crucial for observers to not only examine the original policy developed by each state, but to note statutory changes and amendments as the policy is modified over time. While state A may have enacted a very limited policy initially, it is also possible that the state's equal opportunity commission was granted greater power and given a broader scope of authority as numerous amendments were introduced at later dates.

Glick and Hays (1991) found that the first states to adopt living will laws generally produced very restrictive (in terms of patient autonomy) right to die policies, while many later adopters enacted far more permissive laws. However, the authors also find that over the course of the diffusion period, ten of the earliest adopters substantially liberalized their policies through amendment. When the content of each state's living will law was scored at the end of the study period, thereby taking account of reinvention through amendment, date of adoption did not appear to be a determinant of policy content, for some early adopters had reinvented to produce some of the most permissive policies in the nation, while other early innovators had very restrictive policies.

Few studies have examined the relationship between date of adoption and policy content, and fewer still have allowed for reinvention through amendment and statutory revision. The study of policy reinvention is relatively new and largely unexplored. This book will contribute to the literature by examining both interstate and intrastate policy reinvention for a single issue over an extended period of time. It will begin, like so many previous studies, by identifying the correlates of the decision to adopt an innovation; but, in contrast to most work, it will also examine cross-sectional variation in the content or substance of these first adoptions. In addition, the research scheme allows for states to revise and amend their original policies, and it will examine influences on the substance of adoptions at the end of the diffusion period being studied. Finally, the manuscript will identify and analyze the adoption of new policy instruments that are distinct from, yet are outgrowths of, existing innovations.

The policy process is not static, but perpetual, and states continually revise their policies and invent new approaches to old problems. In the following section, a typology of policy innovations is offered in order to distinguish between the various ways in which state legislatures innovate and reinvent during the diffusion process.

A TYPOLOGY OF LEGISLATIVE POLICY INNOVATIONS[1]

As previously mentioned, most innovation research focuses on the correlates of the date of adoption of a given policy; these studies make the implicit assumption that all states adopt a uniform policy. However, as the research on reinvention demonstrates, this assumption is often unwarranted, and, as a result, substantial variation in state policy outputs goes unconsidered. But it is this variation that has the greatest potential to inform our understanding of the policy process. Policy content varies across governmental units and over time, and there are numerous ways in which states innovate and reinvent.

Table 2.1 displays the different ways in which states may adopt an innovation. The rows are labeled by order in the diffusion process, and the columns denote differences in adoption type. The double vertical lines dividing columns 3 and 4 differentiate adoptions of a new policy from later adoptions of a related, yet new and distinct, policy instrument.

Consider the cells in the second column. The first state to enact a given type of policy is said to produce the <u>core innovation</u>. All other states which produce a similar law after the core innovation is adopted are considered to be later adopters. Later adopters may pass a law identical to the core innovation; such a law is a <u>subsequent identical innovation</u>. Most previous work on innovation assumes this type of adoption during diffusion, and in many cases, states appear to have exactly replicated core innovations. For example, the 1931 California Fair Trade Law was copied almost verbatim by twenty states; indeed, ten of these states copied two typographical errors that appeared in the core California law (Grether 1937, 19-20).

While close emulation may occur during the diffusion process, it is important to understand that later adopters often work within political and economic environments very different from that of the core innovator;

later adopters also have the benefit of being able to observe the core adoption's impact. As a result, states may appreciably alter or modify core adoptions to better suit their own needs or to remedy perceived flaws or weaknesses in the core policy. When a state deviates from the core innovation by making substantive (as opposed to trivial or semantic) changes, additions or deletions, then the resulting policy is a <u>subsequent reinvented innovation</u>.

Table 2.1
A Classification of Innovations

Diffusion Order	First Policy		New Policy Instrument	
	First time adoption of innovation	Unit's modification of its first innovation	First time adoption of new policy instrument	Unit's modification of its new policy instrument
First unit to adopt	*Core Innovation*	*Renovated Reinvention*	*Core Tangential Innovation*	*Renovated Reinvention*
Later adopters	*Subsequent Identical or Reinvented Innovation*	*Renovated Reinvention*	*Subsequent Identical or Reinvented Tangential Innovation*	*Renovated Reinvention*

Reinvention may occur not only when each state adopts an innovation for the first time (a process that can be thought of as interstate reinvention), it may also take place at another (intrastate) level. In fact, even when the initial diffusion process appears to be totally complete (i.e., all 50 states have some version of the core innovation), policy reinvention may continue. After making its first adoption, a state may decide to change its policy through amendment or statutory revision; this process has been referred to as "reinvention through renovation" (Glick 1992, 49). Both cells in the third column of Table 1 are labeled <u>renovated reinvention</u>. A single state may engage in this process more than once; conceivably, a state could reinvent the same general policy on an annual basis. Other states may reinvent their policies numerous times before laggard states even adopt for the first time.

As social and technological conditions change, and as states gain experience in a policy area, it may become apparent that the core innovation and its subsequent adoptions and reinventions have been rendered obsolete or need to be augmented by a new type of policy. When a state adopts a new means (policy instrument) to achieve the same general ends being sought through an existing policy, the state enacts a tangential innovation. As the fourth column of Table 1 indicates, there are three types of these innovations. The first state to adopt the new policy instrument produces the core tangential innovation. The remaining states may enact the exact same policy (subsequent identical tangential innovation) or may tailor the policy to better suit their needs (subsequent reinvented tangential innovation). And, as shown in the last column of the table, each state may amend its tangential policy over time, thereby producing a new class of renovated reinventions.

A hypothetical example may prove illustrative. To reduce the incidence of teen pregnancy the state of New York enacts a law requiring pregnancy prevention seminars to be conducted annually in all public high schools. The policy requires that students be given basic facts regarding reproduction and be informed of the various birth control options. The year after New York adopts the core innovation, two more states adopt pregnancy prevention programs. Nebraska's policy, a subsequent identical innovation, is indistinguishable from New York's. Louisiana, however, produces a law that requires its schools to conduct classes that stress abstinence as the only certain way to avoid pregnancy; the law disallows the mention of other forms of birth control. Louisiana's law is a subsequent reinvented innovation. Three years later, in response to pressure from concerned citizens and organized interests, Nebraska amends its policy to require parental permission for students to attend the annual prevention seminars. Nebraska's amended policy is a renovated reinvention.

In the ten years following the passage of New York's core innovation, forty-one states adopt pregnancy prevention programs. However, despite these programs, most states have witnessed steady or increased teen pregnancy rates. Legislators in New Jersey, frustrated by the perceived failure of their program, narrowly approve a new approach to the problem. New Jersey adopts a law that awards a modest college (or vocational/technical) scholarship to each student who has not parented a child at the time she or he graduates from high school. This innovation involves the use of a new policy instrument to tackle an old problem. In the following year, Michigan and Ohio adopt New Jersey's policy verbatim. In the same year, Texas adopts a very similar scholarship program, but makes the scholarship program available not just to high school graduates, but to all persons under 21 who pass a high school equivalency exam prior to becoming parents. The New Jersey policy is the core tangential innovation. Michigan and Ohio adopt subsequent identical tangential innovations, and the Texas policy is a subsequent reinvented tangential innovation. Two years later, Texas adopts a renovated reinvention when it makes the scholarship available to all teen mothers who give their child up for adoption.

In the case of the right to die, the 1976 California Natural Death Act, which produced the nation's first living will law, is the core innovation. The forty-six states which approved living will laws after California, produced subsequent innovations. In 1982, Delaware approved a health care proxy law designed to overcome some of the deficiencies of the living will approach to planning; this proxy law was the core tangential innovation, and it was followed by forty-seven subsequent tangential innovations (most were reinvented, but a few were nearly identical). Similarly, surrogate decision making statutes also qualify as tangential innovations.

The above classification scheme applies to all types of public policies. However, this book is confined to one specific class of policies: permissive policies. In the following section, the meaning of permissive policies is discussed, and a theory of legislative innovation and reinvention is presented.

PERMISSIVE POLICIES AND LEGISLATIVE INNOVATION

In order to facilitate the analysis of public policy, scholars have developed a number of classification schemes. Lowi's (1964) familiar typology disaggregates policies intro three main types: regulatory, distributive and redistributive. Other researchers have modified and expanded Lowi's categorization, but most of these works still bear a close resemblance to Lowi's original scheme (Froman 1968; Hayes 1981; Ripley and Franklin 1987; Salisbury 1968).

Permissive policies can loosely be described as regulatory policies. However, they really do not fit neatly into any existing typology; therefore, they should be treated as a separate and distinct type of policy. Johnson and Canon (1984) define permissive policies as those which allow citizens and consumers to exercise new rights and to avail themselves to new products and services designed to advance those rights (see also Glick 1994).[2] Examples of such permissive policies include the right of women to choose abortion, the right of individuals to consume alcohol or view pornography, and the right of citizens to refuse unwanted medical treatment.

The Decision to Adopt: Core Innovations

Permissive laws may challenge existing mores and values; therefore, these policies often prove controversial. The first issue this theory must consider concerns why states adopt permissive innovations when they do, and why some states are innovators while others remain nonadopters. Previous research stresses the importance of socioeconomic factors such as wealth and urbanization; however, these studies have focused almost exclusively on economic policies. Permissive policies are characterized by high ideological conflict and low economic costs (Hays 1995), and therefore do not have a major impact on socioeconomic conditions in a state, and debate usually is conducted in moral, as opposed to economic, terms. Indeed, Mooney and Lee (1995) found that traditional socio-economic variables had no effect on states' adoptions of abortion regulations in the pre-Roe era, and Glick and Hays (1995) found a similar null relationship in their study of living will adoptions. If the traditional forces are not at work, then it is necessary to identify those factors that do influence adoption of permissive policies.

Degree of Controversy: Opposition and Support.

Savage (1985) has demonstrated an inverse relationship between issue fragility and rate of diffusion, where fragility denotes the existence (real or perceived) of organized opposition to a policy. Similarly, Hays (1995) found that, in a short period of time, most states adopted relatively noncontroversial laws such as child abuse reporting requirements and crime victim compensation statutes. However, Hays also found that for a highly controversial policy, public campaign funding legislation, fewer than half of the states innovated over a fifteen year period. Level of controversy clearly affects both the likelihood and rate of adoption of policies. Because permissive policies are always controversial, careful attention must be given to the balance of power between opponents and supporters of a policy.

For any given permissive policy, the strength of groups that object to the policy weighs heavily on the calculus of risk-averse legislators. The effect of those who oppose a policy on moral grounds is juxtaposed by the number of citizens having membership in groups that are likely to utilize the services created by the proposed policy. For example, Mooney and Lee (1995) found that the size of both the Catholic and fundamentalist Protestant population in a state inhibited the adoption of abortion reforms, whereas female workforce participation and strength of organized medicine were factors that promoted legalization.

For living will laws, I hypothesize that the size of a state's Catholic population should be inversely related to its likelihood of adoption. The individual state Catholic Conferences were instrumental and highly successful in blocking early right-to-die proposals (Glick 1992). However, it should also be noted that, in 1982, the National Conference of Catholic Bishops (NCCB), acknowledging that the push for living will laws had gained momentum in the states, approved a major change in political strategy. Rather than flatly opposing all living will laws, state lobbyists were encouraged to support bills that contained very restrictive provisions (Glick 1992). This approach was widely utilized in the 1983 legislative session; lobbying for the most limited policies possible, Catholic Conferences hoped to restrict citizens' access to, and reliance upon, living wills (Glick 1992; Glick and Hays 1995). This suggests a piecewise interaction hypothesis: the size of state's Catholic population has a greater effect in inhibiting living will adoptions in the years preceding the NCCB's strategic switch than in the years after state-level Catholic lobbies began supporting "diluted" statutes. In other words, a structural break is expected to occur in 1983.

Groups that stand to benefit the most from living will laws are senior citizens and organized medicine. Lobbyists for various geriatric organizations, including AARP, can be expected to support right to die laws because advance directives are most likely to be utilized by aging patients in the nursing home setting. Medical practitioners and providers should support living wills statutes because these policies often release professionals from liability while allowing decision making to take place within the informal parameters of the patient-family-doctor relationship.[3]

Institutional Determinants: State Legislatures.
Also of interest is the influence of "institutional" or "structural" variables. Institutional configurations regulate options for agenda setting and innovation, and some state legislatures are better suited to create new policies than are others. In the aggregate, demand for permissive policies is more likely to be converted into policy outputs in states with professionalized legislatures (Bowman and Kearney 1988; Carmines 1974). Professional legislatures have longer sessions, and professionalism increases the resources available to legislators, especially in terms of personal and committee staff.

However, permissive policies differ substantially from the distributive and redistributive issues examined in previous studies. Permissive policies involve moral absolutes (Meier 1994), juxtapose actors disinclined to compromise on fundamental issues (Moen 1984, Mooney and Lee 1995), and are not characterized by a high degree of technical complexity (Gormley 1986). For the re-election oriented legislator, permissive innovation always produces winners and losers, guaranteeing negative feedback from the latter. The costs of supporting morality-based policy should be higher for the full-time, professional legislator than for the part-time, "citizen" representative. The latter have less to lose by supporting new (and highly salient) legislation, and the former have more to gain by circumnavigating controversial initiatives.

Therefore, on balance, legislative professionalism should be inversely related to willingness to innovate.

Political Determinants.
The electoral environment of a state influences policy making. District-level party competition, state election cycles, and the presence or absence of divided government are important correlates of innovation. Level of competition between parties impacts electoral security and should affect the likelihood of legislators adopting controversial policies; interparty competition should be negatively related to a state's propensity to innovate. In a given year, the presence of an election also decreases the willingness of legislators to take stands on tough issues. Berry and Berry (1992) found that states were less likely to adopt controversial tax policies in election years than in non-election years, and Mooney and Lee (1995) reached a similar conclusion regarding the passage of abortion reforms. Finally, ease of policy making is facilitated by one-party control of both chambers of a state legislature as well as the state's gubernatorial office. States should be less likely to adopt permissive policies in periods of divided government than in periods of one-party control.

Horizontal Influences: Interstate Diffusion.
For a given policy, once a state adopts a core innovation, all other states are at risk for adoption. Evidence suggests that states look to their neighbors for guidance (Foster 1978; Freeman 1985; Savage 1981). Therefore, states geographically proximate to the core adopter are likely to follow suit and adopt the innovation. Once a policy begins to diffuse in a region, there is often a growing feeling that the policy's "time has come" (Savage 1985). Decision makers may begin to believe that adoption is inevitable and, therefore, decide to jump on the innovation bandwagon. During the diffusion process, a state's propensity to adopt increases as more neighboring states adopt the policy.

Not only is the act, by a neighboring state, of adopting a policy important, but the content of such adoptions can also be expected to affect how influential the state's law will be in influencing its neighbors. A weak or "half-hearted" policy (i.e., one full of restrictions or prohibitions) should not have nearly the same impact as a deep or "committed" policy.

States whose neighbors have adopted comprehensive permissive policies should be more likely to innovate than are states whose neighbors have either not adopted an innovation or who have enacted weak innovations. Similarly, as the total number of states in the nation to adopt a policy increases, so does the pressure for remaining states to adopt. Indeed, the most common approach to the study of innovation across disciplines is the analysis of adoption distribution curves (Musmann and Kennedy 1989). Rogers's (1962) social learning theory describes three phases of diffusion. In the first stage, innovation precedes slowly, and only a few units adopt the policy. In the second period, the "take-off" phase, nonadopting units gauge the experiences of the early adopters, and as the benefits and advantages of the policy become clear, there is a quick burst of many adoptions. Finally, the third period is marked by a slow "mopping up" of the remaining nonadopters. Evidence from a number of studies supports Rogers's theory. For example, Gray (1973) finds that for many policies, the frequency of innovation over time appears to closely approximate the normal (bell-shaped) distribution. When aggregated over time, innovation patterns resemble the "S"-shape of the cumulative normal distribution. Permissive core innovations can be expected to diffuse in such a manner, as these innovations are "new commodities," and some state legislators should be willing to "test the water" and "get in early," while lawmakers in other states will wait to gauge the experiences of these first policy trailblazers.

Horizontal Influences: Intergovernmental Actors.
Once the innovation cycle is underway, concerns often arise regarding the lack of uniformity of policies and the concomitant disparity in individual rights across states. Intergovernmental organizations such as the National Governor's Association (NGA), the National Conference of State Legislators (NCSL), and the National Conference Commission on Uniform State Laws (NCCUSL) often press for guidelines and homogeneity. Jacob (1988) found that the rapid adoption of no-fault divorce laws by all fifty states was greatly facilitated by the NCCUSL's drafting of a uniform law. To state legislators considering an innovation, such "national" advocacy may add legitimacy to a proposed policy and provide additional justification for adoption.

The NCCUSL approved a model living will law in 1985. Therefore, all things being equal, the probability of legislative adoption should be greater in the pre-1985 period than in the post-1985 period. It is also reasonable to speculate that the emergence of this NCCUSL policy should interact with regional diffusion trends. Specifically, once an intergovernmental recommendation has been made, the influence of neighboring states will likely be diminished. I propose another piecewise interaction hypothesis: states are more influenced by the adoptions of neighboring states in the pre-NCCUSL period than they are after the Commissioners published the model law.

As alluded to previously, the mere adoption of a permissive policy may be only the beginning of a lengthy battle. A policy's content is also important if it is to be effective in promoting its goals and being accessible to state residents. Accordingly, attention now shifts to explanations of variation in policy content and to the process of reinvention through renovation.

Content of First Adoptions

Date of adoption is an important determinant of the content of state innovations. The first state(s) to adopt an innovation takes a bold step, as the policy is unprecedented. In such a situation, opposition is likely to be high, and legislators may be highly skeptical. Kingdon (1984) notes that when promoting a new idea, policy proponents often invest a good deal of time and energy in "softening up" both elites and masses. In order to assuage the fears of concerned or wavering elites, bill sponsors often make concessions and adopt provisions limiting the policy's scope or impact. Therefore, early adopters can be expected to adopt fairly limited or restricted policies.

After early innovators have "broken the ice," later adopters may be afforded greater latitude in specifying a policy's stringency and scope. Later adopters can be expected to develop more extensive or permissive policies than do early innovators for a number of reasons. First, it is possible that later adopters have been criticized for their delay in addressing the issue, and the problem may have reached a critical point in many of these states. In this case, later adopters may attempt to pacify issue publics and justify their dilatory response to the issue by adopting an extensive and far-reaching policy. Second, laggard states should have learned from the experience and reinvention efforts of earlier adopters. Because they may have been avoiding an issue for a while, legislators in later-adopting states may wish to "get the matter over with in one swoop" and "be done with it" by avoiding the pitfalls or prohibitions that necessitated policy renovation in the early-adopting states.

The limited evidence on policy reinvention supports the above hypothesis. Mooney and Lee (1995) found that, on balance, later adopters produced more permissive abortion reforms than did early adopters, and Glick and Hays (1991) found a positive relationship between date of adoption (i.e., number of years since the first adoption) and living will facility scores.

Reinvention Through Renovation: Core Innovations

Once a state adopts an innovation, it usually modifies or alters its policy over time. Favorable conditions often promote early adoption, yet early adopters often enact weak first policies. However, once a policy is intact and later adopters have produced more extensive innovations, early adopters can be expected to gradually liberalize their policies through reinvention. Therefore, as long as the conditions that promote adoption remain favorable over time, early adopters should be expected to produce renovated reinventions that keep pace with or exceed the "permissiveness" of the adoptions of other states.

A state's propensity to renovate[4] its core innovation should be conditioned by the same factors that led it to adopt the innovation in the first place. In addition, I hypothesize that as the time since an innovation was first approved increases, so does the likelihood of renovation; this reflects the belief that policies that were once "cutting edge" invariably need to be modified in order to stay with the times. Similarly, states, even early adopters, look to their neighbors and to regional leaders for renovation cues. Once it becomes evident that a state's extant policy is less facilitative than the policies found in nearby states, the pressure to renovate is felt.

In addition to renovating their core adoptions, state legislators may also have the option of looking at entirely new policy means altogether. Amending an innovation is one alternative, but the same policy problems or limitations that drive lawmakers to renovate a statute may also encourage these officials to consider tangential innovations. As discussed in the next section, tangential innovations can be expected to diffuse at a quicker rate than core innovations.

The Decision to Adopt: Tangential Innovations

After a given general policy is adopted, it may become apparent that, regardless of how many reinventions and modifications are added, the policy falls short of achieving all of its desired goals. New policy mechanisms or legislative tools may be needed to get the job done. Tangential innovations supplement, and may replace, the original innovation. The same political and institutional factors that promote adoption of the first type of innovation can be expected to increase the propensity to enact a tangential innovation. In addition, states that have already adopted the original innovation are more likely to adopt the tangential innovation than are states that have not yet innovated in the policy area. The former have demonstrated a willingness to innovate and are more likely to correct or supplement the original policy with a tangential innovation than are the latter. Moreover, having developed a reputation for leadership in the policy area, early innovators during the diffusion of the original policy are likely to continue in their leadership role during the diffusion of the tangential policy.

However, it is important to note that during this second phase of innovation, the early "first-round" innovators do not have a monopoly on policy leadership; in some instances different states may emerge as the core and early tangential innovators. At the point in time that entrepreneurs begin promoting a tangential innovation, the states with the most liberal or extensive first policies should be the most likely to adopt tangential innovations. While they may not have been leaders in the first phase, as time progresses, some states may demonstrate, through renovation, the greatest commitment to the program goals (i.e., have the most extensive or permissive policies). On the other hand, it is also possible that early innovators in the first phase continuously amend their original legislation, and are, therefore, in a position to continue their leadership role in promoting the tangential innovations.

The crucial point is that the content (i.e., level of permissiveness) of a state's existing core innovation should be positively related to its likelihood of adopting a tangential innovation. In the case of refusal of treatment legislation, the strength or level of facility of a state's living will law should be positively related to its legislature's willingness to adopt a health care proxy law or surrogate decision making statute. For surrogate policies (these were the last legislative innovations to "take off"), likelihood of innovation should be a function not only of the content of a state's living will law, but it should also be influenced in the same way by the provisions of its health care proxy statute.

As the case with core policies, tangential innovations may also receive a "boost" from the adoption of intergovernmental model laws. In 1989 the NCCUSL approved a model proxy/durable power of attorney statute, and in 1991 the organization endorsed and published a model surrogate policy. Adoption of these types of tangential innovations should be greater in post-NCCUSL adoption years than in the years preceding action by the Commissioners' Conference. The impact of regional policy influences should also be mitigated in the periods following the approval of these model laws.

All things being equal, tangential innovations should not prove nearly as contentious as their predecessor core innovations. Tangential diffusion can be expected to proceed at an accelerated rate, as lawmakers may be able to portray these policies as routine and noncontroversial outgrowths of a core innovation. While the fundamental tenets of social learning theory still apply, the diffusion curves for tangential policies should be "shortened" (i.e., when plotted cumulatively, these adoptions should approximate an "S"-curve, but the tails of the distributions should be much smaller than they were for core innovations, reflecting the rapid rate of dissemination of the new policy mechanisms).

Content of Tangential Innovations

It is clear that date of adoption of the first innovation should be an important correlate of the decision to adopt a tangential innovation. This variable should also prove important in determining the content of a state's first adoption of a new policy instrument (tangential innovation). Early adopters face the formidable task of "breaking the ice" and, therefore, usually enact limited tangential policies. Later adopters benefit from the "softening up" efforts of early innovators, and later adopters enjoy greater leeway in determining a policy's scope and stringency.

As the case with core innovations, early innovators that have adopted limited policies can be expected to gradually liberalize their policies over time. Therefore, as long as the political and institutional conditions that facilitate enactment of tangential policies remain favorable over time, early adopters should be expected to generate renovated reinventions that match or exceed the permissiveness of the tangential policies in other states.

Reinvention Through Renovation: Tangential Policies

The same political, institutional and horizontal variables that were responsible for promoting the adoption of tangential innovations should also be positively related to the likelihood of renovation. Also important are tangential policy developments in other states. The amount of time elapsed since a tangential policy was adopted in a state is hypothesized to be positively related to policy renovation, and the further the level of permissiveness of a state's tangential policy falls below the levels in nearby states, the more likely legislators are to approve amendments to the tangential policy.

Because diffusion of tangential policies is expected to be accelerated, and because states learned from previous mistakes when evaluating their core policies, there should be less need to renovate tangential policies. Health care proxy laws and surrogate statutes should be subject to considerably less amendment and revision than are living will laws.

Of course, there is no guarantee that all states legislatures will adopt certain types of permissive policies. Risk averse lawmakers often go to great lengths to avoid taking action on the most controversial of issues. Sometimes state judiciaries must field difficult questions and promulgate policy guidelines. In the next section, a theory of judicial innovation and reinvention is presented.

PERMISSIVE POLICIES: JUDICIAL INNOVATION

As reactive actors, courts differ from legislatures in their ability to make policy. Judiciaries cannot actively "seek-out" disputes for resolution nor can they exercise their prerogative of judicial review until such time as justiciable cases reach their jurisdictions. Once a case is before a state tribunal, justices often show tremendous restraint in formulating their opinions (e.g., ruling on the most narrow facets of the case in order to avoid invoking constitutional principles, declaring cases moot, etc.). Most cases never even make it to court due to a variety of factors (e.g., settlements, conflict avoidance, pre-trial mediation), and of that small group of cases that do make it to a court of original jurisdiction, only a handful are granted appellate review. Appellate justices, particularly in courts of last resort, enjoy considerable discretion in granting petitions for review or *certiorari*; only a very select number of cases are granted such an audience. The politics of judicial innovation are inextricably linked to the appellate review process. The following section begins with a discussion of judicial innovation, and then a number of theoretical propositions are offered in an attempt to identify the determinants of innovation, the factors affecting the likelihood of judicial policy renovation, and the correlates of the content of judicial decisions.

The Concept of Judicial Innovation

As previously defined, an innovation is any idea new to a potential adopter; this definition applies to judicial decisions as well as to legislative policies. However, there are important differences that distinguish innovation efforts in these two branches of state governments. First, state legislatures have ultimate statutory authority, whereas there are multiple tiers in state court systems. Any new policy approved by a legislative body constitutes an innovation, but only the decisions issued by state appellate

A Theory of Policy Adoption and Reinvention 45

courts are controlling authority in their respective jurisdictions. This means that only decisions by appellate courts, as opposed to trial courts of original jurisdiction, can qualify as innovations.[5] Also important is the fact that any time an appellate court, when hearing a case of first impression, rules on the substantive permissive issue at bar and sets any type of guidelines (no matter how narrow the court's focus) to govern related controversies in the state, judicial innovation takes place. This means that if a state supreme court, for example, rules that there is no legal basis for allowing surrogates to direct the discontinuance of life-supports on behalf of an incompetent patient, the court has adopted an innovation. By ruling that no rights exist, the court has effectively produced a decision, much the same way it would have innovated if it determined that a patient's common law right to freedom from unwanted bodily-intrusion warranted surrogate decision-making under certain circumstances.[6]

In this book, I am primarily concerned with judicial surrogate innovations. Although state courts have rich histories of addressing the legality of refusal of treatment when such action was requested by competent patients (e.g., blood transfusions for adult Jehova's Witnesses), these cases, except when the lives of minors were implicated, have almost invariably affirmed the right to decline treatment (see Chapter 5). Surrogate decision making cases, by contrast, are unique to the latter half of the twentieth century and involve the creation of a new class of rights and new policy mechanisms for exercising those rights.

Bearing the above discussion of judicial innovation in mind, the following section attempts to identify the determinants of judicial innovation. Many "new" judicial, political and institutional variables are considered.

The Decision to Adopt: Judicial Innovations

<u>Degree of Controversy: Opposition, Support and Interest Aggregation.</u>
Although their avenues of influence are limited in the judicial arena, pressure groups do have a number of options available to them when attempting to influence judicial outcomes. Scholars have long recognized the importance of interest groups in sponsoring "test cases," providing

legal advice and pro bono representation to potential litigants, and aiding government attorneys in civil actions (Truman 1951; Vose 1958). Recent efforts have focused on the importance of filing *amicus curiae* briefs. Although there is little evidence directly linking friend of the court briefs with judicial policy outcomes, the volume of such briefs filed in federal and state appellate cases has risen dramatically over the past several decades (O'Connor and Epstein 1982; Epstein 1994). In addition, recent evidence indicates that the presence of an *amicus* brief greatly enhances the likelihood that a case will be granted *certiorari* (Caldeira and Wright 1994).

All of the above methods of influence can be utilized in permissive policy litigation. Therefore, I hypothesize that the effect of those who oppose a policy on moral grounds is juxtaposed by the number of citizens having membership in groups that are likely to utilize the services created by the proposed policy. In the case of the right to die, the size of a state's Catholic population should be inversely related to adoption, whereas the size of a state's medical community and geriatric population should each be positively related to the likelihood of judicial innovation.

Institutional Determinants: Judicial Variables.

The U.S. Constitution empowers each individual state to set up its own judicial system, and this experiment in American federalism has resulted in a diverse array of structural arrangements. For example, some states have a dual-tiered system comprised of courts of original jurisdiction and a court of last resort. Other states have three- or four-tiered systems, with intermediate appellate courts positioned to hear appeals in various geographic regions (circuits). The presence of an intermediate appellate court should be positively related to the likelihood of judicial innovation for a number of reasons. First, these intermediate bodies help to guarantee that more appeals will be heard in the state; courts of last resort are often so busy dealing with mandatory cases (e.g., death penalty cases and cases over which these supreme courts have original jurisdiction) that there is little room on their dockets for additional cases. Intermediate appellate courts increase the discretionary caseload available to courts of last resort. In addition, research findings garnered from "cue theory" suggest that *certiorari* is more likely when there is conflict between judicial authorities

A Theory of Policy Adoption and Reinvention

(Ulmer 1984); when an intermediate appellate court overturns the decision of a lower court, this may send a message to supreme court justices that this is a case rife for final disposition. It also warrants mentioning that, even if a case does not reach a court of last resort in a state, intermediate appellate courts can produce judicial innovations.

The extent of judicial professionalism and prestige is another important variable. Some state judiciaries are staffed by career justices, many of whom have attended Ivy League law schools and have distinguished themselves in private practice before accepting their judgeships; other states offer considerably lower salaries, have a high rate of turnover, and are less successful in recruiting accomplished lawyers and scholars to their benches. There is a direct correlation between professionalism and prestige (Jacob 1996). Research by Caldeira (1984, 1988) suggests that in making and justifying policy choices, state courts are particularly reliant upon precedents handed down in other jurisdictions. Networks of communication have been identified, with some state courts emerging as leaders and others as followers. Previous researchers have found evidence of less-professionalized judiciaries taking cues from more reputed courts in other states during the diffusion of judicial reforms (Canon and Baum 1981) and in the diffusion of different judicial doctrines (Baum and Canon 1982). All things being equal, a state court of last resort's reputation for judicial leadership should be positively related to its likelihood of innovation. States with reputed judiciaries are more likely to innovate early in a given policy area, while less-reputed tribunals are more likely to be laggard adopters.

Previous research on state courts has stressed the importance of judicial selection (e.g., Glick and Emmert 1987), but many scholars concede that, in the aggregate, method of selection does not have major implications for public policy outputs (Jacob 1996). However, for permissive policies, whether a judge is appointed or elected should be a major consideration when considering the determinants of judicial innovation. Permissive policies, as previously discussed, divide issue publics and always invite some threat of electoral retribution. And scholars have found that state judges respond to contours in public opinion when ruling on morality-based policies (Brace and Hall 1995; Kuklinski and Stanga 1979). Elected judges should be more leery of adopting controversial policy innovations than are justices in states that do not require them to stand for re-election.

The amount of prior related case activity in a state should be another important correlate of appellate innovation. The first time a certain issue appears before a state trial court, appellate review may be unlikely to be granted. But as a corpus of decisions by lower courts in a state begins to emerge and grow, a state's high court justices may begin to realize the importance of addressing the issue. In addition, lower courts are likely to render different verdicts in these cases and to rely on different standards and precedents in formulating their opinions; this type of intrastate judicial conflict may invite appellate resolution.

While there is no shortage of studies examining the behavior of state courts and state legislators, little substantive political science research has examined the roles of attorney generals in the policy process.

Institutional Determinants: Attorney Generals.
Attorney generals impact the policy process, particularly judicial policy making, in a number of important ways. First, these officials often issue advisory opinions that guide district attorneys and practitioners in a state on whether or not the state should intervene in a given policy area or object to a particular practice. In addition, state attorney generals are often parties to lawsuits and make decisions on whether or not to appeal cases to which the state or "the people" are a party. This willingness to push for litigation can increase the likelihood of *certiorari*; in fact, previous studies have found that justices are more likely to grant requests for review when a governmental official or state is a party to a lawsuit (Songer 1979; Teger 1980; Ulmer 1983).

Method of selection should be of crucial importance, as elected attorney generals should be more disinclined to bring controversial, high-profile lawsuits than are appointed officials in other states. Indeed, a recent study found that attorney generals who had to stand for re-election were less likely to initiate state lawsuits against big tobacco than were attorneys who could not be removed from office without cause (Winder, LaPlatt, and Carter 1999).

A Theory of Policy Adoption and Reinvention

Horizontal Influences.
State appellate courts have been found to influence one another during the diffusion process. The judicial reputation hypothesis discussed in the previous section assumes that certain state courts earn reputations as national leaders and that the tribunals in other jurisdictions take cues from these elite judicial pathfinders. The notion that "state appellate courts are open to influence from other courts regardless of location" receives support from an important study of the diffusion of judicial tort innovations (Canon and Baum 1981, 984). However, other scholars have found that regionalism figures prominently in the diffusion of precedents among state supreme courts (Caldeira 1983, 1985); in a series of studies, Harris (1979, 1980, 1982) reports that sectional and regional patterns were of primary importance in shaping judicial diffusion curves.

State courts should be expected to accord greater weight to the decisions and innovative opinions of courts in nearby states than to those handed down in other parts of the nation. As the number of permissive judicial adoptions by a state's regional neighbors increases, so too should the likelihood of such an appellate policy in the given state. Not only are justices likely to take cues from their neighbors, but policy entrepreneurs in a given state are also likely to be influenced and inspired by successes in nearby states when crafting their own litigation strategies and promoting test cases.

Vertical Influences.
The power of judicial review is the ultimate means of federal judicial influence over the content of state appellate decisions. Because permissive policies often involve the exercise of individual liberties and civil rights, these types of cases are likely to eventually reach the U.S. Supreme Court. Once the high court has ruled on a matter, its holding is controlling authority throughout the nation. When the Supreme Court issues a ruling finding constitutional protections for flag burning, for example, state courts are obligated to adopt the position of the Supreme Court.

However, it is also important to note that in recent years, the U.S. Supreme Court has backed away from issuing the sweeping and uncompromised rulings that characterized the more judicially active courts found during the heyday of the civil rights movement. The high court is paying greater deference to the Tenth Amendment to the U.S. Constitution and allowing states greater latitude in placing limits on the exercise of civil liberties. When Supreme Court justices issue a ruling that essentially allows states to determine the appropriate boundaries of a given policy, different judicial outcomes are likely to be found across the states. Indeed, recent evidence on the "new judicial federalism" suggests that many state courts are now finding constitutional protections and guarantees of civil liberties that are more expansive and permissive than the rights recognized by federal courts (Kincaid 1994).

The Supreme Court's 1990 ruling in *Cruzan* is somewhat innocuous in nature. The justices found a constitutional liberty interest that allows competent individuals to refuse unwanted life supports, but the majority made clear its belief that states were empowered to place reasonable restrictions and safeguards on the practice of surrogate decision-making. The impact of *Cruzan* should be limited in scope; by recognizing a constitutional basis for the decision to decline treatment, the high court may have encouraged review and adoption by state appellate courts, but the fact that *Cruzan* upholds state restrictions and does not endorse any procedural or evidentiary requirements may also suggest that it is of only limited value to state justices. Adoption should be more likely in the post-*Cruzan* era than in the pre-*Cruzan* period; however, the the 1990 decision should have only a limited-to-modest impact.

I also propose a piecewise interaction hypothesis: regional influence should decline in the wake of a federal policy directive. The strength of this impact, however, is conditioned by the nature of the court's ruling. A limited ruling, such as *Cruzan*, should have only a limited effect in supplanting or diminishing horizontal influences.

Judicial Renovation

Like legislatures, state appellate courts are capable of engaging in reinvention through renovation. However, the concept of judicial renovation warrants special attention. Because courts, in making policy, must tailor the scope of their holding to the specific facts and circumstances of the cases before them, justices rarely issue comprehensive opinions that anticipate additional contingencies and

A Theory of Policy Adoption and Reinvention 51

applications. Judicial renovation occurs when justices strike down or make a substantive modification to a previous state innovation (precedent); in order for a decision to qualify as a renovation, a court must alter the legal basis of its previous decision or otherwise change evidentiary requirements or procedural standards. Extensions of a previous decision to a new set of facts is not renovation unless the court also departs from the fundamental tenor of its previous decision.

In the case of the right to die, let us assume that a state court of last resort issues a ruling that finds a constitutional basis for medical decision making by surrogates, but that the decision requires clear and convincing evidence of an incompetent patient's wishes be presented to a probate judge before a nontreatment decision can be implemented. This decision (assuming this was a case of first impression in the state) qualifies as a judicial innovation. Now suppose that, two years after this policy was adopted, the court hears a new case and, upon deciding that its previous evidentiary requirement was too stringent, approves a best interests of the patient standard and abandons the requirement of prior judicial approval when all parties to a nontreatment decision are in agreement as to the propriety of withdrawing life-supports. This subsequent case qualifies as a judicial renovation because the court made a substantive change to its prior holding. However, suppose that in the original innovative opinion, the state court limited its holding to cases involving incompetent patients sustained by artificial respirators, and in a subsequent case ruled that its previously established procedures should also be extended to situations involving incompetent patients being kept alive through renal dialysis treatments. Because it did not alter the fundamental directive contained in its original innovation, the dialysis decision does not qualify as a renovation (it would, however, be subsumed under the broader category of reinvention).[7]

The Decision to Renovate.
The same factors that lead a court to adopt a judicial innovation should also contribute to its likelihood of renovating its policy. In addition, it is also reasonable to speculate that, because state courts take cues from regional leaders, justices are more likely to consider renovation when their extant policy "falls behind" the more permissive policies approved in

neighboring states. In addition, as renovation is predominately a progressive phenomenon (i.e., policies usually grow more facilitative and permissive over time), the length of time since the approval of a state's original innovation should be positively related to its likelihood of judicial renovation.

Although there are clear reasons to expect judicial renovation to occur, renovation probably occurs less often in the judicial, than in the legislative, arena. Once a court has adopted a rationale, lower court justices in the state are likely to apply the precedent to future situations and contingencies, reducing the need for appeals. When lower courts reach a decision that is consistent with the spirit of a high court's innovation (i.e., is a logical extension of the judicial policy to a new set of facts), the absence of conflict may decrease the likelihood of *certiorari*, even when appeals are filed.

Content of Judicial Innovations.
Date of policy adoption should be positively related to the extent of policy facility or permissiveness. Early courts are likely to proceed cautiously in charting previously unnavigated waters, while later adopters benefit from the "softening up" efforts of the early innovators. By the time the diffusion cycle is essentially complete, early innovators can be expected to have renovated their policies to keep pace with regional and national trends. Date of adoption should affect the content of first policies, but not of later ones.

As suggested by the case vignettes in Chapter 1, judicial and legislative policy making do not take place independently of one another. Rather, judges and legislators are cognizant of developments that have taken place or that are under consideration in other branches of their state's government. The following section offers a brief theory of how this interaction affects permissive policy innovation.

JUDICIAL AND LEGISLATIVE INNOVATION

There are numerous ways in which the decisions of courts can alter legislative behavior, and the reverse holds true as well. In order to specify how innovations in one institution influence decisions in another, it is necessary to first examine the motivations of office-holders in each of these institutions. Legislators continuously look to their prospects for re-election; this means that they are, as previously discussed, risk-averse and disinclined to take actions that invite the threat of electoral retribution. State justices, by contrast, are not nearly as wary of controversy as are their policy-making counterparts in state assemblies. Indeed, appellate justices at the state and federal levels appear to be motivated by a desire to resolve controversies and create policy. The large body of findings from the "cue theory" literature suggests that the presence of a controversial case involving conflict or permissive policy issues (e.g., civil rights and civil liberties, rights of criminal defendants, privacy rights, equal protections of the law) actually increases the likelihood of review by supreme courts (Tanenhaus 1981; Teger and Kosinski 1980; Ulmer 1983). All other things being equal, state justices should be less risk-averse than are state legislators.

Judicial Influences on Legislative Behavior

Owing to their controversial nature, permissive policies always threaten to exact political costs from elected legislators. Nondecisions and policy inaction are commonplace in state assemblies. It is reasonable to assume that many legislators wish to avoid addressing highly salient and controversial issues if at all possible. One alternative is to allow a state judiciary to "tackle" a social problem, thereby taking "the heat" off of legislators. Indeed, a "deep" and highly facilitative judicial innovation can effectively limit the need for subsequent legislative action, especially when a state court identifies constitutional liberties that cannot be abridged by statute. The presence of a facilitative permissive policy in a state should be inversely related to the likelihood of legislative innovation on a given issue. By the same logic, the absence of a judicial innovation (or the presence of a weak or limited judicial policy) means that the social problem in question will go unresolved, and pressure for legislative adoption will continue to mount.

Before taking any definitive policy action, legislators are likely to look for signs of future judicial adoption. If the conditions are ripe for judicial adoption, legislators are likely to "hold off" on expending political capital by supporting a controversial policy. Two heuristic aids can be used by legislators to gauge the likelihood of judicial innovation. First, as the number of cases involving the given policy increases in state courts, lawmakers are likely to assume that appellate review is soon to follow. In addition, lawmakers are likely to look at judicial developments in nearby states, hoping that an increase in judicial adoptions in neighboring states will forecast the emergence of the issue on their own state's appellate judicial agenda. In the absence of any judicial developments in the state, it is likely that the social problem will reach a "critical point," thereby necessitating legislative action.

The same logic should apply to the willingness of legislators to renovate an existing policy. Once a court has taken up an issue, legislators may wish to defer to judicial fiat and avoid amending or liberalizing the controversial policy. Judicial action begets legislative inaction.

Legislative Influences on Judicial Behavior

There are two different possibilities regarding the impact of legislative adoptions on decision making by state judiciaries. The first is that state justices may view certain permissive policies as better suited to legislative resolution; arguing that legislatures comprised of elected representatives are better equipped to convert constituency preferences into policy outcomes, justices may refuse to take up an issue, especially if the state legislature has already innovated in a policy area. The second possibility, however, is that legislative innovations are likely to invite lawsuits challenging statutory restrictions. When this happens, justices may see the opportunity to exercise their discretion and power of judicial review. I believe the latter scenario is likely to prevail in the majority of cases. Statutes invite litigation, thereby increasing the opportunities for judicial review and innovation.

It should be stressed that few previous studies have attempted to link judicial and legislative policy making using an innovation framework.[8] I believe my theoretical expectations are justified and tenable; however, the study of legislative-judicial interaction during the diffusion process is relatively nascent, and the research approach used in Chapter 6 to explore

A Theory of Policy Adoption and Reinvention

this phenomenon is as much inductive in nature as it is deductive. Only through detailed exploration of a policy area can we garner results that allow for the construction of a more comprehensive and complete theory of the policy process.

CHAPTER 3
Research Design and Methods

INTRODUCTION

This chapter is designed to provide a parsimonious sketch of the research design. The discussion in the following sections is supplemented by a number of appendices contained at the end of the text. Appendix A lists all of the statutes that were used to score the legislative innovations and renovations. Appendix B contains tables that present, in summary fashion, the measurement operations and data sources used for each of the substantive variables contained in the empirical models. The coding schemes for the policy facility scores appear in Appendix C, and the cases that qualify as appellate innovations or renovations are cited in Appendix D.

LEGISLATIVE INNOVATION AND REINVENTION

The Decision to Adopt

The first models concern the decision to adopt each of the three types of right to die policies. In the interest of brevity, and because they closely parallel the theory section, the hypotheses are not explicitly stated. As the same independent variables are used in all three adoption models, a single econometric specification is presented, and causal direction is indicated by the "+" or "-" sign preceding the variable. Variables that are unique to the proxy and surrogate statutes are discussed in the text.

The models are estimated using Event History Analysis (EHA), a pooled time-series technique (Allison 1984). The time period under study is 1976-1994 for living will laws, 1982-1994 for proxy laws, and 1977-1994 for surrogate statutes. The unit of analysis is "state-years," and the data are stacked cross-sectionally over time. Observations begin with the period of the first adoption, and each state is dropped from the given data set after it adopts the particular type of innovation under investigation. States that never adopt an innovation remain in the data set through 1994.

The theory suggests the following model:

$$\begin{aligned}\text{Adoption}_{i,t} = \Phi(&-b_1\%\text{Catholic}_{i,t} + b_2\text{Piecewise 1983 Catholic Interaction}_{i,t} \\&+ b_3\text{Senior Citizens}_{i,t} + b_4\text{Physicians}_{i,t} - b_5\text{Legislative Salary}_{i,t} \\&+ b_6\text{Interparty Competition}_{i,t} - b_7\text{Electoral Threat}_{i,t} \\&- b_8\text{Divided Government}_{i,t} - b_9\text{Regional Facility}_{i,t-1} \\&- b_{10}\text{Piecewise Regional Facility Interaction}_{i,t-1})\end{aligned}$$

where the dependent variable of interest, $\text{Adoption}_{i,t}$, is the probability that state i will adopt a right-to-die law in year t, and Φ indicates the cumulative logistic distribution function. This equation takes the form of a discrete-time logit model. $\text{Adoption}_{i,t}$ is a dummy variable coded 1 if state i adopts a law in year t, and is coded 0 if the state does not adopt in that year.

$\%\text{Catholic}_{i,t}$ is the term that reflects the size of a state's Catholic population, and is measured as the percentage of a state's citizens that are Catholic. $\text{Senior Citizens}_{i,t}$ is the percentage of a state's residents who are over the age of sixty-five, and $\text{Physicians}_{i,t}$ is the number of medical doctors per 100,000 persons. The first variable is expected to yield a negative coefficient, while the signs of the latter two coefficients should be positive. The hypotheses reflect the belief that Catholics should be opposed to right-to-die laws, while senior citizens and medical practitioners are the two groups most likely to demand and benefit from such laws.[1]

Recall from Chapter 2 that, prior to 1983, state-level Catholic delegations actively lobbied against all living will proposals. However, in late 1983, following a surge of liberal court decisions, the National Conference of Catholic Bishops endorsed a new lobbying approach: rather than opposing living will laws, Catholic lobbyists would draft and sponsor their own health care proxy and living will laws and attempt to

Research Design and Methods 59

place restrictive provisions in any new laws. Piecewise 1983 Catholic Interaction$_{i,t}$ is calculated using the following formula:

$$(\%Catholic_{i,t} - \%Catholic_{i,1983}) * (0 \text{ if } 1983 \text{ or before}, 1 \text{ if after})$$

The inclusion of this variable allows a piecewise linear regression approach to testing the hypothesis that the influence of the Catholic Church in blocking innovation waned after 1983 (Glick 1992; Glick and Smith 1995).[2]

Legislative Salary$_{i,t}$ denotes the extent to which a state's legislature is professionalized; this variable is operationalized as the mean legislative salary (i.e., the salary for non-leadership positions) plus per diem expenses, expressed for all years in constant 1982 dollars.[3] Electoral Threat$_{i,t}$ measures electoral activity in year t using Mooney and Lee's (1995) state legislative election index; the index increases from 0 by the fraction of each of the following actors up for election in a given year: state House of Representatives, state Senate, and incumbent governor. Both variables are hypothesized to have a negative effect on a state's likelihood of adopting an innovation.

Divided Government$_{i,t}$ is a dummy variable indicating the existence of divided government; it is coded 0 for years when both of a state's legislative chambers and the gubernatorial office are controlled by a single party, 1 otherwise.[4] Interparty Competition$_{i,t}$ is the folded-Ranney party control index; annual figures are obtained by way of a five-year moving average transformation of the scores calculated by Bibby and colleagues (4th through 6th eds. of *Politics in the American States*) for the periods 1989-94, 1981-88 and 1975-80.[5] Positive coefficients are expected for both of these variables.

A facility index is created for each policy (see the following section and Appendix C), with high scores indicating very permissive policies and low scores denoting fairly restrictive ones. Regional Facility$_{i,t-1}$ is the mean facility score of states in the previous year (excluding the state in question) in the one of the nine U.S. Census Bureaus in which a state is found (with nonadopters in the region scored as zero). This is a measure of "neighborhood" influence, similar to that calculated by Mooney and Lee (1995). It is expected to yield a positive coefficient.

Piecewise Regional Facility Interaction$_{i,t-1}$ is a variable that measures the relative impact of regional policy influences on adoption in the years following the adoption of model NCCUSL laws. Recall that the Commissioners approved laws in the early months of 1985, 1989 and 1991 endorsing living will laws, durable power of attorney laws and surrogate decision-making laws, respectively. The following measures are calculated:

1985 (Living Will) Interaction Term =
(Regional Facility$_{t-1}$ - state i's lagged 1985 Facility Score)

1989 (Proxy) Interaction Term =
(Regional Facility$_{t-1}$ - state i's lagged 1989 Facility Score)

1991 (Surrogate) Interaction Term =
(Regional Facility$_{t-1}$ - state i's lagged 1991 Facility Score)

The 1985 term is included in the living will model, the 1989 term in the health care proxy adoption model, and the 1991 term is used in the surrogate models. Each of these measures are used to test the hypothesis that a structural break occurred in the effect of regional facility on adoption following the NCCUSL model adoption. If one of these interaction term's coefficients is statistically significant, this means that the null hypothesis of no structural break can be rejected. The inclusion of these interaction terms affects the substantive interpretation of the regional facility score variables as well. The coefficient of the former term captures the impact of regional policy trends in the year prior to the NCCUSL adoption; in order to gauge the impact of regional trends in the period after the model law intervention, it is necessary to add the regional facility score coefficients and the interaction term coefficients.[6]

<u>Tangential Innovations: Proxy and Surrogate Laws</u>.
The variables listed in the equation at the top of this section are included in all three legislative models. In addition, because the theory predicts that once a core innovation is adopted it facilitates the adoption of tangential innovations, a state's lagged living will facility score is included in the proxy and surrogate models. The coefficients of these variables are

Research Design and Methods

expected to be positive, reflecting the belief that states with permissive living will laws should be more likely to approve tangential innovations than should states with weak or no living will laws in place. I also include a lagged proxy score in the surrogate model for the same reason.

Facility Scores.

For each of the three policy types, I have created a scheme to score policies based on their level of facility (i.e., how easy the policy is to use and how many individuals and circumstances it encompasses). Each of the coding schemes is presented in Appendix C. All three policies are scored on provisions relating to ease of drafting and execution, implementation requirements and scope of coverage, and enforcement procedures. There are seventeen types of provisions that are examined for living will laws, eighteen for health care proxy policies and twelve for surrogate decision making statutes. Points are awarded depending on the content of each provision. For example, a statute that places a time limit on the validity of a living will is awarded no points, while a statute that specifies no such expiration date receives one point; the logic underlying this assignment scheme is that time limitations contribute to the inflexibility of advance directives (i.e., many persons will either forget, or be unable, to re-execute a document after the passage of five or seven years), and that statutes that impose no such limitations allow for greater use of advance directives at the end of life. Similarly, statutes are scored on their construction of "triggering conditions," the diagnostic conditions under which treatment may be withdrawn of withheld. In some states, declarants' nontreatment wishes may only be implemented in the event of a "terminal" illness (i.e., one from which death is expected within a specified time period, with or without the administration of life-sustaining treatment); because such requirements exclude persons in persistent vegetative states and a host of other individuals who may wish to decline "non-terminal" therapies (e.g., dialysis and chemotherapy), these types of provision are awarded zero facility points. A statute that explicitly recognizes conditions such as PVS, irreversible coma, and permanent unconsciousness as valid triggering conditions is awarded three facility points, and a law that allows the draftee of a directive to specify the precise triggering conditions under which she or he would like to decline treatment is awarded five points.

(Note that the triggering provisions are weighted more heavily that are the time limitation provisions; the disproportionate emphasis on the former reflects my belief that expansive triggering conditions contribute more to overall levels of policy facility than do provisions conferring unlimited time validity on documents.) All of the points for a given policy type are added together to create the total facility scores; high scores denote permissive and facilitative policies, while low scores suggest weak and limited laws.

In identifying the various provisions to be included in the facility score indexes, I relied on two sources. First, I reviewed the medical and legal literature on right to die statutes, and I identified the specific types of provisions that consistently emerged as important in the eyes of health care practitioners and legal scholars. Second, Glick and Hays (1991) created a facility index for living will laws, and their codebook proved an invaluable source; indeed, for the living will index, I used fourteen of the same provisions that these authors did (although I assigned different weights to the policy options) and supplemented these fourteen items with three additional ones stressed in the literature. The living will index furnished the foundation for the health care proxy and surrogate decision making indexes, as I only needed to make modest additions and deletions in order to construct these latter two measures. As a validity check, I correlated the first adoption scores calculated by Glick and Hays with my own such scores for the period 1976-1989 (the time period studied by Glick and Hays), and the zero-order correlation coefficient was a robust .96, suggesting that my living will index was measuring the same facility concept assessed in the earlier study.

A facility score was calculated for each state and for each policy. This process is relatively straightforward when calculating a state's original statute. However, most states renovated their laws over time by adding amendments. This meant that facility scores had to be re-calculated each time this occurred. In order to track the changes over time it was necessary to obtain copies of the bills that were passed by state legislatures in each of the years that amendments were approved. This process can prove complicated. Fortunately, the dates of amendments and the legislative citations are included in the legislative history lines of these statutes. While most law libraries, even full depositories, do not retain enrolled

Research Design and Methods

bills for more than a few years, the University of Houston's law library has an extensive (microfilmed) collection of bills approved in the legislative sessions of all fifty states that extends back to 1971. I was able to obtain copies of all right to die statutes and all amendments offered during the study period, and a score was recorded for each state in each year. In order to check for reliability in coding, I enlisted the aid of three undergraduate research assists and two political scientists. Using the coding schemes in Appendix C, these individuals calculated facility scores for each state's first policy (they did not score amendments). When their scores were compared with mine, the results indicated few major deviations. (The coefficient of inter-coder reliability was .94 for living will laws, .93 for health care proxy laws and .89 for surrogate statutes.)

The Decision to Renovate

To account for states' decisions to amend their existing policies, state's were scored on whether or not they renovated their existing policies. Once a state adopted a statute, it was assumed to be at risk for renovation. Renovation was treated as a multiple, recurring event, with renovation being theoretically possible in each year following the first statutory adoption. A simple logistic regression model is estimated to explain variation in the decisions to renovate. The following econometric specification is offered:

$$\text{Renovation}_{i,t} = \Phi(-b_1\%\text{Catholic}_{i,t} + b_2\text{Piecewise 1983 Catholic Interaction}_{i,t} + b_3\text{Senior Citizens}_{i,t} + b_4\text{Physicians}_{i,t} - b_5\text{Legislative Salary}_{i,t} + b_6\text{Interparty Competition}_{i,t} - b_7\text{Electoral Threat}_{i,t} - b_8\text{Divided Government}_{i,t} - b_9\text{Regional Facility}_{i,t-1} - b_{10}\text{Regional Distance}_{i,t-1} + b_{11}\text{Time Since Adoption}_{i,t})$$

Most of the variables are the same as those offered in the EHA models above; two "new" variables warrant discussion, however. First, Regional Distance$_{i,t-1}$ measures how a state's policy compares to those of its neighbors. It is calculated by taking a state's facility score and subtracting it from its regional facility score; the coefficient of this variable should have a negative sign, indicating that the further below regional standards a state's policy falls, the more likely it is to renovate its policy. Time Since Adoption$_{i,t}$ is simply the number of years elapsed since a state adopted its statute; this variable is hypothesized to have a positive impact on likelihood of renovation.

Variation in Policy Content Over Time

In order to determine how date of adoption influences policy content, two simple bivariate OLS regression models are estimated. First, for each policy type, a state's first policy facility score is regressed on date of adoption (date of adoption is calculated by subtracting 100 from the last two digits of the year of adoption). The results are expected to reveal that early innovators produced more restrictive policies than later innovators. However, once the first model is re-estimated using each state's scores at the end of the study period (i.e., the 1994 facility scores), the relationship between date of adoption and policy content should be considerably diminished, evidencing a pattern of reinvention through renovation, whereby early adopters brought their policies into harmony with those of other states.

JUDICIAL INNOVATION AND RENOVATION

The Decision to Adopt

Another event history analysis is used to account for adoption of judicial surrogate policies by state appellate courts. Only those cases that specifically create a policy governing decision making by surrogates (as opposed to refusal by competent patients) constitute judicial innovations. Following the theory outlined in the previous chapter, the following specification is presented:

$$\text{Adoption}_{i,t} = \Phi(-b_1\%\text{Catholic}_{i,t} + b_2\text{Senior Citizens}_{i,t} + b_3\text{Physicians}_{i,t}$$
$$- b_4\text{Elected AG}_{i,t} + b_5\text{Cumulative State Cases}_{i,t-1} + b6\text{IAC}_{i,t}$$
$$- b_7\text{Elected Judges}_{i,t} + b_8\text{Judicial Reputation}_{i,t} + b_9\text{Population}_{i,t-1}$$
$$+ b_{10}\text{Regional Facility}_{i,t-1} - b_{11}\text{Piecewise Regional Facility}$$
$$\text{Interaction}_{i,t-1})$$

Elected $AG_{i,t}$ is a dummy variable coded 1 if a state's Attorney General is elected by the citizens, 0 if this is an appointed office. Elected Judges$_{i,t}$ is also scored 1 if justices on the state's court of last resort must stand for re-election, 0 if they are appointed, selected by the legislature or only stand for a single retention election under a merit plan. Each of these variable is expected to yield a negative coefficient, as the theory predicts that appointed justices should be less likely to approve an innovation than are those who do not suffer prospects of electoral retribution. Cumulative State Cases$_{i,t-1}$ is a count of all previous appellate decisions that address the right to refuse medical treatment previously adopted during the study period; only the "ultimate" opinion is counted for a single state (i.e., a case that reaches an intermediate appellate court and the court of last resort is not counted twice). This variable is expected to have a positive effect on judicial innovation. The presence of an intermediate appellate court is similarly expected to increase prospects for adoption; $IAC_{i,t}$ is a dummy variable coded 1 if a state has at least one level of intermediate appellate courts, 0 if it only has trial courts and a court of last resort. Judicial Reputation$_{i,t}$ is Caldeira's (1988) citation score, which counts the number of times opinions by a state's high court have been cited by courts in other jurisdictions; it is expected to yield a positive coefficient. Population$_{i,t-1}$ is simply the number of residents inside a state's border; it is included as a control variable, as it seems reasonable to suggest that large states will produce more cases and that courts in these states will, therefore, have more opportunities to make policies than will courts in smaller states.

Regional Facility$_{i,t-1}$ is the mean facility score of all other states in a given state's census region. Piecewise Regional Facility Interaction$_{i,t-1}$ is a piecewise interaction term that taps the impact of regional policy trends on likelihood of adoption following the U.S. Supreme Court's 1990 ruling in *Cruzan*; a negative and statistically significant coefficient would be evidence of a structural break that occurred in the post-*Cruzan* years. This term is calculated using the following formula:

(Lagged regional judicial facility score - lagged 1990 mean regional facility score) * (0 if 1990 or before, 1 if after)

If this interaction term's coefficient is statistically significant, the null hypothesis of no structural break can be rejected. As the case with the legislative models, the inclusion of an interaction terms affects the substantive interpretation of the regional facility score variable. The coefficient of the piecewise interaction term captures the impact of regional policy trends in the years prior to the *Cruzan* decision; in order to gauge the impact of regional trends in the period after the U.S. Supreme Court's intervention, it is necessary to sum the regional facility score coefficient and the interaction term coefficient.

<u>Judicial Facility Scores</u>.
The process of constructing a facility index is considerably different when judicial, as opposed to legislative, policies are the topic of consideration. Measurement schemes for the former must be simple and limited to only those particular legal issues that must be addressed by all innovating courts. Legislative indexes, by contrast, may score statutes on all of the provisions that might conceivably be addressed by lawmakers. Legislators have the ability to create a policy designed to anticipate all future contingencies, whereas courts are reactive actors who must tailor their analyses and policy prescriptions to the specific legal questions at bar in a given case. When creating a surrogate decision making policy, there are three issues that must be addressed in an appellate opinion: the legal basis of the right to refuse treatment, the evidentiary standard to be satisfied prior to approving a nontreatment decision, and the inclusion or absence of a requirement of formal judicial involvement in uncontested cases. While there are many additional factors that many courts addressed (e.g., the requirement that a nontreatment decision be confirmed by two independent neurologists or by an institutional ethics committee or state ombudsman for the elderly), not all courts addressed these issues or had the opportunity to rule on such points. Therefore, the judicial facility index is limited to three simple, yet very important, dimensions of decision making by surrogates. The fact that these, and only these, three considerations are consistently discussed in almost all law articles on judicial right to die policies is further support for the validity of the index. Although no intercoder reliability approach was utilized, I was able to compare my coding decisions with articles in legal journals discussing a

Research Design and Methods

particular case and with the state-by-state judicial summaries furnished by Choice in Dying (1997); coding of judicial opinions proved to be relatively straightforward, and there were very few cases on which my interpretation of a decision differed from those of other analysts. (The specific policy options and corresponding points appear in Appendix C, and interstate variation in the substantive legal principles is discussed in detail in Chapter 5.)

The Decision to Renovate

Judicial renovation occurs when a state's appellate court alters the legal or substantive basis of that state's previously adopted judicial surrogate policy. An opinion is scored as a renovation whenever it results in a change to the state's judicial surrogate facility score. Once a given state adopts a judicial innovation, it is considered to be at risk for approving renovations throughout the remainder of the study period. The following specification is suggested:

Renovation$_{i,t}$ = Φ(-b$_1$%Catholic$_{i,t}$ + b$_2$Senior Citizens$_{i,t}$ + b$_3$Physicians$_{i,t}$
- b$_4$Elected AG$_{i,t}$ + b$_5$Cumulative State Cases$_{i,t-1}$ + b6IAC$_{i,t}$
- b$_7$Elected Judges$_{i,t}$ + b$_8$Judicial Reputation$_{i,t}$ + b$_9$Population$_{i,t-1}$
+ b$_{10}$Regional Facility$_{i,t-1}$ - b$_{11}$Regional Distance$_{i,t-1}$
+ b$_{12}$Time Since Adoption$_{i,t}$)

The same variables used in the judicial EHA model are used again, and the last two variables in the equation measure how far a state's extant judicial policy falls above or below the policies in neighboring states (Regional Distance$_{i,t-1}$) and the length of time that has elapsed since the adoption of a state's first policy (Time Since Adoption$_{i,t}$).

Variation in Policy Content Over Time

In order to determine how date of adoption influences policy content, two simple bivariate ordered probit models are estimated. A state's first judicial policy facility score is regressed on date of adoption (date of adoption is calculated by subtracting 100 from the last two digits of the year of adoption). The results are expected to reveal that early judicial innovators produced more restrictive policies than did later adopting tribunals. However, once the first model is re-estimated using each state's scores at the end of the study period (i.e., the 1994 judicial facility scores), the relationship between date of adoption and policy content should be attenuated, suggesting a pattern of reinvention through renovation, whereby early adopters brought their policies into harmony with those of the courts in other states.

Case Studies

In order to supplement the quantitative models estimated above, detailed cases studies of judicial policy making in six states are presented in Chapter 5. These states were selected because they are illustrative of the varied approaches used by appellate courts in different states and because they help the reader gain a better understanding of the specific legal principles (and resulting policy implications) invoked by state justices. In selecting the states to be included in this section, I was not guided by a concern for obtaining a representative sample of all states that produced appellate policies. (Such an approach would prove difficult, given the fact that many states produced only one policy, whereas only a handful of states extensively refined their judicial policies.) Rather, I selected five states from the same geographic region (the northwest); courts in each of these states adopted and reinvented judicial surrogate policies. Justices on the high courts of each of these states were clearly cognizant of the legal developments that were afoot in neighboring jurisdictions. Although geographically proximate to one another, there is tremendous institutional variation in the structure of these state court systems. The courts of last resort in Massachusetts and Maine are reputed as highly professionalized, with judicial citation scores of 49 and 47, respectively (Caldeira 1988).[7] Tribunals in New York (36) and New Jersey (36) have moderate scores, and Connecticut's judiciary is one of the least reputed in the nation (18). In short, I chose five states from the same part of the country, but which have varied types of judiciaries which produced different right to die policy outcomes. By way of contrast, I also include Minnesota as an example of a state which produced only one single, yet highly facilitative, judicial innovation. Taken together, the approaches approved by the courts in these six states cover the full range of judicial policies approved by the twenty-three states whose appellate courts produced surrogate decision-making policies.

INTEGRATED MODELS

Judicial Influences on Legislative Adoption and Renovation

Each of the three legislative EHA models is re-estimated, with the cumulative intrastate cases, regional judicial facility score, and current state judicial facility scores included in the right hand side of the equations. To combat multicollinearity and to allow for a more parsimonious presentation of results, the predicted probabilities generated in the first legislative models are substituted for all of the substantive regressors included in the original runs. This exact same approach is used in re-estimating the legislative renovation models. The econometric specifications are presented below.

Leg. Adoption$_{i,t}$ =Φ(+b$_1$Predicted Probabilites$_{i,t}$ - b$_2$Cumulative State Cases$_{i,t-1}$ - b$_3$Regional Judicial Facility$_{i,t-1}$ - b$_4$ Judicial Facility$_{i,t-1}$)

Leg. Renovation$_{i,t}$ =Φ(+b$_1$Predicted Probabilites$_{i,t}$ - b$_2$Cumulative State Cases$_{i,t-1}$ - b$_3$Regional Judicial Facility$_{i,t-1}$ - b$_4$Judicial Facility$_{i,t-1}$)

Note that the coefficients of all the substantive regressors are hypothesized to be negative in direction, reflecting the theoretical assumptions made in the previous chapter: judicial innovation (or the possibility of judicial innovation) deters legislative innovation.

Legislative Influences on Judicial Adoption and Renovation

The judicial EHA model is estimated in a similar fashion, with a state's lagged legislative facility score, lagged regional legislative facility score, and predicted probabilities from the first estimation included as regressors. An identical approach is used to estimate the likelihood of renovation by state judiciaries. The econometric specifications are:

Jud. Adoption$_{i,t}$ = Φ(+b$_1$Predicted Probabilites$_{i,t}$ + b$_2$Regional Leg. Facility$_{i,t-1}$ + b$_3$ Leg. Facility$_{i,t-1}$)

Jud. Renovation$_{i,t}$ = Φ(+b$_1$Predicted Probabilites$_{i,t}$ + b$_2$Regional Leg. Facility$_{i,t-1}$ + b$_3$ Leg. Facility$_{i,t-1}$)

Consistent with the previously discussed hypothesis that legislative innovation and reinvention should fuel opportunities for judicial innovation and reinvention, the coefficients of each of the two substative regressors are hypothesized to be positive.

Case Studies

In order to supplement the results from the above models and to compensate for the fact that the statistical analyses may mask the many varied ways in which courts and legislatures may interact, six case studies are presented in Chapter 6. The selection of these six states reflects a number of considerations. First, both the courts and legislatures in these states were active in producing right to die policies, and there is clear evidence of judicial-legislative interaction in all six states. Additionally, there are three primary types of patterns that emerged in the fifty states: judicial dominance, legislative dominance, and mutual reinforcement. I selected two states that fit each of the above classifications. In pairing these states, I attempted to make sure that the states were matched or "mismatched" on key institutional variables. Table 3.1 reports each state's score on Caldeira's (1988) judicial reputation measure and each state's mean legislative salary for the study period (reported in 1982 constant dollars).

Indiana and Maryland both evidenced patterns of judicial leadership followed by legislative adoptions that did not challenge or supplant the extant judicial policies; both of these states have modestly professionalized legislatures, yet Maryland has a highly reputed state judiciary, while Indiana's Supreme Court rates low on this measure. By holding these states constant on the legislative dimension, it is possible to see how two very different state courts established themselves as policy leaders at the intrastate-level. In Ohio and Missouri, legislative innovation preceded judicial policymaking, and state courts adopted a posture of deference to legislative intent; both of these states rate moderately high in terms of judicial reputation, but Ohio's General Assembly is more professionalized than Missouri's. Illinois and Washington are included because they were host to a pattern of "mutually reinforcing innovation," whereby courts and legislatures reinforced one another in the adoption and reinvention process. Washington has one of the most prestigious court systems in the nation, but a citizen legislature; Illinois, by contrast, has a professionalized legislature but only a moderately-reputed judiciary.

The policy making process in each of these states is described in detail in Chapter 6, and the varied patterns are compared and contrasted. This qualitative approach provides a nice complement to the quantitative models estimated previously in that chapter.

Table 3.1
States Included in Judicial-Legislative Case Studies

State	Dominant Institution	Judicial Reputation	Legislative Salary
Indiana	Courts	Low (27)	$16,614
Maryland	Courts	High (47)	$23,390
Missouri	Legislature	Moderately High (39)	$19,546
Ohio	Legislature	Moderately High (44)	$26,328
Illinois	Neither	Moderate (41)	$43,165
Washington	Neither	High (49)	$16,677

The first three chapters have outlined the research questions, theory and research design, and the following four chapters report the results from the empirical investigations. First, however, it is necessary to discuss the unique contribution this research makes to the previous studies on right to die policy making in the American states.

Contribution to Previous Research

Research on right to die innovation has received a good deal of attention in recent years. In his seminal work on the topic, Glick (1992) utilizes agenda setting and innovation frameworks to trace the origins of policymaking in the American states; he identifies a number of key influences on the decisions of state legislatures to adopt living will laws, documents variation in the growing frequency of judicial policy innovations, and presents several case studies which suggest the importance of the legislative-judicial nexus in policy making in the U.S. federal system. Glick and Hays (1991) identify the importance of policy reinvention and renovation, and their analysis of living will statutes and amendments demonstrates the crucial link between date of adoption and the content of public policies. Hays and Glick (1997) further contribute to this literature by performing an event history analysis of living will adoptions, and they identify a number of important correlates of policy adoption.

The research in this book owes a large theoretical and conceptual debt to the work of these scholars. In the pages that follow, I build upon their efforts by extending research on right to die policymaking to new types of policies and to later periods in time. It should be stressed that my research is not a simple replication of Hays and Glick's earlier models. Rather, I offer a number of original theoretical propositions and methodological techniques that are not utilized in the previous research.

My research most closely parallels that of Glick and Hays in Chapter 4, which examines the determinants of legislative innovation and renovation. Like Glick and Hays (1997), I perform an event history analysis of the determinant of living will adoptions; however, in addition to expanding the time period under study (and thereby allowing for many new policy adoptions), I also utilize seven different independent variables and a different theoretical framework, central to which are horizontal variables (e.g., annual regional policy trends and NCCUSL adoptions). In addition to examining living wills, I also analyze two other types of right to die policies (i.e., "tangential innovations") that have received scant attention in the empirical literature: health care proxy laws and surrogate decision making statutes. When attempting to account for the adoption

Research Design and Methods

patterns of these later innovations, I explore the effect of prior adoptions and renovations (e.g., living wills) on the tangential policies; policy innovation and reinvention is thus conceptualized as a continuous cycle. And, in addition to allowing for reinvention through renovation by comparing the content of first and last adoptions, as Glick and Hays (1991) have done, I also estimate models that attempt to account for variation in the rate of policy renovations.

Glick (1992, 1994) details numerous ways in which courts made policy on the right to die. I attempt to expand on his efforts by offering and estimating an empirical model of judicial innovation. My specification contains a number of variables and factors not previously used in any published study of judicial innovation; moreover, I also provide a model that attempts to account for variation in the decisions by state judiciaries to modify and alter previous judicial policies.

My empirical investigation concludes with an analysis of the impact of legislative innovation on judicial innovation, and vice versa. Where Glick (1992) and Hays and Glick (1997) estimate the impact of increasing litigation on the likelihood of a state adopting a living will innovation, I explore the impact of the content of judicial innovations on the likelihood of legislative adoption, and I investigate the reverse process as well. I also offer a number of original case studies to further "flush out" the dynamics of legislative-judicial interaction in the policy making process in the American states.

The next chapter reports the results from the models of legislative adoption and renovation. Like previous scholars, I find that certain political variables affect policy production on the right to die. However, I also find that numerous "new" variables have important effects, with patterns of adoption and influence varying across policy types.

CHAPTER 4
Legislative Innovation and Reinvention

THE ADVENT OF LEGISLATIVE POLICY-MAKING

Although the first refusal of treatment statute in the United States was not approved until 1976, efforts to promote right to die laws extend back at least a full century (Glick 1992, 53-54). The issue, however, gained greater recognition in the United States in the post-war era, a period in which advances in medical technology were dramatically increasing the ability of medical practitioners to extend life and prolong the dying process. Major antecedents to the first legislative policies include a papal declaration; the formation of the Euthanasia Educational Council and similar groups intent on promoting refusal of treatment; the creation of the Hastings Center and the Kennedy Institute on Ethics (research centers designed to consider frontier issues in biomedical ethics); hearings by the U.S. Senate Committee on Aging; numerous proposals and declarations issued by prestigious organizations such as the Harvard Medical School, the American Medical Association, and the American Hospital Association (Glick 1992, 67).

The issue gained increased attention in the professional medical agenda and soon came to occupy a prominent place on the American mass agenda. By 1967, policy proponents were drafting right to die proposals and lobbying state legislative bodies (Glick 1992, 64-74). It was not until 1976, however, that the first legislative right to die policy was enacted.

The California Natural Death Act: The Core Innovation

Following several years of failed attempts at policy passage, the California General Assembly adopted the nation's core policy innovation in 1976 (California Natural Death Act, California Health and Safety Code §§7185 to 7194.5). This landmark living will law precipitated an onslaught of similar proposals before legislatures in nearly all fifty states.

Like most early innovations, the California law met with tremendous opposition, and policy proponents (particularly the California Catholic Conference) were granted considerable concessions in exchange for their "neutrality" on the issue. (For a detailed analysis of the events leading to the drafting and adoption of this law, see Glick 1992, pp. 93-104.) The 1976 policy was extremely limited in scope. First, a valid living will could only be executed fourteen days after two physicians concurred on a diagnosis of "terminal" illness; excluded from the statute's definition of "terminal" were persistent vegetative states and irreversible comas. Directives were not valid unless witnessed by at least two individuals who were unrelated to the declarant and not affiliated with any medical facility or company; in addition, in order for the document to be executed in a nursing home setting (i.e., where most individuals are diagnosed as dying), a state ombudsman for the elderly was required to verify that the declarant was of sound mind and operating free from coercion. Directives had to follow the exact format specified by the statute; declarants were not allowed to specify personal instructions or anticipate possible contingencies/vagaries. Once executed pursuant to these requirements, a living will was valid for only a five year period. The statute invalidated directives in the event of pregnancy, did not recognize out-of-state declarations, and contained no "comply or transfer" provision. It was silent on the use of artificial nutrition and hydration.

While California's living will was the first policy in the nation, it was also the most restrictive. Despite repeated attempts to bring the statute in to line with the more facilitative policies in other states and with the NCCUSL's Model Living Will (the NCCUSL resolution is discussed in greater detail later in the chapter), legislative reinvention proved difficult. In 1988, both chambers of the legislature passed amendments that would have substantially liberalized the policy; however, the bill was vetoed by

Legislative Innovation and Reinvention

conservative Governor George Deukmejian, and there was insufficient support to obtain the supermajority of votes needed for an override. It was not until 1991 that the statute was successfully reinvented; in that year the policy was brought into harmony with the most of the guidelines adopted by the NCCUSL.

The Three Policy Types: Chapter Overview

California's 1976 law constituted the core right to die policy innovation. The forty-six states which adopted living will policies after California produced subsequent innovations. The theory developed in Chapter 2 and operationalized in Chapter 3 suggests that a number of institutional, political and horizontal variables accounted for the diffusion of these living will policies; accordingly, an event history model is estimated and discussed in the next section. Because the policy process rarely ends with the adoption of a new law, as evidenced by the repeated efforts of California lawmakers to amend the state's living will law, the determinants and extent of "reinvention through renovation" are also analyzed in several additional models in the living will section.

Beginning in the early 1980s, many states began supplementing their living will policies with new policy instruments designed to overcome some of the limitations inherent in the former policy. Health care proxy laws, a tangential innovation, created a means through which individuals could appoint an "agent" to make medical decisions in the event of future incompetency or unconsciousness. California continued in its innovative role in 1983 when it adopted a durable power of attorney for health care law. (Only one state, Delaware, had previously allowed individuals to name a proxy; California was the first to specify a power of attorney format.) The diffusion and renovation of these subsequent innovations are examined in the next portion of the Chapter, and the results from the proxy models are compared and contrasted with their living will predecessors.

Advance directives do little to advance the rights of persons who have not executed these documents, and a number of states (although not California) have gradually approved the use of a third type of policy to allow the family members of affected patients to make decisions about (non)treatment issues. Surrogate decision-making statutes, another tangential innovation, are analyzed in the fourth section of the chapter. As the living will was the first refusal of treatment law to be produced in the U.S., the following section begins with a discussion of the diffusion of this innovation.

LIVING WILL LAWS

Policy Diffusion

Table 4.1 displays the date when each state adopted its first living will law. The distribution curves (see Figure 4.1) reveal that, in 1977, seven states followed closely on California's heels in adopting policies (four of the states neighbored California); this mini-surge was followed by a five year lull, during which time only five new statutes were passed. 1983 and 1984 mark a period of heightened activity (or "take-off point"), with adoptions by nine states. 1985, the year in which the NCCUSL approved and released its model living will law, was a watershed year; thirteen state legislatures adopted policies. This burst is followed by a gradual "mopping up" of the twelve laggard adopters from 1986-1992. (To date, Massachusetts, Michigan and New York have not adopted living will statutes.) When plotted cumulatively, the diffusion curve closely approximates the "S"-shape of the cumulative normal distribution function, fitting the social learning theory posited by Rogers (1962). In order to account for the variation in the dates of adoption, the results of an event history analysis are discussed in the following section.

Table 4.1
Dates of Adoption of Living Will Laws

Year	States
76	CA
77	AR, ID, NV, NM, NC, OR, TX
78	
79	KS, WA
80	
81	AL
82	DE, VT
83	IL, VA, WI
84	FL, GA, LA, MS, WV, WY
85	AZ, CO, CT, IN, IA, ME, MD, MO, MT, NH, OK, TN, UT
86	AK, HI, SC
87	
88	
89	MN, ND
90	KY
91	NJ, OH, RI, SD
92	NE, PA
93	
94	

Figure 4.1
Adoption of Living Will Laws

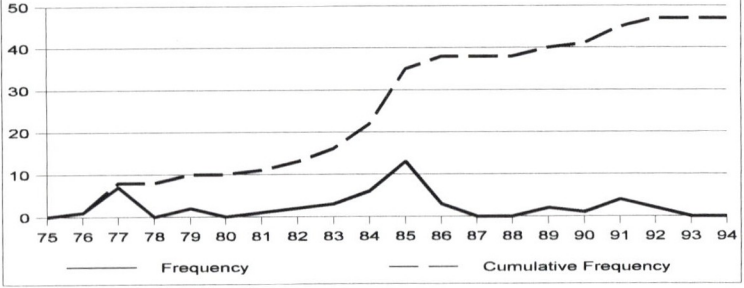

Table 4.2
Annual Hazard Rates for Adoption of Living Will Laws

Year	Risk Set[a]	Adoptions	Hazard[b]
1976	49	1	.0204
1977	48	7	.1458
1978	41	0	.0000
1979	41	2	.0488
1980	39	0	.0000
1981	39	1	.0256
1982	38	2	.0526
1983	36	3	.0833
1984	33	6	.1818
1985	27	13	.4815
1986	14	3	.2143
1987	11	0	.0000
1988	11	0	.0000
1989	11	2	.1818
1990	9	1	.1111
1991	8	4	.5000
1992	4	1	.2500
1993	3	0	.0000
1994	3	0	.0000

[a] Risk Set is the total number of states (excluding Nebraska) that have not previously adopted a living will law.
[b] Hazard Rate = Adoptions/Risk Set.

Table 4.3
Event History Analysis of the Determinants of Living Will Adoptions

Variable	MLE (Wald)	Impact[a]
% Catholic	-3.8048** (4.2967)	-.1289
Piecewise 1983 % Cath int.[b]	-2.6956 (.0513)	-.0068
Divided Government	-.6484 (2.2597)	-.0065[c]
Physicians	.8924* (3.1185)	.1114
Electoral Threat Index	-.5278*** (8.6858)	-.1422
Interparty Competition	3.3125 (2.1010)	.0863
Legislative Salary	-.000030* (3.4700)	-.1041
Senior Citizens	.0904 (1.2415)	.0534
Mean Regional Facil. Score$_{t-1}$	.1210*** (8.5413)	.2645
Piecewise 1985 Facility Int.[d]	-.1096 (2.0601)	-.1281
Constant	-6.1847*** (7.4597)	

Model χ^2 (10 d.f.) = 38.142***
Initial log likelihood = -150.166   Final log likelihood = -131.095

Number of Cases = 466; Cases Scored as Adoption = 46 (9.9%)
Maximum likelihood estimation of a logit model of the probability of a state adopting a living will law in a given year.
[a] Impact is the change in the predicted probability of adoption after changing the independent variable from one standard deviation below its mean to one standard deviation above its mean, holding all other continuous independent variables at their means and the divided government variable at 0.
[b] (Current % Catholic score - 1983 % Catholic score) * (0 if 1983 or before, 1 if after).
[c] Change in predicted probability after switching the divided government dummy variables's score from 0 (unified control) to 1 (divided control).
[d] (Lagged regional facility score - lagged 1985 score) * (0 if 1985 or before, 1 if after).
* Significant at .10 α-level in a two-tailed test; **.05; ***.01.

Event History Analysis: Likelihood of Adoption[1]

Table 4.2 displays the annual hazard rates for the adoption of living will laws, and Table 4.3 reports the results from the logistic regression analysis. As indicated in the latter table, the overall model is statistically significant at better that 99.9% confidence, and five of the substantive coefficients are significant at conventional levels of inference. Institutional, political and horizontal variables all affected the likelihood of adoption in a manner consistent with theoretical expectations.

<u>Degree of Controversy: Opposition, Support, and Interest Aggregation</u>. The percent Catholic variable captures the effect of the size of a state's Catholic population prior to, and including, 1983. The coefficient is negative and statistically significant, and the impact score (which reflects a 12.89% decrease in predicted probability of adoption after changing the variable from one standard deviation below its mean to one standard deviation above its mean, holding all other independent variables at their means) reflects the strength of the Catholic lobby and State Catholic Conferences in preventing innovation during this early period.

Recall from Chapter 2 that, prior to 1983, state-level Catholic delegations actively lobbied against all living will proposals. However, in late 1983, following a surge of liberal court decisions, the National Conference of Catholic Bishops endorsed a new lobbying approach: rather than opposing living will laws, Catholic lobbyists would draft and sponsor their own health care proxy and living will laws and attempt to place restrictive prohibitions in any new laws. The results of the analysis, as evidenced by the negative and statistically insignificant coefficient of the piecewise interaction term, indicate, however, that there was no structural break occurring in 1983 (varying the cutpoint year by plus and minus one does not substantially alter the results). Rather, the size of a state's Catholic population continued to be inversely related to the adoption of living will laws throughout the diffusion period.

When compared to the impact of the Catholic lobby, other organized interests are comparatively weak. Individual physicians were instrumental in drafting and supporting proposals in some states (Glick 1992), but the AMA and other organized medical groups did not aggressively pursue a coordinated push for legislation. (As discussed in Chapter 5, medical groups generally approved of policies that promoted provider discretion in the treatment setting, while opposing complicated regulatory frameworks that erected procedural hurdles.) The number of physicians in a state, a rough proxy of the strength of the state's medical lobby, is positively related to innovation. A one standard deviation shift in this variables's distribution results in, *ceteris paribus*, an 11% increase in the likelihood of adopting a living will law.

Senior citizens groups do not appear to have played a major role in promoting the right to die, despite the fact that most potential "consumers" of living wills are over the age of fifty-five. The coefficient for this variable, while positive, is statistically insignificant, perhaps reflecting the ambivalence of AARP and other organized groups representing aging populations. (Indeed, as discussed in the *amicus* section of the next chapter, seniors groups often maintained a low profile on this controversial issue, occasionally advocating precautionary policy measures designed to avoid elder abuse and coercion at the end of life.)

Institutional Determinants: Legislative Professionalism.
As hypothesized, legislative professionalism is inversely related to probability of adoption. The negative and statistically significant coefficient for the salary variable marshals support for the hypothesis that citizen-legislators are less risk-averse than their full-time counterparts in more professionalized states. A perusal of Table 4.1 reveals that, although highly professionalized California enacted the core innovation in 1976, most of the first subsequent innovations in 1977 were undertaken by states not typically reputed as "leaders" in the innovation literature (e.g., Arkansas, Idaho, Nevada, New Mexico, North Carolina, and Texas). Indeed, the impact score of -.1041 indicates that, all things being equal, a one standard deviation shift in legislative professionalism results in a 10.41% decrease in probability of adoption.

Political Determinants.
By far the most important political variable is the electoral threat index. The negative coefficient indicates that innovation was significantly less likely in periods when large numbers of lawmakers were up for re-

election. The impact score indicates that, holding all other factors constant, the probability of adoption is 14.22% percent lower during periods when two-thirds of elected offices were being contested than it is in years when no officials had to run for re-election. The adoption of a right to die law always has the potential to awaken issue publics, and lawmakers clearly have a preference for taking action during periods in which the effects of negative feedback can be minimized.

The other two political variables, interparty competition and divided government, while yielding coefficients in the hypothesized directions, did not prove to be as important as the threat of electoral retribution. Interparty competition is positively related to adoption, while innovation appears less likely in periods of divided government; however, neither of these coefficients is statistically significant.

Horizontal Influences.
The regional influence hypothesis receives the greatest support from the results of the event history analysis. The adoption of permissive living will policies by neighboring states clearly increases the pressure on nonadopters to innovate. In the pre-1986 period, all other things being equal, a shift of 1 standard deviation in the previous year's regional facility score increased the probability of adoption by 26.45 percent. Moreover, this variable remains important even after the NCCUSL adopted its model living will law. The fact that the piecewise interaction term is statistically insignificant means that we cannot reject the null hypothesis that no structural break occurred following the model law's publication.[2] Regional patterns were a pervasive force throughout the diffusion cycle.

It should also be noted that the NCCUSL's resolution justified and facilitated policy adoption for many states. When the EHA model was re-estimated to include a dummy variable scored 1 if 1985 or after, 0 if 1984 or earlier, the results indicated that probability of adoption increased by 28.85 percent after the draft law was promulgated (due to multicollinearity the regional score and interaction variables had to be excluded from this analysis).

Horizontal factors clearly claimed the lion's share of explanatory power in the above analysis. However, the adoption of a living will policy

Legislative Innovation and Reinvention

marked only the beginning of policy making on the right to die. Many states amended their initial policies in subsequent years in response to regional trends, political pressures and policy considerations. These renovation efforts are discussed in the following section.

Reinvention Through Renovation

Table 4.4 shows how each state's living will policy changed over time. A comparison of the mean score for first policies (18.11 points) with mean 1994 score (23.74 points) is telling evidence of facilitative reinvention through renovation. Indeed, 33 states increased their scores over time, with an overall mean increase of 5.65 points. Only 14 states chose not to revise their policies following adoption; 19 states renovated only once, while 11 states reinvented twice, and 3 states amended their policies in 3 separate years. In order to explain why some states renovated while others did not, the results of a logistic regression model are presented next.

<u>Logistic Regression Analysis: Likelihood of Renovation.</u>
Table 4.5 reports the MLE coefficients from an analysis of whether or not a state renovated its policy once it had adopted an innovation. The model is statistically significant at better than 99.9% confidence, and the results indicate that most of the factors that accounted for the variation in the diffusion of first innovations do not emerge as major determinants of renovation. In fact, only two variables are statistically significant and in the hypothesized direction; one is a "new" variable, and the other was insignificant in the EHA.

While the percentage Catholic population in the pre-1984 years did not have a major impact on reinvention, this variable is extremely important in the years following the 1983 strategy adoption of the National Conference of Catholic Bishops. The negative and statistically significant coefficient of the piecewise interaction term indicates that a structural break occurred, with the Catholic lobby exerting a good deal of influence in the post-1983 period. When this result is considered in tandem with the EHA results, an interesting caveat is suggested: not only were the state Catholic conferences successful at stalling or blocking the adoption of living will policies, they were also effective at precluding the adoption of facilitative amendments to the original policies. The strategy of supporting limited policies was coupled with a staunch opposition to policy liberalization.

The size of state's Catholic population notwithstanding, regional pressures were clearly the most important determinants of renovation. The lagged regional distance score indicates that the further a state's facility score was below the regional mean, the more likely the state was to amend its policy; states with below average scores felt pressure to renovate, presumably in order to bring their policy into harmony with regional trends, while states with scores above average were less likely to reinvent. All else held constant, a one standard deviation increase in a state's regional facility score in a given year resulted in an increased probability of adoption in the following year of 33.3%.

Table 4.4
Initial and Amended Living Will Facility Scores

State	Adopt Year	First Score	Final Score	Gain	# of Amds.
AL	1981	20	20	0	0
AK	1986	25	25	0	0
AZ	1985	17	27	+10	2
AR	1977	17	26	+9	1
CA	1976	10	26	+16	1
CO	1985	14	20	+6	1
CT	1985	10	22	+12	1
DE	1982	15	16	+1	1
FL	1984	17	26	+9	2
GA	1984	12	25	+13	3
HI	1986	16	25	+9	1
ID	1977	12	22	+10	2
IL	1983	14	25	+11	1
IN	1985	16	21	+5	1
IA	1985	16	24	+8	1
KS	1979	21	21	0	0
KY	1990	15	24	+9	1
LA	1984	20	27	+7	2
ME	1985	22	31	+9	2
MD	1985	18	28	+10	1

Table 4.4 (continued)
Initial and Amended Living Will Facility Scores

State	Adopt Year	First Score	Final Score	Gain	# of Amds.
MN	1989	26	26	0	0
MS	1984	24	24	0	0
MO	1985	19	19	0	0
MT	1985	22	22	0	0
NE	1992	24	24	0	0
NV	1977	17	26	+9	1
NH	1985	12	22	+10	2
NJ	1991	29	29	0	0
NM	1977	16	20	+4	1
NC	1977	14	19	+5	1
ND	1989	17	22	+5	1
OH	1991	23	23	0	0
OK	1985	14	27	+13	3
OR	1977	12	23	+11	2
PA	1992	26	26	0	0
RI	1991	25	25	0	0
SC	1986	13	20	+7	2
SD	1991	25	25	0	0
TN	1985	25	29	+4	1
TX	1977	13	20	+7	3
UT	1985	22	26	+4	1
VT	1982	18	18	0	0
VA	1983	22	28	+6	2
WA	1979	19	24	+5	1
WV	1984	20	22	+2	1
WI	1983	14	25	+11	2
WY	1984	17	25	+8	2

First Score: $\mu = 18.11$ $\sigma = 4.75$
Final Score: $\mu = 23.74$ $\sigma = 3.23$
Gain Score: $\mu = +5.65$ $\sigma = 4.65$

Table 4.5
Determinants of Living Will Renovations

Variable	MLE (Wald)	Impact[a]
% Catholic	-.0721	-.0022
	(.0013)	
Piecewise 1983 % Cath int.[b]	-27.2325***	-.0528
	(10.214)	
Divided Government	-.4353	-.0439[c]
	(1.4688)	
Physicians	-.5389	-.0616
	(1.1171)	
Electoral Threat Index	-.2604*	-.0614
	(3.1247)	
Interparty Competition	.2692	.0073
	(.0209)	
Legislative Salary	.0000159	.0504
	(.9065)	
Senior Citizens	.0042	.0144
	(.0029)	
Distance From Region. Score$_{t-1}$[d]	-.1501***	-.3330
	(22.3106)	
Years Since First Adoption	-.0305	-.0097
	(.5850)	
Constant	-.8081	
	(.1463)	

Model χ^2 (10 d.f.) = 34.854***
Initial log likelihood = -158.824   Final log likelihood = -141.397
Number of Cases = 466; Cases Scored as Renovation = 50 (10.7%)

Maximum likelihood estimation of a logit model of the probability of a state amending an extant living will law in a given year.
[a] Impact is the change in the predicted probability of renovation after changing the variable from 1 s.d. below its mean to 1 s.d. above its mean, holding all other continuous variables at their means and the divided government dummy variable at 0.
[b] (Current % Catholic score - 1983 % Catholic score) * (0 if 1983 or before, 1 if after).
[c] Change in predicted probability after switching divided government from 0 (unified control) to 1 (divided control).
[d] State's lagged facility score - lagged regional facility score.
* Significant at .10 α-level in a two-tailed test; **.05; ***.01.

Renovation: Increased Facility Over Time.

Renovation at the intrastate level was an exclusively facilitative process; without exception, every state to amend its policy did so in a manner that resulted in liberalizing its living will policy. Mean scores and standard deviations are reported for each year in the diffusion period (see Table 4.6) and are plotted in Figure 4.2. Facility scores increased steadily over time, but reinvention, as evidenced by the rising and falling standard deviation curve, was uneven. Disparity in policy content increased through the 1980s, with laws becoming slightly more homogeneous in the early 1990s.

The results from the regression of living will facility scores on date of adoption are reported in Table 4.7. In keeping with expectations, date of adoption is inversely related to policy liberalism. Later adopters enacted more permissive first policies than did early innovators. This simple bivariate model explains nearly 33% of the variation in facility scores. However, when the model is re-estimated using each state's 1994 (renovated) scores, the impact of date of adoption decreases considerably. While the coefficient is still negative, its diminished magnitude suggests that early innovators substantially reinvented their policies over time.

With a standard deviation of 3.23 points in 1994 (refer to Table 4.6), it is clear that living will laws differ across states on a number of key dimensions. States have enacted markedly different rules governing drafting and execution requirements, implementation procedures and scope of coverage, and enforcement mechanisms. Figures 4.3 through 4.10 detail variation in statutory provisions. A cursory comparison of first and final policies reveals that states eventually abandoned some of their most restrictive requirements, but have retained additional provisions that inhibit execution and limit individual choice. Three specific aspects of living will laws are discussed in the next section.

Table 4.6
Living Will Facility Scores: 1976-1994

Year	N	μ	σ
1976	1	10.00	--
1977	8	13.88	2.59
1978	8	13.88	2.59
1979	10	15.50	3.44
1980	10	15.50	3.44
1981	11	15.91	3.53
1982	13	16.00	3.29
1983	16	16.38	3.28
1984	22	16.91	3.29
1985	35	17.20	3.71
1986	38	17.34	3.75
1987	38	17.89	4.11
1988	38	18.16	4.06
1989	40	18.67	4.28
1990	41	18.95	4.34
1991	45	21.82	4.11
1992	47	22.81	3.93
1993	47	23.40	3.60
1994	47	23.74	3.23

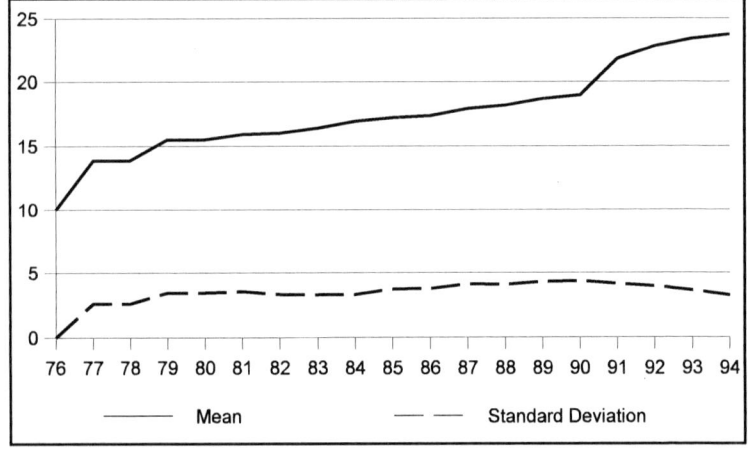

Figure 4.2
Living Will Facility Scores: 1976-1994

Table 4.7
OLS Regression of Living Will Facility Scores on Date of Adoption

Model 1: Initial Adoption		Model 2: 1994 (Reinvented) Score	
Variable	**Coefficient (t-ratio)**	**Variable**	**Coefficient (t-ratio)**
Adoption Date	-.6084*** (-4.655)	Adoption Date	-.1947* (-1.866)
$R^2 = .325$		$R^2 = .072$	

* Significant at .10 α-level in a two-tailed test; ***.001.
(constants not reported)

Drafting and Execution Requirements.
The first living will policies contained a number of rules that made advance directives difficult to complete for the lay person, particularly in the clinical setting. For example, the California core innovation and four of the 1977 laws contained re-execution requirements; essentially this meant that a living will could be drafted at any time, but had to be re-executed (i.e., re-drafted and certified) once a patient was diagnosed as terminally ill. Such a procedural hurdle meant that many patients, particularly those who either became demented in long-term geriatric health care facilities or who were rendered incompetent as the result of accident or sudden onset of illness, would be unable to avail themselves of the living will option.

The difficulties of the re-execution requirements were undoubtedly compounded by their companion provision: the expiration date. Seven of the early adopters placed either five or seven year limits on the length of time for which a living will was valid, after which time the directive had to be redrafted or recertified. These time limits had the potential to prove particularly troublesome for patients in nursing homes. These two requirements were clearly granted as concessions to right-to-die opponents in the 1970s; however, once the early adopters "broke the ice," later innovators abandoned these particularly restrictive requirements. The fact that no state to adopt a policy after 1982 included a re-execution or expiration rule is telling; moreover, all seven states that adopted either or both of these policies approved amendments in the 1980s or 1990s that eliminated these restrictions.

The amount of discretion afforded to living will declarants also varied considerably across states (see Figure 4.3). States that have opted for the "inflexible" format provide a sample document in the text of their statutes and require that all declarants use this exact form, with no additions or deletions permitted. An option that (at least implicitly) grants greater latitude to individuals in articulating their preferences is the "semi-flexible" format; in this instance the enabling statute does not contain language precluding the use of personalized instructions, nor does it explicitly authorize such addendums to the statutory document. A "personalized" format may utilize one of several approaches designed to allow individuals to custom tailor their directive in accordance with their personal wishes; some living will forms use "checklists" of treatment options and triggering conditions, while others include a space in the sample document for personal directions, and other statutes prescribe no sample form at all, requiring individuals to create their own documents. As figure 4.3 shows, of the eight states to originally use the inflexible format, only one (Ohio) has retained it; the vast majority of states (thirty-eight) have moved to the personalized model.

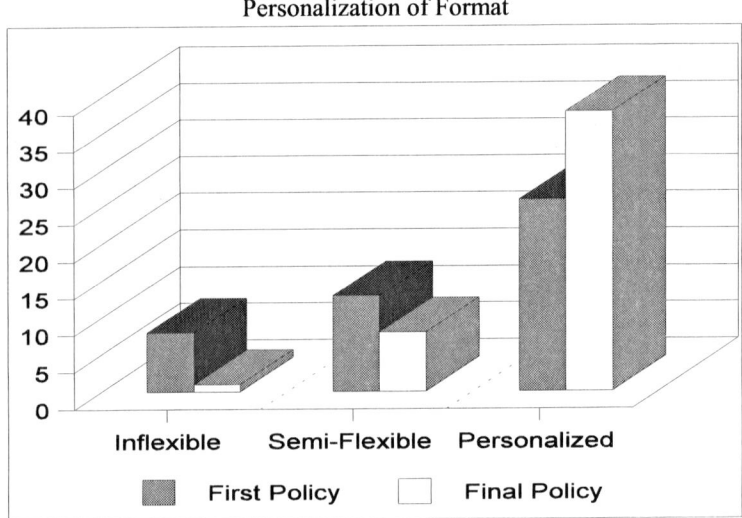

Figure 4.3
Personalization of Format

Also of concern to right-to-die advocates are the witnessing requirements that apply to living wills. As Figure 4.4 indicates, some states require or have required that directives be "officiated" (e.g., prepared by a probate attorney; notarized; certified by a court official; or, in nursing homes, authorized by a state official, such as an ombudsman for the elderly). Such procedural safeguards, no matter how well-intentioned, decrease the ability or willingness of individuals to prepare living wills; of the fifteen states to require such witnessing, five have renovated their policies to allow for less rigorous certification. Sixteen states have settled on "institutional" rules that preclude caregivers, health care staff, insurance representatives and a declarant's fellow patients from witnessing the signing of a directive. Most states now place "standard" probate restrictions on witnessing (e.g., banning a patient's family members and estate beneficiaries from the process), but Mississippi requires no witnessing when a document is handwritten and signed by a declarant.

Figure 4.4
Witnessing Requirements

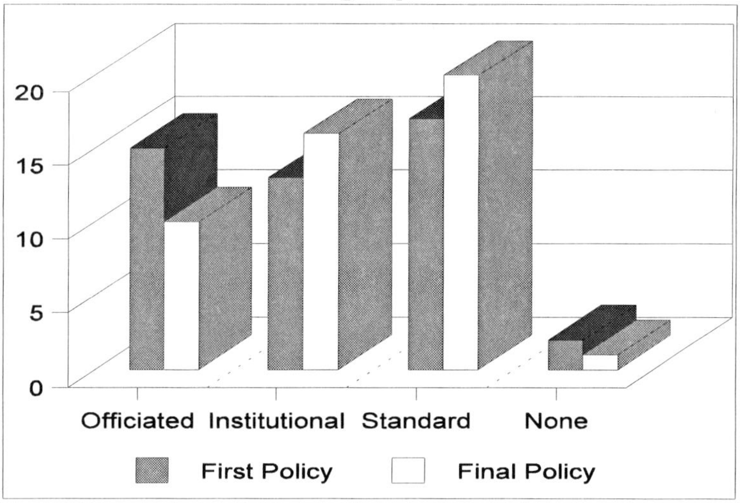

Most states have also created policies that contain medical filing requirements and revocation procedures. As time progressed, drafting and execution requirements became more facilitative, as evidenced by the distributions in Figure 4.5. But preparation formalities are only the "tip of the iceberg" as far as policy analysts are concerned. Even more important to the facility of a state's overall policy are the implementation requirements, which cover when, and under what conditions, life-sustaining procedures can be declined.

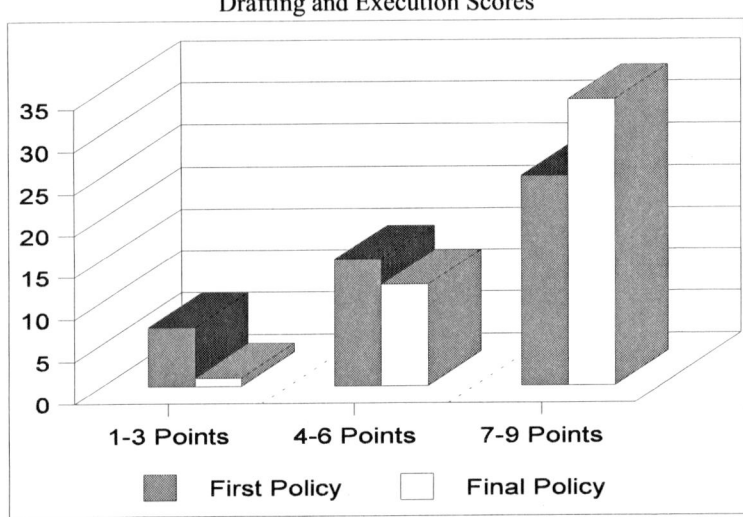

Figure 4.5
Drafting and Execution Scores

Implementation Requirements.
The two most important (and heavily weighted in the facility index) provisions are triggering requirements and rules governing the withdrawal of artificial nutrition and hydration. The former specifies when the conditions of a living will can be activated. Most first statutes contained very specific definitions of terms such as "terminal illness" and "qualified patient;" excluded from the scope of these constructions were persistent vegetative states and permanent unconsciousness. Consider the definition of "terminal condition" as it appears in the Missouri statute:

> An incurable or irreversible condition which, in the opinion of the attending physician, is such that death will occur in a short period of time regardless of the application of medical procedures (Mo. Ann. Stat. §459.010(6)).

This definition explicitly limits the option to decline treatment to only a subset of the many patients who receive a variety of (often unwanted) life-prolonging treatments at the end of a cognitive, sapient life. Of the forty states which enacted original policies with restrictive definitions, twenty-six have renovated their policies to cover PVS and similar conditions; fourteen states still cling to their original, limited language, however (see Figure 4.6).

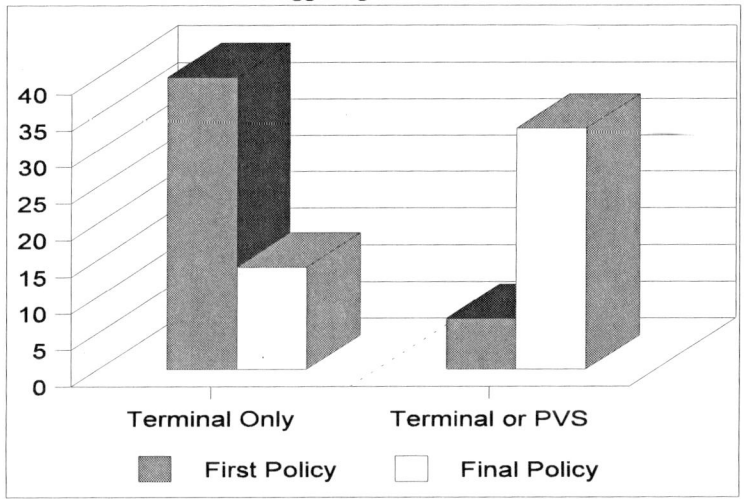

Figure 4.6
Triggering Conditions

The use of nasogastric and implanted feeding tubes to deliver sustenance to unconscious and/or severely debilitated patients is standard medical practice, at least when there is hope for recovery. However, as shown in Figure 4.7, many states have placed "all-out" moratoriums on the discontinuation of this type of treatment, even when a diagnosis indicates that there is no substantive chance of recovery to a conscious state. Indeed, seventeen states had such requirements in their original laws. Similarly, several states have opted for more ambiguous language, requiring sustenance delivery whenever an attending physician deemed such treatment necessary to provide "palliative" or "comfort care." For example, in 1985 Maryland legislators approved the following mandatory provision in their statutory sample living will:

...I direct that such [life-sustaining procedures] be withdrawn or withheld, and that I be permitted to die naturally with only the administration of medication, the administration of food and water, and the administration of any medical procedure deemed necessary to provide comfort care or alleviate pain (Md. Health-Gen. Code Ann. §§5-6012).

It was unclear whether "food and water" referred to orally administered sustenance (e.g., by syringe) or to intubated feedings; this ambiguity was further compounded by the "comfort care" provision, as the statute failed to specifically define this term, leaving it open to considerable interpretation. Fortunately, in May of 1993, the Maryland General Assembly altered the statute. In that session lawmakers, in addition to relaxing witnessing requirements, rescinding a pregnancy disqualification and expanding the scope of triggering conditions, also approved language which made it legal for declarants to specifically direct the withdrawal of artificial nourishment. Thirty-four states now allow for such an "explicit" instruction, and twenty-six of those statutes had to be renovated in order to guarantee this right. A handful of states, nine to be exact, have retained

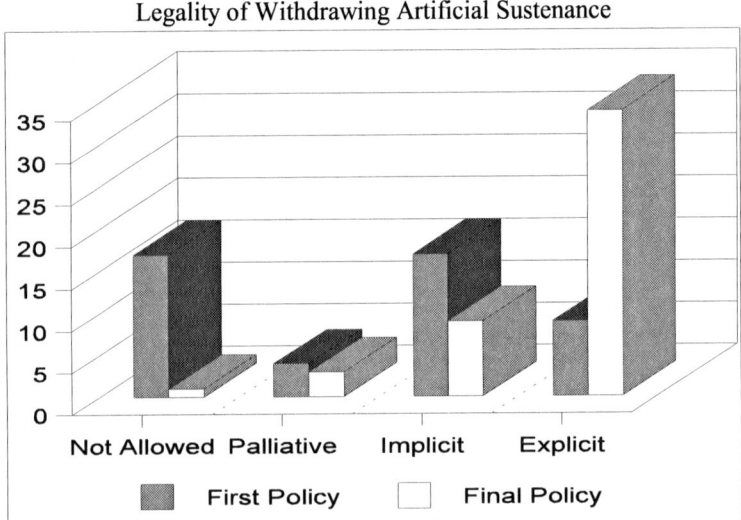

Figure 4.7
Legality of Withdrawing Artificial Sustenance

laws which "implicitly" allow for sustenance discontinuation (e.g., the statutes do not differentiate between sustenance and other life-prolonging therapies such as respirators and renal dialysis). At the end of 1994, only four states retained policies with outright or ambiguous hydration and nutrition clauses; the majority of states renovated their policies.

Figure 4.8
Out-of-State Declarations

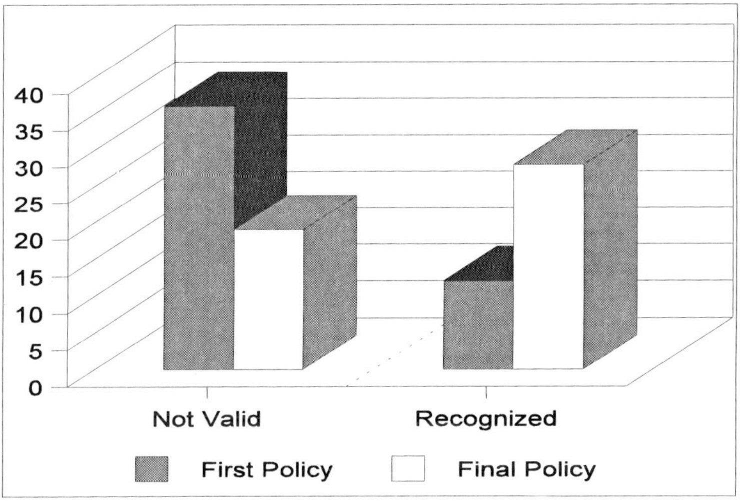

A number of factors appear to have contributed to renovation efforts. State courts liberally interpreted statutes or found constitutional protections that expanded statutory rights (see Chapter 5), states responded to horizontal pressures, and the NCCUSL's model living will law was extremely facilitative in its proposed rules and definitions. The importance of this latter influence can be seen when considering portability requirements. Few states originally drafted laws that recognized living wills drafted in other jurisdictions. Prior to 1985, only three states had such a provision; however, after the NCCUSL law, twenty-eight states approved reciprocity clauses (see Figure 4.8). In terms of implementation rules, states also renovated policies relating to pregnancy restrictions, challenges from "objecting" parties, and waiting periods (the amount of time a "qualified" patient must wait before having her or his wishes effectuated). Figure 4.9 shows the dramatic reinvention of implementation requirements over the course of the diffusion period.

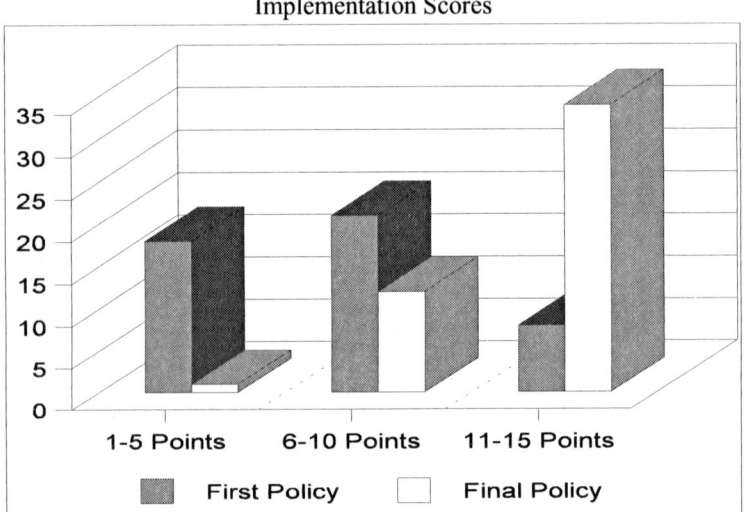

Figure 4.9
Implementation Scores

Enforcement Provisions.

A statute conferring new rights and privileges is all but meaningless unless it is accompanied by guarantees of those rights and mechanisms designed to enforce their exercise by individuals. Almost all states (forty-four out of forty-seven) require providers to comply with the terms of a patient's living will or to allow for the transfer of the patient to a compliant facility or caregiver. However, twenty-six states prescribe no penalties for institutional noncompliance, while nine states deem such actions on the part of physicians to be "unprofessional conduct," and six states impose civil penalties, and another six prescribe criminal penalties. There has been surprisingly little renovation in terms of penalties for noncompliance; only six states have liberalized their policies over time.

Almost all states have clauses in their living will statutes that confer immunity upon caregivers acting in "good faith" and that protect the terms of life insurance policies (by making clear that refusal of treatment is not suicide, an action which invalidates many policies). Similarly most states prescribe civil or criminal penalties for "bad faith" or deception on the part of any party to a nontreatment decision. Nevertheless, most states adopted these clauses in their original statutes. As Figure 4.10 shows, very little renovation has occurred in terms of making living wills enforceable.

Figure 4.10
Enforcement Scores

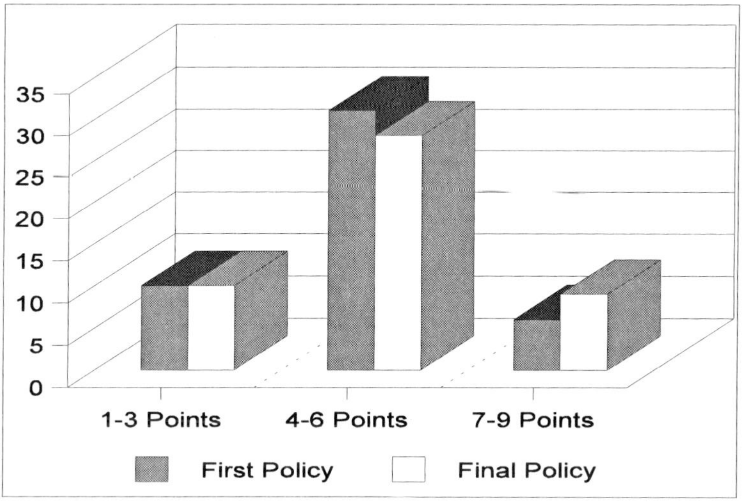

[Bar chart showing First Policy and Final Policy values across three categories:
- 1-3 Points: approximately 12 (First Policy) and 12 (Final Policy)
- 4-6 Points: approximately 33 (First Policy) and 30 (Final Policy)
- 7-9 Points: approximately 8 (First Policy) and 11 (Final Policy)]

The dramatic policy renovation that characterized living wills is but one part of the broader process known as policy reinvention. As states amended their original living will laws, many also began to seek alternatives to these policy instruments by adopting new statutory mechanisms designed to promote patient self-determination at the end of life. The following section describes the adoption and renovation of one such type of tangential innovation: the health care proxy/durable power of attorney.

HEALTH CARE PROXY STATUTES

The Delaware Health Care Decisions Act:
Core Tangential Innovation

In 1982 Delaware's General Assembly enacted the Health Care Decisions Act (or "Death With Dignity Act") (Delaware Code Title §§2501 to 2517). This adoption is significant not simply because Delaware became the twelfth state to give statutory recognition to living wills, but because the statute was the first in the nation allowing individuals to appoint health care proxies. Specifically, the statute, which resembled most other early living wills in almost all other respects, contained a lengthy clause which allowed the declarant of a living will to appoint a health care agent to either enforce the living will or make decisions on behalf of the declarant in the event of the latter's incompetency. The sample living will document contained a specific space for individuals to include the name, address and phone number of their health care agent.

With this simple expansion of the living will, Delaware lawmakers pioneered the first health care proxy law in the nation. Many analysts (e.g., Meisel 1995) credit California with adopting the first health care proxy law; however, legislators in Sacramento approved a durable power of attorney law in 1984, a full year after Delaware's law was approved by the General Assembly and signed by the governor.[3]

Like most core innovations, the original Delaware statute is fairly restrictive. In terms of drafting and execution, directives expire after ten years (this provision was stricken in the following legislative session); the witnessing requirements are among the most demanding in the nation, and the provisions governing proxy appointment are not fully explained in the sample living will document (although they are delineated in the statute) nor are alternate proxies recognized. The statute fails to include PVS in its definitions of "comatose" and "terminal;" however, proxies are (implicitly) allowed to interpret this type of triggering condition. The law makes no specific mention of artificial nutrition and hydration. Directives are invalid in the event of pregnancy, can be "blocked" by concerned parties objecting to the treatment decision and, if executed in another state, are not recognized in Delaware. In addition, there are no provisions requiring providers to comply or transfer with a directive. While Delaware legislators took a bold step by adopting the first proxy innovation, they have not, over the remainder of the twelve-year study period, liberalized or renovated the policy. It was later adopters that approved more permissive policies and/or liberalized their proxy statutes through renovation.

As discussed in the following sections, the diffusion and renovation of the subsequent tangential innovation (proxy laws) bears some similarities to the patterns characterizing living reinvention; however, the differences are more striking than the commonalities. The adoption and renovation of health care agent policies was, when compared to their living will predecessors, considerably smoother and less rife with controversy.

Policy Diffusion

Table 4.8 displays the date when each state adopted its first health care proxy law. Delaware's adoption in 1982 was followed by two subsequent tangential innovations in 1983, three in 1984, and four in 1985. With the exception of 1988, adoptions took place in every year through 1993. Between the four years 1989 and 1992 (the NCCUSL approved a model health care agent law in early 1989) thirty-one states innovated. The diffusion patterns depicted in Figure 4.11 offer a sharp contrast to those for living will laws. When plotted cumulatively, the resulting adoption curve for DPA's bears little resemblance to the "S-"-shape that characterized the previous policy; instead, the diffusion curve is almost a straight line, with forty-eight states adopting the innovation within the span of a single decade. There is a "short burst" of adoptions, followed by a rapid and encompassing "take-off" phase in which a majority of states innovate; there is no period characterized by a gradual "mopping up" of laggard adopters. (To date, Alabama and Alaska have not adopted proxy laws.)

Table 4.8
Dates of Adoption of Health Care Proxy Laws

76	77	78	79	80	81	82	83	84	85	86	87	88	89	90	91	92	93	94
						DE	CA	FL	IN	ID	AR		KS	GA	CT	AZ	MD	
							VA	LA	IA	RI	IL		ME	KY	MO	CO		
								WY	TX		NV		MN	MA	MT	HI		
									UT		VT		NM	MI	NH	**NE**		
													OH	MS	NJ	OK		
													OR	NY	NC	PA		
													WI	SD	ND	SC		
														TN		WA		
														WV				

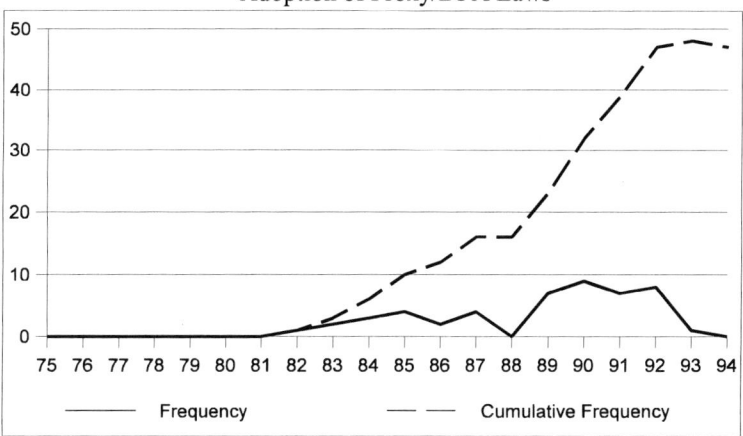

Figure 4.11
Adoption of Proxy/DPA Laws

Table 4.9
Annual Hazard Rates for Adoption of Health Care Proxy Laws

Year	Risk Set[a]	Adoptions	Hazard[b]
1982	49	1	.0204
1983	48	2	.0417
1984	46	3	.0652
1985	43	4	.0930
1986	39	2	.0513
1987	37	4	.1081
1988	33	0	.0000
1989	33	7	.2121
1990	26	9	.3462
1991	17	7	.4118
1992	10	7	.7000
1993	3	1	.3333
1994	2	0	.0000

[a] Risk Set is the total number of states (excluding Nebraska) that have not previously adopted a health care proxy law.
[b] Hazard Rate = Adoptions/Risk Set.

Event History Analysis: Likelihood of Adoption

Table 4.9 reports the hazard rates for the adoption of health care proxy laws (note the uneven hazard rates in the post-1989 period), and Table 4.10 displays the results of the event history analysis. Recall that the theory developed in Chapter 2 suggests that tangential innovations should be characterized by less controversy than original innovations. This is clearly the case. With the exception of the interparty competition variable, which is positive and significant, no other intrastate variables have a major effect on likelihood of innovation.

Of particular interest is the positive (but insignificant) coefficient for the percent Catholic variable; this may reflect the changing strategy of Church leaders in the early 1980's. By 1984, state Catholic conferences were proposing their own (restrictive) durable power of attorney statutes. Many of the DPA laws adopted contain language advising declarants and their agents of the right to seek spiritual guidance prior to implementing a nontreatment decision, and some statutes even contain sample documents that provide a space for declarants to list the name (and contact information) of their religious leaders. It bears mentioning that the three states which have not adopted living will policies (Massachusetts, Michigan and New York) all have Catholic populations well-above the national average; all three of these states approved DPA laws in 1990.

Once again, horizontal influences appear to play the preponderant role in explaining adoptions. The coefficient of the regional facility score is positive and statistically significant; in the years prior to 1990, a one standard deviation increase in a state's regional facility score increases its probability of adoption in the following year by 22.44%. The small size and statistical insignificance of the piecewise interaction term's positive coefficient indicates that regional influences continued to be important in the years following the NCCSUL's model DPA law publication.

As the case with living wills, the NCCUSL resolution also stimulated the adoption of health care proxy laws. When the above model was re-estimated with a dummy variable capturing the pre- and post-NCCUSL effects (with the regional and interaction terms dropped), the results indicate that after the adoption of the model law in 1989, likelihood of innovation increased by 28.85%, holding all other variables at their means.

Table 4.10
Event History Analysis of the Determinants of Proxy Adoptions

Variable	MLE (Wald)	Impact[a]
% Catholic	.6064	.0199
	(.1047)	
Divided Government	-.6472	-.0648[b]
	(2.4320)	
Physicians	.1301	.0158
	(.0758)	
Electoral Threat Index	-.1271	-.0337
	(.6904)	
Interparty Competition	4.8028**	.1225
	(3.9627)	
Legislative Salary	-.000012	-.0405
	(.5480)	
Senior Citizens	.1269	.0734
	(2.0078)	
Mean Regional Facil. Score$_{t-1}$	.1247***	.2244
	(10.0861)	
Piecewise 1989 Facility Int.[c]	.0332	.0343
	(.4522)	
Living Will Facility Score$_{t-1}$	-.0041	-.0105
	(.0290)	
Constant	-5.463***	

Model χ^2 (10 d.f.) = 39.381***
Initial log likelihood = -142.982   Final log likelihood = -123.2915

Number of Cases = 386; Cases Scored as Adoption = 47 (12.18%)
Maximum likelihood estimation of a logit model of the probability of a state adopting a health care proxy law in a given year.
[a] Impact is the change in the predicted probability of adoption after changing the independent variable from one standard deviation below its mean to one standard deviation above its mean, holding all other continuous independent variables at their means and the divided government variable at 0.
[b] Change in predicted probability after switching the divided government dummy variables's score from 0 (unified control) to 1 (divided control).
[c] (Lagged regional facility score - lagged 1989 score) * (0 if 1989 or before, 1 if after).
* Significant at .10 α-level in a two-tailed test; **.05; ***.01.

Surprisingly, a state's prior living will innovation does not appear to have influenced its willingness to adopt a proxy law. The theory suggests that once a state has adopted a core or subsequent core innovation (e.g., a living will policy), the adoption of a tangential innovation (e.g., DPA policy) is expedited by the fact that policy sponsors can market the proposal as a routine outgrowth of extant state policy. While the quick pace of proxy diffusion suggests that policy entrepreneurs may in fact have been successful at downplaying the controversy surrounding DPA's, the presence or absence of a facilitative living will law did not appreciably increase the probability of innovation. In fact, the coefficient in question is small in value, negative and statistically insignificant.

Although only two variables proved important in the EHA, the overall model is statistically significant at better than 99.9% confidence; in fact, the DPA model has a better goodness-of-fit than its living will cousin.[4] Not only did diffusion occur faster for the tangential innovations but, as shown in the next section, policy renovation, while present, was not nearly as pronounced for DPA's as it was for living wills.

Reinvention Through Renovation

Table 4.11
Initial and Amended Health Care Proxy Scores

State	Adopt Year	First Score	Final Score	Gain	# of Amds.
AZ	1992	26	26	0	0
AR	1987	25	25	0	0
CA	1983	16	23	+7	3
CO	1992	22	22	0	0
CT	1991	17	17	0	0
DE	1982	17	18	+1	1
FL	1984	16	24	+8	2
GA	1990	26	26	0	0
HI	1992	19	19	0	0
ID	1986	8	24	+16	1
IL	1987	27	27	0	0
IN	1985	14	26	+12	2
IA	1985	15	23	+8	1
KS	1989	18	19	+1	1

Table 4.11(continued)
Initial and Amended Health Care Proxy Scores

State	Adopt Year	First Score	Final Score	Gain	# of Amds.
KY	1990	21	21	0	0
LA	1984	19	22	+3	2
ME	1989	29	29	0	0
MD	1993	29	29	0	0
MA	1990	24	24	0	0
MI	1990	19	19	0	0
MN	1989	24	27	+3	1
MS	1990	19	20	+1	1
MO	1991	22	22	0	0
MT	1991	22	22	0	0
NE	1992	26	26	0	0
NV	1987	15	22	+7	1
NH	1991	24	24	0	0
NJ	1991	30	30	0	0
NM	1989	16	16	0	0
NY	1990	25	25	0	0
NC	1991	22	22	0	0
ND	1991	23	23	0	0
OH	1989	13	18	+5	1
OK	1992	23	23	0	0
OR	1989	21	27	+6	1
PA	1992	24	24	0	0
RI	1986	15	26	+11	3
SC	1992	23	23	0	0
SD	1990	16	17	+1	1
TN	1990	19	19	0	0
TX	1985	19	22	+3	1
UT	1985	22	26	+4	1
VT	1987	22	22	0	0
VA	1983	21	29	+8	3
WA	1992	20	20	0	0
WV	1990	20	20	0	0
WI	1989	25	25	0	0
WY	1984	14	25	+11	2

First Score: = 20.67   = 4.66
Final Score: = 23.08   = 3.43
Gain Score: = +2.42   = 4.02

Table 4.12
Determinants of Health Care Proxy Renovations

Variable	MLE (Wald)	Impact[a]
% Catholic	2.4331 (1.4773)	.0533
Divided Government	.2292 (.2315)	.0211[b]
Physicians	-.5890 (.6889)	-.0304
Electoral Threat Index	-.2555 (1.7746)	-.0448
Interparty Competition	-.7896 (.0980)	-.0132
Legislative Salary	-.0000041 (.0434)	-.0092
Senior Citizens	.0091 (.0085)	.0035
Distance From Region. Score$_{t-1}$[c]	-.0222 (.4145)	-.0254
Years Since First Adoption	.2337*** (9.4540)	.1064
Constant	-1.5549 (.2949)	

Model χ^2 (9 d.f.) = 16.363*
Initial log likelihood = -89.843   Final log likelihood = -81.661

Number of Cases = 251; Cases Scored as Renovation = 29 (11.6%)
Maximum likelihood estimation of a logit model of the probability of a state amending a proxy law in a given year, given that it had previously adopted such a statute.
[a] Impact is the change in the predicted probability of renovation after changing the independent variable from one standard deviation below its mean to one standard deviation above its mean, holding all other continuous independent variables at their means and the divided government variable at 0.
[b] Change in predicted probability after switching the divided government dummy variables's score from 0 (unified control) to 1 (divided control).
[c] State's lagged facility score - lagged regional facility score.
* Significant at .10 α-level in a two-tailed test; **.05; ***.01.

Table 4.11 reports the initial and amended health care proxy scores for each state. As with living will laws, there is evidence of reinvention through amendment; early adopters, for the most part, increased their facility scores over time. However, only nineteen states (i.e., fewer than 40%) altered their tangential innovations. Of these states that did renovate, twelve did so on only one occasion; four states approved amendments in two subsequent years, and only three states renovated in three separate years. The majority of states were content with their first policies. The following section attempts to account for the decisions of lawmakers to amend their innovations or to retain the status quo.

Logistic Regression Analysis: Likelihood of Renovation.
Table 4.12 reports the MLE coefficients from an analysis of whether or not a state renovated its policy once it had adopted an innovation. The overall model is only statistically significant at better than 90% confidence, and only a single variable proved to be an important predictor of renovation. As the number of years elapsed since a state's first health care proxy adoption increased, so did the likelihood of policy renovation, suggesting that early innovators were far more likely to revise their policies than were later adopters. This relationship is significant at greater than 99.9% confidence, and, all things being equal, once four years had elapsed since a state's first passage, the chance of reinvention increased by just over 10%.

None of the other variables proved terribly important in explaining renovation. While regional pressures appeared important in increasing a state's propensity to adopt a DPA law, they do not appear to play a substantive role in stimulating policy revision. Similarly, interest groups, political environment and institutional structure all appear to have null effects. The limited findings from the above regression model should be placed in context; indeed, as discussed in the next section, there is considerably less time-serial variation in proxy scores than there is for living will scores.

Increased Facility Over Time.
The mean score for first adoptions is 20.67, and the mean 1994 score increases to 23.08, with the average increase ("gain" score) being 2.42

points (see Table 4.11). Table 4.13 and Figure 4.12 depict the average facility scores for each year in the diffusion period. The mean score increases slightly from 1982 to 1983, but then the mean begins to vacillate at slightly lower levels for the next four years (the standard deviation increases over this time period, suggesting growing interstate disparity). From 1988 through the end of the study period, scores increase steadily over time, and some degree of policy homogenization occured, as evidenced by the falling standard deviation values.

Table 4.14 reports the results of the OLS regression of facility scores on date of adoption. The coefficient for the independent variable is negative, significant at better than the .001 α-level, and accounts for 25.6% of the variation in the dependent variable.

The earliest policies were more restrictive than those produced later in time. However, almost all of the lowest scores were increased through amendment; when the model is re-estimated for the 1994 scores, the influence of date of adoption is negligible. Early innovators enacted amendments resulting in policies that were on par with those of later adopters. For first policies, the lowest score was 8 points (Idaho) and the highest score was 29 (claimed by Maryland and Maine), yielding a range of 21 points. By the end of 1994, the lowest score was 16 points (New Mexico), and many states had scores at or approaching the maximum 29 points; the range at the end of the study period was only 13 points.

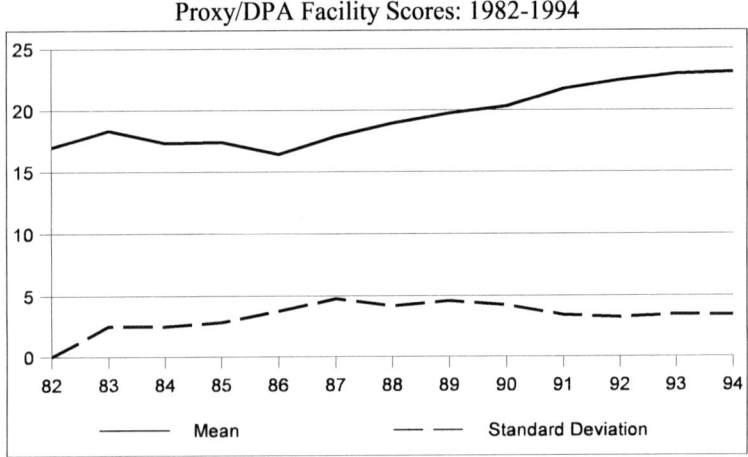

Figure 4.12
Proxy/DPA Facility Scores: 1982-1994

Table 4.13
Proxy/DPA Facility Scores: 1982-1994

Year	N	μ	σ
1982	1	17.00	--
1983	3	18.33	2.52
1984	6	17.33	2.50
1985	10	17.40	2.84
1986	12	16.42	3.75
1987	16	17.88	4.76
1988	16	18.94	4.15
1989	23	19.74	4.59
1990	32	20.31	4.20
1991	39	21.74	3.42
1992	47	22.45	3.22
1993	48	22.94	3.46
1994	48	23.08	3.43

Table 4.14
OLS Regression of Proxy/DPA Scores on Date of Adoption

Model 1: Initial Adoption		Model 2: 1994 (Reinvented) Score	
Variable	**Coefficient (t-ratio)**	**Variable**	**Coefficient (t-ratio)**
Adoption Date	-.7935*** (-3.976)	Adoption Date	.1129 (.6670)
$R^2 = .256$		$R^2 = .010$	

*** Significant at .001 α-level in a two-tailed test.
(constants not reported)

Policy renovation occurred along the same dimensions as it did for living will laws. Drafting and execution provisions that were liberalized included witnessing requirements, personalization of format, and the abandonment of expiration dates. One additional concern that affects proxy laws, which does not apply to living wills, is the possibility that an appointed proxy might die or become incapacitated before the declarant does. Fortunately many states began allowing the appointment of "alternate" proxies (i.e., individuals appointed to make decisions in the event the "primary" agent is no longer able to represent the principal). Figure 4.13 shows that only fifteen states included such provisions in their first laws but, by the end of the study period, thirty-three states recognized proxy appointments (i.e., eighteen states renovated their statutes).

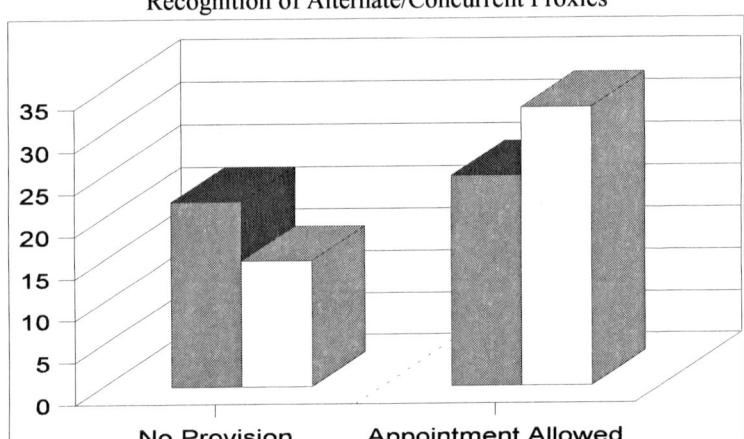

Figure 4.13
Recognition of Alternate/Concurrent Proxies

In terms of implementation requirements, policies were renovated to allow agents to direct the discontinuation of artificial feeding and to allow principals to specify the triggering conditions for ending treatment. Figure 4.14 shows that, while over half of the states originally excluded PVS from their lists of qualifying conditions, by 1994 most states recognized this condition and gave declarants the option of permitting nontreatment in the event of this and similar diagnoses. Following the NCCUSL's 1989 recommendations, many policies were also changed to eliminate diagnostic waiting periods and to make directives portable. Few changes, however, were made to statutory enforcement and liability provisions.

Figure 4.14
Triggering Conditions

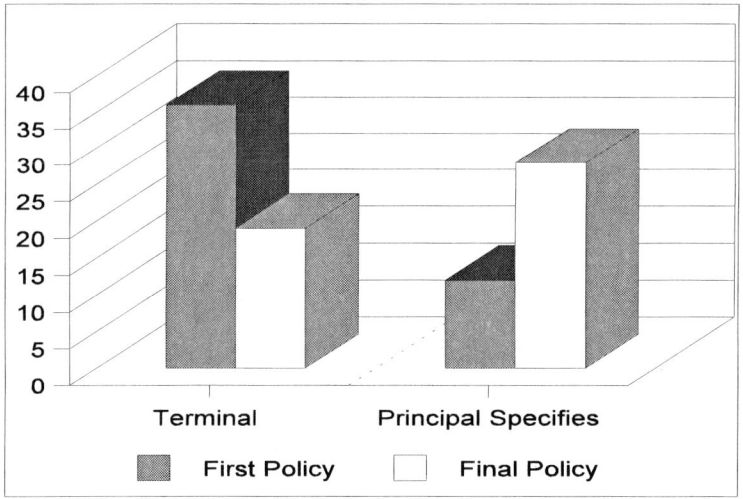

Presently, all but two states have health care proxy laws. As discussed in Chapter 2, these advance directives options have successfully overcome some of the limitations of living will policies, including offering declarants greater flexibility and reducing the fear of provider-liability in the clinical setting. However, practitioners and policy advocates alike have grown increasingly troubled by the fundamental limitation of both living will and health care agent directives: the majority of U.S. citizens have not executed such a document, meaning that, in the event of accident or tragedy, many persons are unable to avail themselves to the new class of rights created by advance directives. A third type of policy, the surrogate decision-making law, has evolved to create procedures through which a patient's family members can make decisions on her or his behalf when no advance directive exists (or cannot be located). The diffusion and renovation of these (apparently extremely controversial) plans are discussed in the next section.

SURROGATE DECISION-MAKING LAWS

Arkansas and North Carolina: Core Tangential Adoptions

Arkansas and North Carolina each innovated in 1977. The latter did so by "tacking on" a short surrogate clause to its first living will policy. The surrogate provisions in the Right to a Natural Death Act (N.C. Gen. Stat. §§90-320 to 90-322) were fairly brief, likely reflecting an attempt to protect informal norms of patient-doctor-family decision-making that probably prevailed in the state at the time. The statute specified that, when members of a terminally ill and incompetent patient's family agreed that treatment should be withdrawn or de-escalated, providers had no obligation to continue life-supports.

The North Carolina law prescribed a "priority list" of potential decision-makers (an ordinal ranking scale of immediate family members), but did not specify a means through which disputes among surrogates of the same priority class could be resolved. It is significant that the statute contained no "physician veto" provision requiring a doctor or health care facility to consent to a nontreatment decision. Even more remarkable is the fact that the legislation permitted an attending physician to discontinue treatment at her or his discretion when a terminally ill patient lacked any immediate family for consultation.

Family members (and physicians) in the Tarheel State were given the authority to implement a nontreatment decision pursuant to the same implementation requirements applicable to living wills; this meant that PVS was not recognized as a valid triggering condition, but that there were also no restrictions on sustenance, nor were there waiting periods, judicial blocking procedures or pregnancy restrictions. Lacking from the statute were any enforcement provisions, but the law was substantially overhauled in 1991.

North Carolina's policy was officially approved (i.e., signed by the governor) almost two months after Arkansas had adopted its own surrogate policy. Although the two states crafted innovative policies that created similar surrogate procedures, the two laws appear to have been crafted independently of one another. The Arkansas Rights of the Terminally Ill Act (Ark. Code Ann. §§20-17-201 to 20-17-217) developed

Legislative Innovation and Reinvention

a set of procedures whereby the immediate family of a minor patient or incompetent adult who had not prepared a living will was empowered to draft and execute a directive on the terminally ill patient's behalf. In effect, the General Assembly of Arkansas adopted the nation's first surrogate decision making law.

The major difference between the Arkansas and North Carolina laws is that the former required family members to formally create an official "post-hoc" document, whereas the latter policy created a rule deregulating decision-making in institutional care settings. One policy was much more "formal" than the other. For example, the Arkansas statute went a step beyond North Carolina's by prescribing a "majority rule" provision to resolve conflicts between family members with the same priority status (e.g., siblings when a patient was widowed or unmarried). Unlike in North Carolina, there is no evidence that policy proponents in Arkansas attempted to covertly attach surrogate provisions to the law. On the contrary, the act contained only two paragraphs detailing the drafting of living wills by competent persons, while two pages of text outlined the rules governing decision making by surrogates. The preamble to the bill specifically noted that the policy was intended to serve dual purposes:

> ...An act to permit an individual to request or refuse in writing medical or surgical means or procedures calculated to prolong his[sic] life; and to authorize such request or refusal by others on behalf of one incompetent or under 18... (Arkansas Acts, No. 897, 1977)

The Arkansas law, like most early policies, contained a narrow definition of terminal illness, a moratorium on the withdrawal of sustenance and specified only minimal enforcement procedures. This landmark law of 1977 was followed by a decade of legislative inactivity on the right to die. It was not until 1987 that the refusal of treatment issue was again placed squarely upon the state's governmental agenda. In that year the title of the act was changed to the Rights of the Terminally Ill *or Permanently Unconscious Act* (italics added), with PVS being explicitly recognized as an appropriate triggering condition. Additional facilitative provisions were added, including a filing requirement and criminal penalties for failure to comply with a nontreatment decision.

Although Arkansas and North Carolina produced extremely permissive and original policies, their adoptions would not seem to have had an immediate impact on lawmakers in other states. First, neither of these states is generally reputed as being an innovative leader, and it is likely that few policy proponents in other states looked to these two southern states for policy cues. In addition, the two adoptions appear to have been very "low key;" in fact, a major search of all mass periodicals in 1977 revealed that, although several articles in major newspapers and magazines reported the adoption of living wills in these states, no journalists appeared to "pick up on" the surrogate provisions contained in the statutes. As discussed in the following section, a good deal of time would elapse before the surrogate model was approved in other jurisdictions.

Policy Diffusion

The diffusion pattern for surrogate decision-making adoptions, depicted in Table 4.15 and Figure 4.15, differs appreciably from the patterns found for the two previous policies. The adoption of surrogate laws was (and remains) a highly controversial endeavor. There was no "quick surge" or "short burst" following the 1977 core tangential innovations. Indeed, a full six years elapsed before the next such statute was approved. The years 1983-1985 can be considered a truncated "take-off" phase with two, three and then five states adopting innovations. Following this mini-surge, three years elapsed before the next adoption. A second surge or "take-off" begins in 1991, following the NCCUSL's endorsement of family decision-making statutes. By 1994, only twenty-four states had adopted innovations. The plot of cumulative adoptions (see the dotted line in Figure 4.15) depicts a pattern of three periods of "bursts followed by lulls."

This episodic and disjointed pattern of adoptions proved difficult to explain in any systematic manner. The results of the event history analysis reveal that most of the "traditional suspects" were not at work in the politics of adopting surrogate laws.

Table 4.15
Dates of Adoption of Surrogate Decision-Making Laws

Year	States
77	AR, NC
78	
79	
80	
81	
82	
83	OR, VA
84	FL, LA, NM
85	CT, IN, IA, TX, UT
86	
87	
88	
89	ME
90	SC
91	IL, MT, NV, OH
92	AZ, CO, WY
93	MD, WV
94	KY

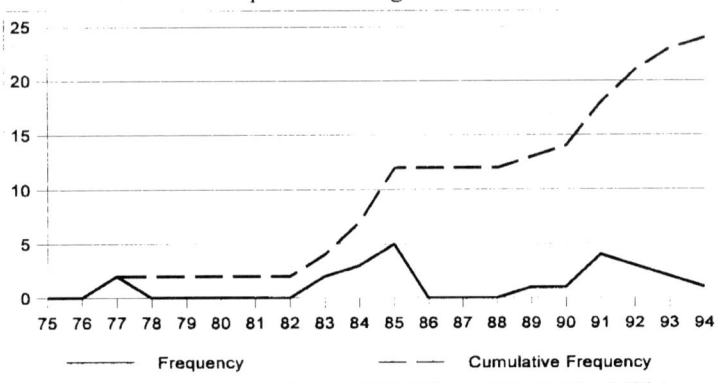

Figure 4.15
Adoption of Surrogate Statutes

Table 4.16
Annual Hazard Rates for Adoption of Surrogate Laws

Year	Risk Set[a]	Adoptions	Hazard[b]
1977	49	2	.0408
1978	47	0	.0000
1979	47	0	.0000
1980	47	0	.0000
1981	47	0	.0000
1982	47	0	.0000
1983	47	2	.0426
1984	45	3	.0667
1985	42	5	.1190
1986	37	0	.0000
1987	37	0	.0000
1988	37	0	.0000
1989	37	1	.0270
1990	36	1	.0278
1991	35	4	.1143
1992	31	3	.0968
1993	28	2	.0714
1994	26	1	.0385

[a]Risk Set is the total number of states (excluding Nebraska) that have not previously adopted a surrogate decision-making law.
[b]Hazard Rate = Adoptions/Risk Set.

Table 4.17
Event History Analysis of the Determinants of Surrogate Adoptions

Variable	MLE (Wald)	Impact[a]
% Catholic	-3.5027	-.0260
	(2.1673)	
Divided Government	-.3095	-.0075[b]
	(.3793)	
Physicians	.8593	.0235
	(2.1247)	
Electoral Threat Index	-.4182*	-.0245
	(3.6012)	
Interparty Competition	2.4260	.0136
	(.7677)	
Legislative Salary	-.000051**	-.0402
	(3.8403)	
Senior Citizens	.1189	.0153
	(1.0340)	
Mean Regional Facil. Score$_{t-1}$	.1015	.0169
	(1.8350)	
Piecewise 1991 Facility Int.[c]	.1699	.0111
	(1.1951)	
Living Will Facility Score$_{t-1}$	.0037	.0003
	(.0176)	
Proxy/DPA Facility Score$_{t-1}$	-.0260	-.0113
	(.6465)	
Constant	-6.8281**	
	(5.6301)	

Model χ^2 (11 d.f.) = 18.773*
Initial log likelihood = -105.224   Final log likelihood = -95.838
Number of Cases = 720; Cases Scored as Adoption = 24 (3.33%)

Maximum likelihood estimation of a logit model of the probability of a state adopting a health care surrogate law in a given year.
[a] Impact is the change in the predicted probability of adoption after changing the independent variable from one s.d. below its mean to one s.d. above its mean, holding all other continuous independent variables at their means and the divided government variable at 0.
[b] Change in predicted probability after switching the divided government dummy variables s score from 0 (unified control) to 1 (divided control).
[c] (Lagged regional facility score - lagged 1991 score) * (0 if 1991 or before, 1 if after).
* Significant at .10 level in a two-tailed test; **.05; ***.01.

Event History Analysis: Likelihood of Adoption

Table 4.16 reports the annual hazard rates (note the uniformly low values), and Table 4.17 displays the results of the model estimation. While most of the coefficients reported in Table 4.17 are in the hypothesized directions, only two are statistically significant.[5] Limited support exists for the electoral threat hypothesis. Although the impact is small in magnitude, it still appears that, all other things being equal, lawmakers are less inclined to produce controversial policies in election years, when the stakes are highest. The results also support the proposition that citizen legislators are more likely to expend political capital on such policies than are career politicians. Indeed, an inspection of the states that have adopted laws (refer to Table 4.15) reveals that the most professionalized and reputed assemblies in the nation (e.g., California and New York) have yet to innovate, while many of the "less renowned" bodies have gone where their more professionalized cousins "fear to tread." In fact, of the twenty-four states to adopt surrogate statutes, fifteen have legislative salaries and total populations below their respective 1994 national medians.

Horizontal pressures do not appear to be nearly as important in this model as they did in the advance directives models, as evidenced by the paltry and statistically insignificant coefficients of the lagged regional facility score variable and 1991 piecewise interaction term. The NCCUSL draft of 1991 played a minor role in stimulating adoption, with nine of the twenty-four states innovating after the passage of the model law. When the EHA model was re-estimated to include a dummy variable capturing the change from the pre- to the post-1991 period (with the two regional variables dropped), the results indicated that states were 4.6% more likely to adopt a surrogate law after the NCCUSL advocated such policies than they were before, all other variables held constant.

The results further suggest that the prior adoptions of a living will and/or DPA law had little to no discernible impact on willingness to approve surrogate statutes. Two explanations may be advanced for why these proposed relationships failed to materialize. First, having previously adopted controversial policies, many politicians may have been reluctant to re-open another right to die "can of worms;" this hesitancy was

Legislative Innovation and Reinvention

possibly compounded by the fact that it may have proved far more difficult in practice to characterize surrogate policies (which allow for the discontinuation of treatment without the express prior approval of a patient) as routine policy revisions than it was, for example, to argue that a DPA statute was a natural and technical extension of a living will policy. Second, a number of state appellate courts handed down rulings that legalized decision making in the absence of an advance directive (see Chapter 5). Once a state's high court created such a policy, many lawmakers may have seen little need (or incentives) to re-open the Pandora's box.

Not only were states reluctant to approve surrogate laws, but, of the states that did adopt these policies, only a handful chose to amend their first laws.

Reinvention Through Renovation

Table 4.18 reports that only nine of the twenty-four adopters reinvented their policies through amendments. Moreover, no state renovated on more than one occasion. This lack of policy revision probably owes most to the controversial nature of surrogate policies and to the late dates at which many of the states innovated. Few traditional forces appear to be at work in driving policy expansion, as discussed in the following section.

<u>Logistic Regression Analysis: Likelihood of Renovation.</u>
The results of the logistic regression analysis displayed in Table 4.19 reveal that only date of first adoption appears to be a correlate of renovation, and the impact score for this factor is not terribly large (.0549). And this finding should be taken lightly, given the fact that the overall model is statistically insignificant at conventional levels of inference and fails to predict a single renovation. Unlike the case with the advance directives policies, electoral threat, legislative professionalism and disparities in regional scores do not appear to propel states toward renovation.

Although few in number, all of the renovation efforts contributed to increased policy facility, as discussed next.

Table 4.18
Initial and Amended Health Care Surrogate Facility Scores

State	Adopt Year	First Score	Final Score	Gain	# of Amds.
AZ	1992	15	15	0	0
AR	1977	14	18	+4	1
CO	1992	14	14	0	0
CT	1985	7	15	+8	1
FL	1984	9	13	+4	1
IL	1991	20	20	0	0
IN	1985	6	11	+5	1
IA	1985	10	18	+8	1
KY	1994	15	15	0	0
LA	1984	14	14	0	0
ME	1989	15	23	+8	1
MD	1993	22	22	0	0
MT	1991	15	15	0	0
NV	1991	19	19	0	0
NM	1984	14	14	0	0
NC	1977	17	20	+3	1
OH	1991	13	13	0	0
OR	1983	13	21	+8	1
SC	1990	15	15	0	0
TX	1985	14	14	0	0
UT	1985	15	15	0	0
VA	1983	15	20	+5	1
WV	1993	21	21	0	0
WY	1992	15	15	0	0

First Score: $\mu = 14.29$ $\sigma = 3.83$
Final Score: $\mu = 16.50$ $\sigma = 3.26$
Gain Score: $\mu = +2.21$ $\sigma = 3.16$

Table 4.19
Determinants of Health Care Surrogate Renovations

Variable	MLE (Wald)	Impact[a]
% Catholic	-.0115 (.0000)	-.0001
Divided Government	.7490 (.8478)	.0361[b]
Physicians	.6562 (.2734)	.0215
Electoral Threat Index	-.3515 (1.0256)	-.0248
Interparty Competition	2.7422 (.3550)	.0186
Legislative Salary	.0000115 (.0246)	.0104
Senior Citizens	.1930 (1.6135)	.0303
Distance From Region. Score$_{t-1}$[c]	-.0773 (.9478)	-.0296
Years Since First Adoption	.1953* (3.0438)	.0549
Constant	-10.0686** (3.9273)	

Model χ^2 (9 d.f.) = 11.018
Initial log likelihood = -34.644   Final log likelihood = -29.135

Number of Cases = 160; Cases Scored as Renovation = 9 (6.0 %)
Maximum likelihood estimation of a logit model of the probability of a state amending a surrogate law in a given year, given that it had previously adopted such a statute.
[a] Impact is the change in the predicted probability of renovation after changing the independent variable from one standard deviation below its mean to one standard deviation above its mean, holding all other continuous independent variables at their means and the divided government variable at 0.
[b] Change in predicted probability after switching the divided government dummy variables's score from 0 (unified control) to 1 (divided control).
[c] State's lagged facility score - lagged regional facility score.
* Significant at .10 α-level in a two-tailed test; **.05; ***.01.

Modestly Increased Facility Over Time.

An examination of the patterns depicted in Table 4.20 and Figure 4.16 indicates that facility scores did not increase steadily over time; rather, mean scores dipped during the 1980's and did not begin increasing until after the NCCUSL draft in 1991.

Table 4.20
Surrogate Facility Scores: 1977-1994

Year	N	μ	σ
1977	2	13.50	.71
...	...	...	...
1983	4	13.75	.96
1984	7	13.14	1.95
1985	12	12.00	3.16
...	...	...	...
1989	13	12.54	3.50
1990	14	12.71	3.43
1991	18	14.94	4.15
1992	21	15.48	3.47
1993	23	16.35	3.82
1994	24	16.50	3.26

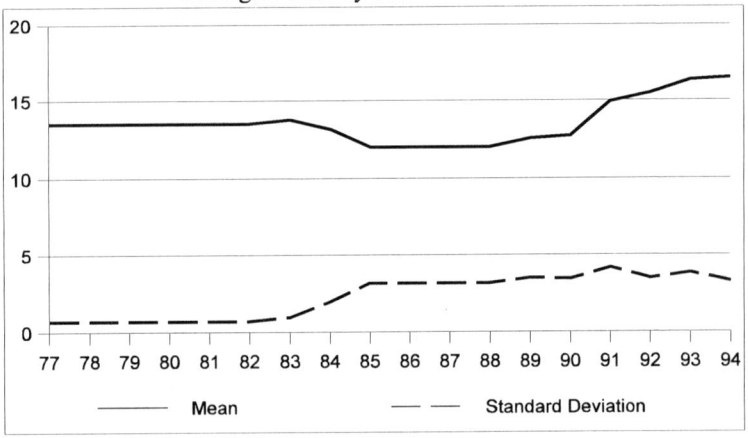

Figure 4.16
Surrogate Facility Scores: 1977-1994

The results of the OLS regression of facility scores on date of adoption reported in Table 4.21 support the notion that policies became more permissive over time. Indeed this independent variable accounts for nearly 25% of the variation in first policy facility, and by 1994 many of the limitations of the earliest laws appear to have been revised, as date of adoption is not a significant regressor, nor does it account for much variation in facility scores across the twenty-four states.

Table 4.21
OLS Regression of Surrogate Facility Scores on Date of Adoption

Model 1: Initial Adoption		*Model 2: 1994 (Reinvented) Score*	
Variable	**Coefficient (t-ratio)**	**Variable**	**Coefficient (t-ratio)**
Adoption Date	-3.908** (-2.70)	Adoption Date	-.0647 (-.476)
$R^2 = .249$		$R^2 = .010$	
** Significant at .05 α-level in a two-tailed test. (constants not reported)			

By the end of 1994, the mean score was a mere 16.5 points (a maximum score of 31 is possible). The adopting states produced fairly restrictive policies and engaged in very limited reinvention through amendment. Given the mean of the 1994 scores, a standard deviation of 3.26 suggests that surrogate laws differ considerably across states.

Many states now have policies that recognize PVS as a legitimate triggering condition and that permit decisionmakers to direct the discontinuance of artificial sustenance. Many of these battles were fought previously or at the same time as they were for the advance directives laws. Figures 4.17 through 4.19 detail some of the provisions, unique to surrogate laws, on which there is wide interstate variation.

Surrogate Eligibility and Conflict Resolution.
Figure 4.17 shows that most states prescribe an ordinal ranking of family members who are eligible to serve as surrogates. However, five statutes

contain imprecise language that seems to assume that a patient's "family," "entire family," or "immediate family" will act as a unified and solitary unit. At least implicitly, these laws would allow a single family member (a distant cousin, for example) to block or forestall the nontreatment decision of the rest of a patient's family. No renovations have been made in terms of delineating priority status among potential surrogates.

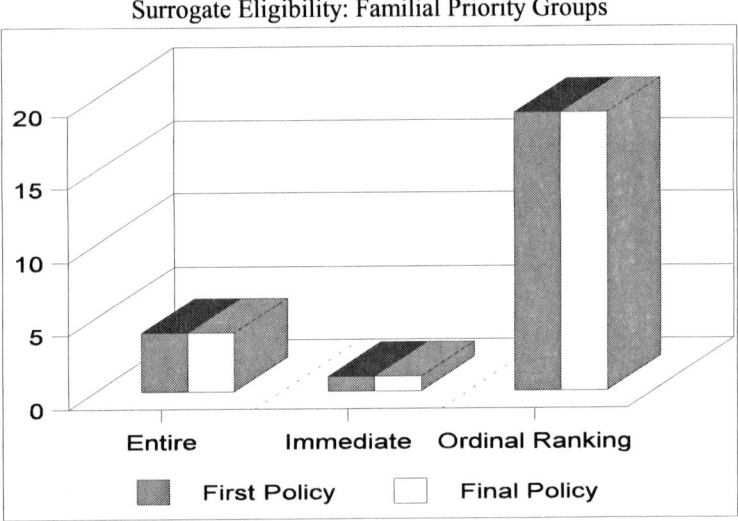

Figure 4.17
Surrogate Eligibility: Familial Priority Groups

Perhaps even more troubling is the failure of many of these statutes to anticipate intra-familial conflict among surrogates of equal priority status (a division between the adult children of an elderly patient, for example). As shown in Figure 4.18, ten states currently allow a single objecting surrogate to nullify the decision of her or his peers/relatives (e.g., if five siblings agree that treatment should be stopped and one disagrees, treatment must be continued). A dozen other states have opted to specify "majority rule" provisions, whereby the decision of the greatest number of surrogates of the same priority class is honored. While these contingency rules may help to break stalemates and expedite medical action (or inaction), they have the potential to lead to a number of undesirable consequences, not the least of which are familial division and the possibility of litigation. Far more helpful are policies that specify a nonconflictual "tie breaker," in which conflicts among surrogates are referred to trained social workers or medical counselors for mediation. Only two states have adopted this latter alternative, and only one state has replaced its minority veto rule with a majority rule provision.

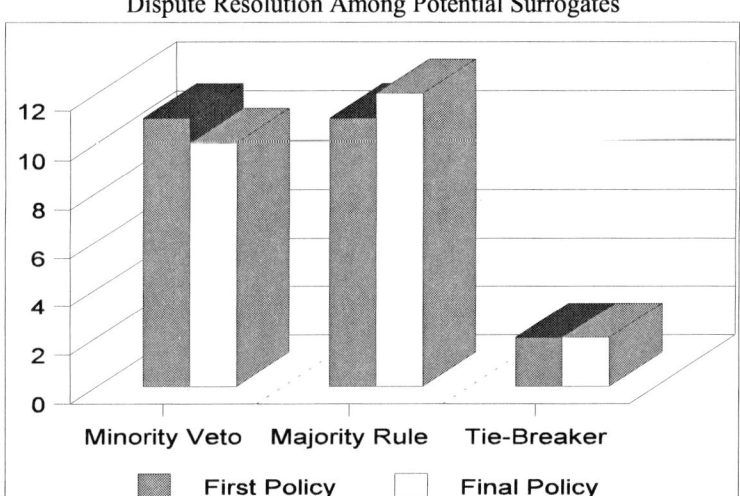

Figure 4.18
Dispute Resolution Among Potential Surrogates

Another potential problem with extant surrogate statutes is that many of them only allow "traditional" relatives (i.e., those related to the patient by blood or through marriage) to serve as surrogates. Excluded from these laws are common law spouses and domestic partners. This lack of recognition can prove particularly problematic for lesbians and gay men; fortunately some states (probably owing to the NCCUSL law's "significant others" clause) have renovated their policies to make them more inclusive (see Figure 4.19).

Efforts to reinvent surrogate policies are likely to continue, as are efforts to promote policy adoption. Such endeavors are likely to take place as part of a concerted effort to overhaul a state's entire right to die "package." In the concluding section, the differences and similarities between, and the "tied fates" of, the three policy types are considered.

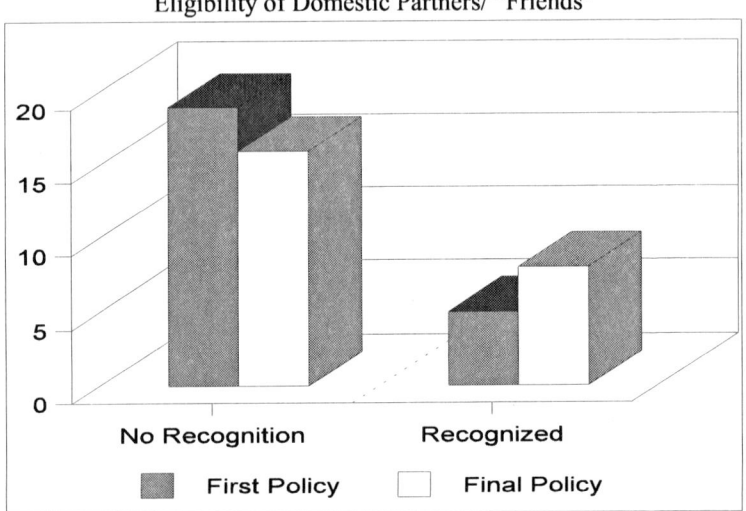

Figure 4.19
Eligibility of Domestic Partners/ "Friends"

CONCLUSION

The diffusion of living will laws conformed most closely to theoretical expectations. In terms of explaining adoptions, levels of support and opposition to policies, electoral threat, and legislative professionalism all affected the propensity of lawmakers to innovate; horizontal influences (patterns in neighboring states and NCCUSL recommendations) exercised the greatest leverage. Health Care Proxy laws disseminated at a much quicker speed than did their living will cousins, and it seems clear that these tangential innovations proved less controversial, with horizontal variables accounting for almost all of the explained variation. Surrogate laws proved to be the most contentious, and these policies moved through the states at an uneven and inconsistent pace, with horizontal factors exerting little influence and political variables explaining only modest amounts of variation.

Legislative Innovation and Reinvention

Perhaps most surprising is the failure of the previous policy innovations to affect later policy adoptions. In the event history analyses for both the DPA and surrogate policies, the presence or absence of a living will policy in the previous year did not increase the likelihood of innovation, nor did the presence of a facilitative DPA law appear to pave the way for the adoption of a surrogate statute. A number of dynamics may be at work in explaining why this is the case.

First, it is possible that lawmakers in some states would have preferred to avoid the thorny refusal-of-treatment issue altogether, but when pressed for demands for a comprehensive statute (e.g., one that legalized advanced directives and decision making by non-appointed surrogates), opted to settle for a revised living will and/or new DPA law, in order to process the issue off of the governmental agenda and to strike a balance between the demands of competing issue publics.

Second, once a state tackled the right to die by adopting an advanced directives law, some legislators may have wished to consider the issue "closed," and policy advocates may have exhausted their resources when attempting gain passage of the first policy type. Indeed, it is entirely likely that many hesitant lawmakers agreed to support a living will or proxy law in exchange for the guarantee that no subsequent "push" be made for a new and more controversial policy type.

Third, as time progressed and all three policy options gained legitimacy and recognition, many states pursued strategies of "dual" or "omnibus" adoptions. By bundling two or more policy proposals together, lawmakers were able to "kill more than one bird with a single stone," while reducing the likelihood that they would have to revisit a controversial right to die proposal.

Table 4.22
Multiple Policy Adoptions in a Single Year

State/Year	Living Will	DPA	Surrogate
Arkansas, 1977	X	---	X
North Carolina, 1977	X	---	X
Delaware, 1982	X	X	---
Virginia, 1983	X	X	X
Florida, 1984	X	X	X
Lousiana, 1984	X	X	X
Wyoming, 1984	X	X	---
Connecticut, 1985	X	---	X
Indiana, 1985	X	X	X
Iowa, 1985	X	X	X
Texas, 1985	---	X	X
Utah, 1985	X	X	X
Maine, 1989	---	X	X
Minnesota, 1989	X	X	---
Kentucky, 1990	X	X	---
Montana, 1991	---	X	X
New Jersey, 1991	X	X	---
Ohio, 1991	X	---	X
Arizona, 1992	---	X	X
Colorado, 1992	---	X	X
Nebraska, 1992	X	X	---
Pennsylvania, 1992	X	X	---
Maryland, 1993	---	X	X

X denotes adoption;   --- denotes no adoption in the listed year.

Legislative Innovation and Reinvention

one or more adoptions in a single session. The most common combination was approving both types of advance directives laws at the same time (utilized by seven states). Six states also approved DPA and surrogate statutes jointly, while four simultaneously passed living will and surrogate laws. Most interesting is the fact that six states were able to "turn the hat trick," by adopting all three policy types in a single legislative session. The prevalence of these combination strategies may contribute a good deal to the explanation of why the lagged "previous policy" variables failed to perform as expected.[6]

Finally, it must be remembered that legislatures are not unitary actors. State judiciaries have been active in creating right to die policies and in interpreting and expanding the statutory creations of legislatures. The nature and extent of judicial policy making is considered in the following chapter, and the interplay between these two branches of government is examined in detail in Chapter 6.

CHAPTER 5
Judicial Innovation and Reinvention

THE RISE OF LITIGATION AND JUDICIAL POLICY-MAKING

Prior to 1976, few cases concerning the refusal of medical treatment had reached the courts of last resort in the American states, and my review of published pre-1970s decisions revealed that these early rulings addressed issues that were only tangentially related to the right to die (e.g., declination of potentially life-saving blood transfusions by Jehova's Witnesses and other religious adherents, approval of lobotomies and radical psycho-therapies for the mentally ill, and protection against involuntary sterilization for prostitutes and other socially-constructed deviants). However, as discussed previously, the post-World War II era was host to dramatic advances in the fight against sickness and disease. And as the potential of modern medicine to extend life through new remedies and artificial techniques increased, so did the ethical quagmires faced by practitioners, patients and their family members. Extant statutes and medical guidelines failed to keep pace with technology, and caregivers were often unsure as to when it was appropriate to terminate or forego death-prolonging therapies. Conflict over "where to draw the line" was inevitable, and state courts were increasingly called upon to resolve disputes and provide guidance to caregivers and other parties to these difficult end-of-life scenarios.

Quinlan: The Core Innovation

1976 was witness to a number of events, including the adoption of the first living will law, elevating the right to die to a position of prominence on the mass and professional agendas. The catalyst for the national debate which began in this year was the widely reported case of a young woman in New Jersey. Sustained by an artificial respirator, 22 year-old Karen Ann Quinlan, who was diagnosed as being in an irreversible and permanently comatose state, was suspended in medical limbo. Her father, Joseph Quinlan, requested that the ventilator be discontinued in order to permit his daughter a natural death. However, Karen's physicians disagreed on the propriety of such a decision, and the fear of liability was at least partially responsible for the hospital's decision to refuse to honor Mr. Quinlan's request without prior judicial approval. The case went to trial, was appealed twice and eventually given an audience by the Supreme Court of New Jersey (*Matter of Quinlan*, 355 A.2d 647, 1976).

Upon considering the facts and the many *amicus* briefs filed by, among others, the county prosecutor, the state Attorney General's Office, and the New Jersey Catholic Conference, the justices produced an innovative and permissive decision. While dismissing "religious freedom" and "cruel and unusual punishment" arguments for withdrawal of treatment, the high court held that both the U.S. Constitution (by virtue of the "penumbra of specific guarantees of the Bill of Rights") and the New Jersey Constitution (Article I, paragraph 1) confer a privacy right "broad enough to encompass a patient's decision to decline medical treatment under certain circumstances" (663). While noting the state's interest in the preservation of life, the Court held that that interest "weakens and the individual's right to privacy grows as the degree of bodily invasion increases and the prognosis dims" (664).

Moreover, the *Quinlan* court prescribed that, in the case of an incompetent patient suffering from a terminal condition, the patient's guardian and/or family could invoke their "best judgement" as to whether the patient would choose to exercise her or his right to privacy. The justices made clear the fact that medical decision making should take place primarily within the "patient-doctor-family relationship," and that court approval of nontreatment decisions would be "inappropriate" and

Judicial Innovation and Reinvention

"impossibly cumbersome" (669). A patient's family members were given license to refuse life-sustaining treatment when the attending physicians, after obtaining the concurrence of the hospital's "ethics committee" or "like body," diagnosed that there was no reasonable possibility of the patient's "return to cognitive and sapient life" (669). For Karen Quinlan, who was in a persistent vegetative state with no possibility of recovery, this decision allowed her father to order discontinuance of the mechanical respirator that was keeping her alive. By conferring immunity upon hospitals and physicians who followed the relatively simple procedures set forth in the opinion, the Court produced the first right-to-die policy in the state and nation.

This ruling was, however, merely the tip of the iceberg. Although Karen Quinlan's feeding tube was removed shortly after the decision, she was successfully weaned from the respirator by nursing staff and, sustained by a feeding tube, was able to breathe on her own for an additional ten years. Because her father never requested that the delivery of artificial sustenance be discontinued, this issue was not before the New Jersey high court in the 1970s. The thorny sustenance question remained dormant until 1983, when an intermediate appellate court in California, relying heavily upon *Quinlan* as precedent, ruled that artificial feeding could be refused like any other form of life-prolonging treatment (*Barber* v. *Superior Court*, 147 Cal. App. 3d 1006, 1983). California's subsequent innovation expanded (reinvented) the *Quinlan* doctrine, and, two years later, the Supreme Court of New Jersey renovated its extant policy to become the second tribunal in the nation to refuse to differentiate between sustenance and "standard" life supports (*In re Conroy*, 98 N.J. 321, 1985). The process of reinvention and renovation was underway, and courts in more and more states were called upon to make policy and settle refusal of treatment disputes.

Gradually Increasing Litigation

The *Quinlan* ruling precipitated an increase in case activity, and similar lawsuits were soon before trial and appellate courts in many other states. Figure 5.1 depicts the growth in refusal of treatment cases across the study period.[1] The number of published state cases heard by trial courts, intermediate appellate tribunals, and courts of last resort in a given year is represented by the short-dashed "frequency" line. This trend line reveals that, in the post-*Quinlan* years, state courts were increasingly called upon to address the legality of medical decision making on behalf of incompetent patients.

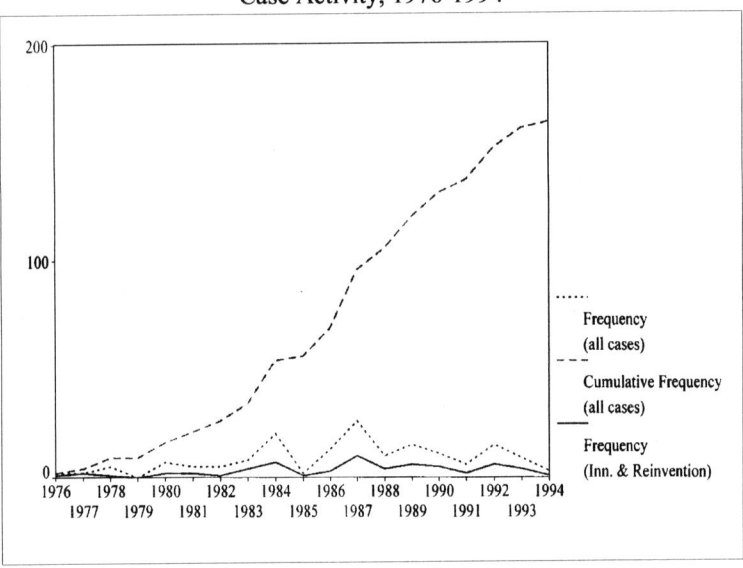

Figure 5.1
Case Activity, 1976-1994

Unlike California's core living will adoption (see Chapter 4), *Quinlan* did not trigger an immediate surge of judicial adoptions in the following year, nor did the core judicial innovation induce hyperlexis or generate an immediate barrage of litigation in other states. Rather, judicial challenges increased with gradual speed through the early 1980s. As the number of permissive decisions grew and a corpus of case law and precedents was created, parties to refusal of treatment disputes (often encouraged and aided by organized interests) showed an increased willingness to take their conflicts to the judicial arena. The mid-1980s, with the exception of 1985, witnessed a dramatic increase in the number of decisions; by 1987, the year of peak case activity, over 100 opinions had been issued by state courts. The right to die continued to occupy space on judicial dockets throughout the remainder of the study period. By the end of 1994, over 165 published decisions directly addressed the legality of discontinuing medical treatment (see the "cumulative frequency" trend in Figure 5.1).

Of course, each case which reached state courts did not result in the creation of a comprehensive right-to-die policy. In fact, only 62 of the 165 decisions (i.e., 37.6 percent) qualified as appellate judicial innovations or reinventions. The "innovation and reinvention frequency" line in Figure 5.1 is nested within the "all cases frequency" line, reflecting the gatekeeping power of appellate courts and the fact that policy entrepreneurs often had to sponsor or support numerous appeals prior to the creation of a substantive judicial policy. Once a judicial innovation was adopted, policy activists and litigants, hoping to resolve ambiguities in previous decisions or to extend/restrict the scope of a ruling, usually pressed for judicial policy expansion and reinvention. Indeed, litigation continues to this day; the right to die became, and in some states, remains, a presence on state judicial agendas.

THE ADOPTION AND DIFFUSION OF SURROGATE DECISION-MAKING POLICIES

Recall from previous chapters that there are two types of right-to-die policies created by state judiciaries. The first involves decision making by competent individuals; almost without exception, courts have ruled that mentally healthy adults have the right to direct their own health care, including the right to refuse treatment, even when such a decision is counter to expert medical advice. Courts have a long history of recognizing this type of patient self-determination, with rulings and common law doctrines that pre-date the post-WWII rise in medical technology.

While rulings that affirm this type of right may be indicative of how a court might handle a more controversial right to die case, decisions involving competent patients are not of primary interest in the present analysis. Rather, this inquiry is concerned with the second class of judicial right to die cases: surrogate decision making laws. These cases, which comprise the vast majority of judicial decisions in the study period, center on the legality of allowing a family member (or, sometimes, a close friend) of a terminally ill and incompetent patient to decline life-prolonging treatment on the latter's behalf. Because most of the patients in these cases have not executed advance directives or clearly articulated their treatment preferences to their caregivers or others, the decision to de-escalate or discontinue life supports is far more controversial than it is in instances involving competent patients. Courts must balance the patient's right to be free from treatment that she or he might have rejected with the state's interest in protecting life and guarding against potential abuse or hasty decisions by potential surrogates. Of the twenty-three states that are governed by a judicially-created surrogate policy, there is tremendous variation in terms of factors such as evidentiary requirements, the legal basis for declination of treatment, and the procedural safeguards to be satisfied in the clinical setting.

Policy Diffusion

Table 5.1 displays the date when each state adopted its first judicial policy governing end-of-life decision-making by surrogates and/or family members of incompetent patients. The distribution curves (see Figure 5.2) reveal that, in 1977, two states followed closely on New Jersey's heels in producing innovative opinions. However, this very short "burst" was followed by two years of inactivity. Diffusion "crept" slowly over the next three years, with only one adoption per year recorded from 1980-1982. In 1983, two states with prestigious and professionalized judiciaries, California and Washington, approved policies, and in the following year, 1984, four additional courts of last resort followed suit. Although it may have looked as if the "take-off" phase had been set in motion in the early 1980s, no such period of rapid growth occurred in the wake of 1984's four adoptions. Instead, no additional state courts innovated in 1985 or 1986, and diffusion proceeded in a disjointed, piecemeal fashion from 1987 through 1994. At the end of the study period, only 23 state appellate courts had created procedures for the implementation of nontreatment decisions made on behalf of incompetent persons.

Table 5.1
Dates of Adoption of Surrogate Policies by State Appellate Courts

		MA						CA	FL GA MN		AZ IA		CT			MI	KY	
NJ	TN			DE	NY	LA	WA	OH		ME	MO	IL		IN	WI	MD	
76	77	78	79	80	81	82	83	84	85	86	87	88	89	90	91	92	93	94

Figure 5.2
Judicial Adoption of Surrogate Decision-Making Policies

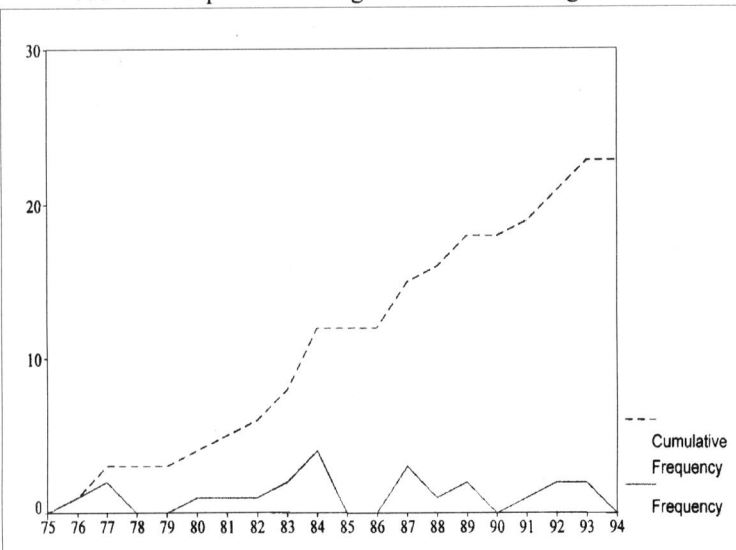

When plotted cumulatively, the pattern of judicial adoptions resembles neither the "S"-shape that characterized the diffusion of living will statutes nor the steep, straight-line pattern that described the rapid approval of durable power of attorney statutes. Instead, judicial policy creation appears to have proceeded in an uneven and random manner. This is not terribly surprising given the reactive nature of courts as policy-makers. Nevertheless, as the following section illustrates, it is possible to explain some of the variation in what may, at first blush, appear to be a random pattern of adoptions. Propensity to innovate was conditioned by a number of political, institutional and exogenous variables.

Event History Analysis: Likelihood of Adoption

Table 5.2 displays the annual hazard rates for adoption of judicial policies, and Table 5.3 reports the results of the event history analysis. As indicated by the results in the latter table, the overall model is statistically significant at better than 99.9% confidence, and seven of the substantive coefficients are significant at conventional levels of inference.[2]

Table 5.2
Annual Hazard Rates for Adoption of Surrogate Policies by Judiciaries

Year	Risk Set[a]	Adoptions	Hazard[b]
1976	50	1	.0200
1977	49	2	.0408
1978	47	0	.0000
1979	47	0	.0000
1980	47	1	.0213
1981	46	1	.0217
1982	45	1	.0222
1983	44	2	.0455
1984	42	4	.0952
1985	38	0	.0000
1986	38	0	.0000
1987	38	3	.0789
1988	35	1	.0286
1989	34	2	.0588
1990	32	0	.0000
1991	32	1	.0313
1992	31	2	.0645
1993	29	2	.0690
1994	27	0	.0000

[a]Risk Set is the total number of states that have not previously adopted a judicial surrogate policy.
[b]Hazard Rate = Adoptions/Risk Set.

Degree of Controversy: Opposition, Support, and Interest Aggregation.
Interest groups have been particularly active in attempting to influence the formation of judicial policy. In addition to providing resources to litigants and monitoring legal developments, some groups have occasionally been direct parties to lawsuits (e.g., *Compassion in Dying* v. *State of Washington*, 850 F.Supp. 1454, 1994). However, the most visible and direct way in which organized interests made their presence known was through the filing of *amicus curiae* briefs. My review of all published refusal of treatment cases from 1976-1994 revealed that about 16 different organizations regularly offered advice to state courts. Activity was greatest for those salient contests in which the stakes were high (i.e., where a court had the potential to produce an opinion that would be

Table 5.3
Event History Analysis of the Determinants of Judicial Adoptions

Variable	MLE/(Wald)	Impact[a]
Elected Attorney General	-2.3069***	-.2123[b]
	(7.8768)	
Cumulative Intrastate Cases$_{t-1}$	1.4976***	.4399
	(10.8892)	
Mean Regional Facil. Score$_{t-1}$	-.4504**	-.0477
	(4.3648)	
Piecewise 1990 Facility Int.[c]	-2.8986**	-.1485
	(5.1828)	
Physicians	1.4263*	.0438
	(3.7643)	
% Catholic	-1.4265	-.0101
	(.4006)	
Intermediate Appellate Court	.1378	.0039[d]
	(.0159)	
Elected Justices	.0481	.0014[e]
	(.0075)	
Senior Citizens	.2299**	.0327
	(3.8971)	
Judicial Reputation	.1417*	.0643
	(3.8157)	
Population	.0000000511	.0152
	(1.2655)	
Constant	-12.8489***	
	(17.1159)	

Model χ^2 (11 d.f.) 44.864***
Initial Log Likelihood -102.820   Final Log Likelihood -80.388

Number of Cases 751; Cases Scored as Adoption 23 (3.1%)
Logit model of the probability of a state appellate court adopting a policy.
[a] Impact is the change in the predicted probability of adoption after changing the independent variable from one s.d. below its mean to one s.d. above its mean, *ceteris paribus*.
[b] Change in predicted probability after switching the attorney general variable's score from 0 (appointed) to 1 (elected by voters).
[c] (Lagged regional facility score - lagged 1990 score) * (0 if 1990 or before, 1 if after)
[d] Change in predicted probability after switching the variable's score from 0 (two-tiered judicial system) to 1 (at least three-tiered judicial system).
[e] Change in predicted probability after switching the variable's score from 0 (appointed or merit plan) to 1 (elected by voters).
* Significant at .10 α-level in a two-tailed test; **.05; ***.01.

controlling authority in a state). While low levels of participation characterized cases before courts of original jurisdiction, once an appeal was granted by an intermediate appellate court, briefs were usually filed by at least one of the major interests on each side of the surrogate decision-making issue. Cases before courts of last resort typically attracted from between six to a dozen separate documents.

Table 5.4
Interest Groups Participating as *Amici*

Right-to-Die Supporters[a]	Pro-Life Groups
*American Civil Liberties Union	Agudah Israel of America
*Choice in Dying	*Americans United for Life
*Concern for Dying	Association for Retarded Citizens
Concerned Taxpayers of America	*State Catholic Conferences
	Catholic Layers Guild
*Society for the Right to Die	*Developmental Disabilities Law Center
Health Care Providers and Medical Organizations	United Handicapped Federation
*American Academy of Neurology	*National Association of Pro-Life Nurses
*American College of Physicians	*National Association for Persons with Severe Handicaps
American Geriatrics Society	
*American Medical Association	*Nursing Home Action Group
*State Hospital Associations	*State Right-to-Life Committees
*State Medical Associations	

Based on a review of all published appellate decisions, 1976-1994.
*Denotes an organization that filed briefs in 10 or more cases
[a] Choice in Dying, Concern for Dying, and the Society for the Right to Die are now all part of the same organization. The latter group changed its name to "Choice in Dying," and it later merged with "Concern for Dying." The reader should note that there are fewer right-to-die groups than there are organizations promoting positions for pro-life interests and organized medicine.

A multitude of different groups and private individuals drafted arguments; however, there were only a handful of national organizations whose presence was observed on a consistent basis in proceedings around the country. Table 5.4 groups the major actors into three categories. Only four organizations served as promoters of the right-to-die movement, while nearly twice as many groups advocated pro-life positions. Despite this lopsided ratio, it should be noted that the two camps participated in relatively equal numbers, and it was extremely rare for one perspective to be represented without being juxtaposed by the other. Health care providers and practitioners, while not participating at the same high rates as the partisan groups, often advocated positions. Generally speaking, the medical groups (e.g., state hospital and medical associations) staked out positions supporting the implementation of nontreatment decisions made within the intimate and informal confines of the family-doctor-patient relationship and opposed attempts to establish formal safeguards and procedural hurdles (e.g., waiting periods, documented approval by institutional review boards, judicial review, etc.). The presence of the medical establishment was almost always felt in civil malpractice actions, suits requesting that providers pay court costs and attorneys' fees, and lawsuits involving hospital bills for allegedly unwanted treatment. Generally speaking, providers supported the creation of policies that deregulated the medical decision making process and conferred immunity upon care-givers acting in good faith, and they opposed those policies that limited provider discretion in the clinical setting.

It is always difficult to assess the impact of briefs on the decision of a court, and only infrequently do justices explicitly acknowledge the role that *amici* played in helping a court majority to its conclusion. On those few occasions when attribution was given to a particular group, it seems clear that courts accorded the greatest weight to physicians and practitioners, particularly the American Medical Association. As the results in Table 5.3 indicate, physicians had the greatest impact of any group of citizens on the decision to adopt a surrogate policy. Although modest in magnitude, the "physicians" coefficient is statistically significant; *ceteris paribus*, when the number of physicians in a state increased from one standard deviation below the interstate mean to one standard deviation above the mean, (i.e., approximately a 67 percent shift in the distribution) likelihood of adoption increased by about 4 percentage points.

The size of a state's Catholic population, a rough proxy of the strength of a state's right-to-life lobby, did not appreciably affect judicial decision-making on the right to die. Indeed, four of the first five innovations were produced by courts in states with high percentages of Catholic parishioners: New Jersey, Massachusetts, Delaware and New York. As discussed in Chapter 4, the state Catholic conferences enjoyed high levels of success in blocking or stalling the adoption of legislative policies. Arguably, this legislative inaction contributed to an increase in the number of suits filed in these states. Policy entrepreneurs simply shifted the venue of conflict from the legislative to the judicial arena, and state justices do not appear to have accorded the same weight to Catholic objectors as did elected lawmakers in their states.

The major right-to-die organizations differ from their opponents in that the former are organized primarily at the national level. Choice in Dying, the organization that formed when the Society for the Right to Die and Concern for Dying merged in the late 1980s, does not maintain state-level chapters and instead relies on a national staff to coordinate all legal actions (Choice in Dying 1997). Accordingly, it is difficult to find a direct measure of the strength of the right to die lobby in a given state.[3]

Another group that would appear to have a direct stake in legal outcomes is senior citizens. Indeed the vast majority of requests for de-escalation of treatment were made on behalf of elderly nursing home residents. However, the American Association of Retired Persons (AARP) has neither sponsored surrogate legislation nor filed briefs in court cases, and no other major group representing seniors has, to date, come forward to influence the content of these controversial policies. Despite the absence of a coordinated geriatric lobby, the size of a state's elderly population was a significant correlate of the decision to approve a judicial policy. It is likely that this reflects the fact that demand for surrogate decision-making was higher in states with aging populations and that this increased demand often precipitated more lawsuits. The impact score for the senior citizens variable is .0327, meaning that a one standard deviation shift in population over the age of 55 produced, on average, a 3.27 percent increase in the likelihood of judicial adoption. The importance of this effect is underscored by the fact that the size of a state's overall population did not emerge as a significant factor in the analysis. Clearly, the age of the citizenry, not the size, is the crucial determinant of right-to-die innovation.

While interests groups were clearly active in attempting to promote and shape judicial policymaking, they do not appear to have been terribly successful at achieving their goals. As discussed in the next section, institutional factors had a much greater impact in determining whether or not appellate courts adopted innovations.

Institutional Determinants: Judicial Variables.
One of the most interesting consequences of the American tradition of judicial federalism is the emergence of very different structural arrangements under which justice is administered in the fifty states. Professionalism and prestige have long been considered important components in regional networks of judicial communication (Caldeira 1988). And the results from the event history analysis suggest that judicial reputation plays an important role in innovation. The impact score for this variable was .0643, suggesting that the most distinguished courts were more likely to be early innovators and that the less renowned tribunals (i.e., those cited least by courts in other states) were more likely to be laggard adopters.

Another important factor was the amount of prior related case activity in a state. In some instances judicial policy emerged in an incremental fashion at the intrastate level. For example, in 1980 the Florida Supreme Court became the first court in the nation to hear a right to die case involving a competent patient. In *Satz* v. *Perlmutter* (379 So.2d 359), the high court issued a very narrow ruling that extended only to the specific facts of the case: a competent, terminally ill adult may refuse artificial respiration. While the justices declined to set guidelines for future cases, they did find a constitutional right to privacy that protects individuals from unwanted, invasive treatment. Because it was limited to instances involving competent adults, the 1980 decision did not qualify as a surrogate adoption; however, the high court had produced a supportive opinion that laid the groundwork for the expansion of patients' rights. In 1984, an intermediate appellate court, relying heavily on the constitutional arguments expressed in *Perlmutter*, extended the right to refuse treatment, vis-a-vis surrogates, to terminally ill patients in PVS (*In Re Guardianship* of *Barry*, 445 So.2d 359). Only four short months after *Barry*, the intermediate appellate court's holding was endorsed by the Florida Supreme Court in a case with similar circumstances. In *John F. Kennedy Hospital* v. *Bludworth* (452 So.2d 921, 1984) the Florida justices adopted the doctrine of substituted judgment and articulated a series of procedures to be followed in the clinical setting. The Florida example is illustrative of a process that occurred in many states: courts at various levels gradually created and extended legal doctrines and policy that allowed individuals to forego death-forestalling medical treatment. This pattern is tapped by the lagged "cumulative intrastate cases" variable; as the number of right to die cases heard by state courts increased, so did the likelihood of a judicial surrogate adoption.[4] The impact score of .4399 is the highest in the model.

The remaining two judicial variables did not prove to be as important. First, although middle-tiered courts in several states produced several important adoptions, in the aggregate, the presence of an intermediate appellate court did not substantially increase the likelihood of adoption, and the vast majority of innovations were pioneered by states' courts of last resort. Secondly, states in which justices were selected and/or retained by popular election were no more or less likely to approve of surrogate decision-making than were states that utilized other methods of judicial selection (e.g., legislative or executive appointment). This pattern is in marked contrast to the results of the statutory adoption models; whereas state legislators were often unwilling to expend political capital on approving controversial policies (particularly in election years), state justices do not appear to have been influenced by the prospect of electoral retribution. This finding is consistent with theoretical expectations, as judicial elections differ from legislative ones on crucial dimensions such as campaign finance and overall visibility; still, this result suggests that right to die cases do not reach the same level of salience as do other controversial social issues that are heard by state judiciaries, such as the death penalty (Brace and Hall 1995).

Institutional Determinants: Attorney Generals.
State attorney generals proved to be extremely important actors in terms of opening or closing windows of opportunity for judicial innovation.

First, these officers often issued advisory opinions that, in practice, guided district attorneys and other local-level prosecutors on whether or not the state should intervene in, or object to, the implementation of nontreatment decisions. In fact, in those cases that reached the appellate level, attorney generals easily brought more suits opposing surrogate decision-making than did any other type of official or organization.

The power to choose to contest nontreatment decisions and to appeal cases was of paramount importance, as many state courts had few or no opportunities to address the legality of ending medical care. Consider the highly-publicized situation in Missouri. In 1983, the parents of Nancy Beth Cruzan, a young woman in a persistent vegetative state, asked that their daughter's life support systems (including the delivery of artificial nutrition and hydration) be discontinued so that she be permitted a natural death. The trial court which heard the case concluded that there was clear and convincing evidence that the patient would not have wanted to be burdened with treatment that had no possibility of restoring her to conscious, meaningful life. Accordingly, the judge ruled that Nancy Cruzan had a constitutional right to liberty and ordered that her nontreatment decision be honored by her providers. Although the nursing home in charge of Ms. Cruzan's care did not appeal the decision, William L. Webster, the elected Attorney General, argued that the decision effectively deprived the patient of her right to life. Webster successfully obtained an injunction blocking the removal of life supports, while his office, acting in concert with the patient's court-appointed guardian *ad litem*, directed the appeal. In 1989 the Missouri Supreme Court ruled against the Cruzans, and, in so doing, articulated a very restrictive policy with a strict evidentiary standard (*Cruzan v. Harmon*, 760 S.W.2d 408). Had Webster not appealed the decision, it is very likely that the high court would never have had the opportunity to produce a policy.

Subsequent developments in the state further highlight the importance of this gatekeeping role. In 1992, Webster's office was again involved in an appeal; this time, the Attorney General objected to the ruling of a lower court which granted an exception to the clear and convincing evidentiary rule for minor patients (*In Re Busalacchi*, No. 73677, excerpted in Choice in Dying 1997). Before the case could be heard, elections for Attorney General were held, and Webster was defeated. His successor, Jay Nixon, petitioned the high court to voluntarily dismiss the case, and the motion was granted in January, 1993 (Choice in Dying 1997), effectively closing a window of opportunity for policy reinvention by the judiciary.

The preceding example accents both the discretionary power which accrues to office holders and the fact that controversial and unpopular position-staking can have electoral consequences for executive-branch officials. The results from the regression analysis suggest that fear of popular retribution weighs mightily on the calculus of risk-averse attorney generals. All other factors held constant, states with elected attorney generals were 21.23 percent less likely to produce judicial innovations than were states utilizing other methods of selection for this office.[5] This finding is important, particularly given the scant attention given to attorney generals, not only in innovation research, but in the broader corpus of state politics literature as well. Research on state-level political processes could benefit from a deeper investigation of the roles of attorney generals.

Horizontal and Vertical Influences.
As discussed in Chapter 2, the United States Supreme Court's 1990 ruling in the *Cruzan* case was essentially innocuous in nature. The learned justices identified a constitutional liberty interest that served as the basis for patient self-determination in health care decision making, but the decision granted tremendous authority to the states in terms of adopting safeguards and standards of evidence. The results from the EHA model suggest that regional diffusion had a greater impact in the post-*Cruzan* era than it did before the opinion was issued, but not in the hypothesized direction.

Counter to theoretical expectations, the coefficient capturing the effects of regional policymaking trends in the 1980s was statistically significant and negative in direction, implying that states actually became less likely to innovate as more of their neighbors adopted and permissively reinvented policies. This effect is magnified in the years after 1990; the statistically significant coefficient for the piecewise interaction term indicates that a structural break occurred in 1990, and, all things being equal, a one standard deviation increase in a state's lagged regional facility score resulted in a decreased probability of adoption of 19.62 percent. Because the *Cruzan* ruling effectively legitimized restrictive prohibitions in state legislative right to die policies, perhaps fewer state courts were willing to consider challenges to extant statutes once the U.S. Supreme Court had ruled, even in spite of facilitative adoptions and renovations by courts in neighboring states.

These findings suggest that, state courts, unlike their legislative counterparts, were not terribly influenced by regional developments. Whereas horizontal variables accounted for the greatest amount of variation in the legislative adoption models, clearly a different dynamic is at work in the diffusion of judicial innovations. Indeed, as discussed in the next section, state appellate justices, while often reliant on precedents from other jurisdictions, also dramatically reinvented policies in a seemingly idiosyncratic matter.

JUDICIAL REINVENTION

The creation of appellate policy required a mixture of chance and strategic timing on the part of litigants and policy entrepreneurs. Once a high court in a state adopted a surrogate policy, that adoption could affect subsequent judicial outcomes in one of two ways. First, the opinion could influence judicial policy making in other state courts (interstate reinvention). In addition, a state court's policy could also contribute to policy expansion, modification or retraction in future decisions within the state (reinvention through renovation). As Table 5.5 indicates, each of these processes was present in the diffusion of judicial innovations. Included in the table are the core innovation, the subsequent reinvented innovations, and policies renovated at the intrastate-level.

An inspection of Table 5.5 supports a number of observations. First, courts were called upon to address the right to die as it applied to a number of different types of individuals (e.g., competent and incompetent patients, minors, and never-competent wards of the states) and a variety of different treatment scenarios ranging from "standard" life supports (e.g., ventilators, respirators, regimens of antibiotics, and dialysis treatments), to DNR and "no code" orders, to the far more controversial treatments involving the artificial delivery of hydration and nutrition.

Table 5.5
Judicial Innovation and Reinvention

Case/Date/State/Court[1]	Treat[2]	Out[3]	Basis[4]	Sur.[5]	Evid.[6]
Quinlan, 8/76, NJ, LR	SLS	+	CON	Yes	SJ
Saickewicz, 11/77, MA, LR	SLS	+	CON	Yes	SJ*
Dockery, 12/77, TN, IAC	SLS	-	----	No	---
Dinnerstein, 6/78, MA, IAC	DNR	+	CON	Yes	SJ
Perlmutter, 1/80, FL, LR	SLS(c)	+	CON	---	---
Spring, 5/80, MA, LR	SLS	+	CON	Yes	SJ
Severns, 9/80, DE, LR	SLS	+	CON	Yes	SJ
Storar, 3/81, NY, LR	SLS	-	CL	No	---
Eichner, 3/81, NY, LR	SLS	+	CL	Yes	CCStrict*
P.V.W., 12/82, LA, LR	SLS	+	CON	Yes	BI*
Colyer, 3/83, WA, LR	SLS	+	CON	Yes	SJ*
Spivey, 9/83, GA, IAC	SLS(c)	+	CON	---	---
Barber, 10/83, CA, IAC	ANH	+	CL	Yes	SJ/BI
Smith, 11/83, NM, LR	SLS	-	STAT	No	---
Barry, 1/84, FL, IAC	SLS	+	CON	Yes	SJ
Shapiro, 5/84, OH, IAC	SLS	+	CON	Yes	SJ*
Bludworth, 5/84, FL, LR	SLS	+	CON	Yes	SJ
L.H.R., 10/84, GA, LR	SLS	+	CON	Yes	SJ
Hamlin, 11/84, WA, LR	SLS	+	CON	Yes	BI
Torres, 11/84, MN, IAC	SLS	+	CON	Yes	BI

Table 5.5(continued)
Judicial Innovation and Renovation

Case/Date/State/Court[1]	Treat[2]	Out[3]	Basis[4]	Sur.[5]	Evid.[6]
Bartling, 12/84, CA, IAC	SLS(c)	+	CON	---	---
Conroy, 1/85, NJ, LR	ANH	+	CON	Yes	BI*
D'Allesandro, 4/86, FL, IAC	ANH	+	CON	Yes	SJ
Bouvia, 6/86, CA, IAC	ANH(c)	+	CON	---	---
Brophy, 9/86, MA, LR	ANH	+	CON	Yes	SJ
Milton, 2/87, OH, LR	SLS(c)	+	CON	---	---
White, 5/87, AL, LR	SLS(c)	+	STAT	---	---
Delio, 6/87, NY, IAC	ANH	+	CL	Yes	CCStrict*
Peter, 6/87, NJ, LR	ANH	+	CON	Yes	SJ
Jobes, 6/87, NJ, LR	ANH	+	CON	Yes	SJ
Farrell, 6/87, NJ, LR	SLS(c)	+	CON	---	---
Rasmussen, 7/87, AZ, LR	ANH	+	CON	Yes	BI
Olds, 10/87, IA, LR	SLS	+	CL	Yes	SJ
Gardner, 12/87, ME, LR	ANH	+	CL	Yes	CCRelax*
Grant, 12/87, WA, LR	ANH	+	CON	Yes	BI
Drabick, 4/88, CA, IAC	ANH	+	CON	Yes	BI
O'Connor, 10/88, NY, LR	ANH	-	CL	Yes	CCStrict*
Cruzan, 11/88, MO, LR	ANH	-	CL	Yes	CCStrict*
Morrison, 11/88, CA, IAC	ANH	+	CON	Yes	BI

Table 5.5(continued)
Judicial Innovation and Renovation

Case/Date/State/Court[1]	Treat[2]	Out[3]	Basis[4]	Sur.[5]	Evid.[6]
McConnell, 1/89, CT, LR	ANH	+	STAT	Yes	CCRelax
Couture, 8/89, OH, IAC	ANH	−	STAT	No	CCRelax*
Westhart, 8/89, CA, IAC	ANH	−	STAT	No	---
Riddlemoser, 10/89, MD, LR	DNR	Moot	---	---	---
Longeway, 11/89, IL, LR	ANH	+	CL	Yes	CCRelax*
McAfee, 11/89, GA, LR	SLS(c)	+	CON	---	---
Fosmire, 1/90, NY, LR	SLS(c)	+	CL	---	---
Swan, 2/90, ME, LR	ANH	+	CL	Yes	CCRelax*
Greenspan, 7/90, IL, LR	ANH	+	CL	Yes	CCRelax*
Browning, 9/90, FL, LR	ANH	+	CON	Yes	SJ
McKay, 11/90, NV, LR	SLS(c)	+	CON	---	---
Moorhouse, 8/91, NJ, IAC	ANH	+	CON	Yes	SJ
Lawrance, 9/91, IN, LR	ANH	+	CON	Yes	BI
L.W., 4/92, WI, LR	ANH	+	CON	Yes	BI
Belcher, 7/92, WV, LR	DNR(c)	+	CL	---	---
Doe, 6/92, GA, LR	DNR	−	STAT	Yes	SJ
Rosebush, 9/92, MI, IAC	SLS	+	CL	Yes	BI
C.A., 10/92, IL, IAC	DNR	+	CL	Yes	BI
Anderson, 11/92, OH, IAC	DNR(c)	+	CL	---	---

Table 5.5(continued)
Judicial Innovation and Renovation

Case/Date/State/Court[1]	Treat[2]	Out[3]	Basis[4]	Sur.[5]	Evid.[6]
Mack, 2/93, MD, LR	ANH	-	CL	Yes	SJ*
Thor, 7/93, CA, LR	ANH(c)	+	CL	---	---
Elston, 7/93, KY, LR	ANH	+	CL	Yes	CCRelax
Doe, 11/93, MA, LR	ANH	+	CON	Yes	BI
Pino, 4/94, FL, IAC	ANH(c)	+	CON	---	---

Table Legend
[1] LR = court of last resort; IAC = intermediate appellate court
[2] Treatment being considered: SLS = standard life-supports; ANH = artificial nutrition and hydration; (c) = competent
[3] Outcome: + = court allowed nontreatment decision; - = court disallowed nontreatment decision
[4] Basis of Decision: CON = constitutional rights; CL = common law rights; STAT = statutory rights
[5] Surrogate Policy: Yes = surrogate policy created or approved; No = surrogate policy denied
[6] Evidentiary Standard: CCStrict = clear and convincing evidentiary standard; CCRelax = clear and convincing standard, but "character" evidence may supplement express intent; SJ= substituted judgment standard; BI = best interests of patient standard;
* = judicial approval required

Secondly, the vast majority of appellate courts to hear these cases produced rulings which approved of the specific nontreatment decisions at bar in the cases. Only in Tennessee did an appellate court issue an opinion that imposed an "all-out" moratorium on decision-making by surrogates (*Dockery* v. *Dockery*, 559 S.W.2d 952, 1977). Once a state court granted *certiorari*, even if it declined to grant the relief being requested by the potential surrogate in the case at bar, the justices almost invariably found that surrogate decision-making would be permissible under certain circumstances. Tribunals that were willing to hear a refusal of treatment case were also willing to make right to die policy; courts that denied review to surrogate cases were perhaps unwilling to enter the political fray surrounding this divisive issue. Thirdly, courts relied upon differing standards and rationales in creating their surrogate decision-

Reinvention Through Renovation

Judicial renovation occurs when a state court substantively "revises" or "updates" its prior innovation. In the case of judicial surrogate policies, renovation occurs when a state court hands down a ruling that in some way alters the central foundations (i.e., changes the evidentiary standards required for discontinuance of treatment, requires prior judicial approval of a nontreatment decision or strikes such a requirement, and/or alters the legal basis of an individual's right to decline treatment) set forth in the state's prior judicial policy.

Table 5.6 displays the dates when states adopted and renovated their surrogate decision-making policies. The single-digit numbers that appear at the "intersection" of a state's abbreviation and the year in which it innovated or renovated denote the state's judicial surrogate facility score. These scores ranged from a low of 0 (decisions by surrogates banned) to a high of 9 (highly facilitative policy). If no decision was handed down in a given year, then no number is recorded for that year; dashes indicate judicial inactivity, and circled values denote renovations. Looking at the first entry in the table, we see that Arizona adopted its first judicial surrogate policy in 1987; with a facility score of 9 points, this decision was highly facilitative, and the policy was not subsequently renovated. The next state in the table, California, reveals a much more active pattern of adoption and renovation. The first policy was created in 1983, and, in the following year, 1984, the policy was renovated and the facility score increased from 7 to 8 points; in 1986, the refusal of treatment issue was again on the judicial decisional agenda in California, but the extant policy was not renovated (i.e., its facility score did not change). In 1988, a renovating opinion was handed down by an appellate court that increased the facility score to 9, and this policy was essentially reaffirmed in another decision by a California appellate court in the following year.

An inspection of Table 5.6 allows the reader to observe the temporal flow of reinvention and to see which states had opportunities to renovate their policies in subsequent decisions. Of the twenty-three states to adopt

156   *Right-to-Die Policies in the American States*

surrogate policies, thirteen either never had an additional case to consider or were unwilling to re-open the surrogate issue by granting a petition for review. Appellate courts in three other states (Florida, Maine, and New York) reviewed cases following the adoption of their first policies, but the tribunals in these states did not abandon the central tenets of their initial rulings. In each of these states, justices applied, without alteration, their prior innovations to new situations and settings or attempted to resolve ambiguities regarding procedural requirements (see the Maine and New York case studies in the next section). Seven states (abbreviations are in bold-faced type in Table 5.6), however, renovated their policies by supplanting holdings in their prior opinions with new doctrines and/or requirements; courts in these states explicitly "overruled" or "replaced" prior decisions that were controlling authority in their respective jurisdictions (see Massachusetts and New Jersey case studies in the next section).

Of these seven renovators, three altered their policies only on one occasion, while the other four states renovated on two separate occasions. A total of eleven judicial renovations occurred over the course of the study

Table 5.6
Temporal Flow of Judicial Adoption and Renovation

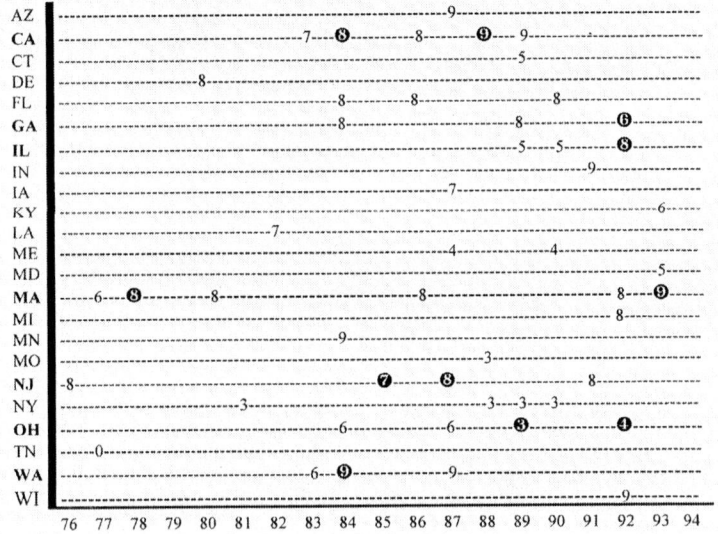

Judicial Innovation and Reinvention

period. Note that twenty-seven cases were heard subsequent to first judicial innovations, meaning that, when pondering whether or not to revise a policy, state appellate courts opted to renovate on 41 percent of these occasions. In an attempt to explain why courts in some states renovated their policies while others did not, the results of a logistic regression analysis are discussed below.

<u>Logistic Regression Analysis: Likelihood of Renovation</u>.
Table 5.7 reports the MLE coefficients from an analysis of whether or not a state renovated its judicial policy once it had adopted a judicial innovation. The results contrast sharply with those from the three legislative renovation models. Neither of the two variables that proved important in statutory renovation, distance from regional score and years since first judicial adoption, proved to be deterministic. In fact, none of the coefficients are statistically significant, and the model fails to predict a single renovation. This lack of findings underscores the episodic and idiosyncratic nature of judicial policy-making on the right to die. Courts are reactive actors, and judges do not enjoy the same opportunities to adopt and renovate policies as do their legislative counterparts. When courts are willing to renovate, it is often due to a chance mix of supporting events and conditions: a situation must exist in which a party to a nontreatment decision contests or challenges the existing right to die policy in the state; someone must bring suit in a court of original jurisdiction; that case (which can not be technically moot) must be appealed by one of the real parties to the contest; an appellate court must determine that significant legal issues need to be resolved in order to grant *certiorari*; and, finally, the particular facts of the case, intrastate changes in legislative policies, interstate changes in judicial policies, new medical evidence, and other factors must conspire, to some degree, in order to convince a court that its previous policy needs to be substantially altered.

Although such renovations seldom occurred, when they did, courts appeared to be more inclined to produce more facilitative policies than they did to specify more restrictive ones.

Table 5.7
Determinants of Judicial Surrogate Renovations

Variable	MLE/(Wald)	Impact[a]
Elected Attorney General	-2.4507	-.4168[b]
	(1.866)	
Cumulative Intrastate Cases$_{t-1}$	-.2866	-.1480
	(2.5088)	
Physicians	2.1285	.1766
	(1.2946)	
% Catholic	-4.2939	-.0875
	(.6344)	
Intermediate Appellate Court	6.2061	.0800[c]
	(.0323)	
Elected Justices	1.6858	.0643[d]
	(1.0645)	
Senior Citizens	-.1417	-.0396
	(.1082)	
Judicial Reputation	.0543	.0632
	(.1453)	
Population	.000000113	.1164
	(1.4674)	
Distance From Region Score$_{t-1}$[e]	.0131	.0057
	(.0070)	
Years Since First Adoption	.1004	.0605
	(.4161)	
Constant	-12.6682	
	(.1318)	

Model χ^2 (11 d.f.) 11.379
Initial Log Likelihood -41.528   Final Log Likelihood -35.839

Number of Cases 182; Cases Scored as Renovation 11 (6.0%)
Maximum likelihood estimation of a logit model of the probability of a state appellate court renovating its extant surrogate policy in a given year.
[a] Impact is the change in the predicted probability of adoption after changing the independent variable from one s.d. below its mean to one s.d. above its mean, *ceteris paribus*.
[b] Change in predicted probability after switching the attorney general variable's score from 0 (appointed) to 1 (elected by voters).
[c] Change in predicted probability after switching the variable's score from 0 (two-tiered judicial system) to 1 (at least three-tiered judicial system).
[d] Change in predicted probability after switching the dummy variable from 0 (appointed or merit plan) to 1 (elected by voters).
[e] State's lagged facility score - lagged regional facility score.
* Significant at .10 α-level in a two-tailed test; **.05; ***.01.

Judicial Innovation and Reinvention

Facility Scores Over Time.
Of the eleven renovative decisions produced by the state appellate courts, only four resulted in lower facility scores, whereas seven resulted in surrogate policies with increased facility (see Table 5.6). Each state's first and final judicial policy scores are displayed in Table 5.8; by the end of the study period, four states had liberally renovated their policies, while only two had place restrictions on their first adoptions. (The Supreme Court of New Jersey decreased its *Quinlan* facility score by one point in 1985, the year in which it tackled the sustenance issue, but, two years later, abandoned a strict evidentiary standard and "relaxed" its facility score back to the *Quinlan* level. The Garden State's 1994 facility score was the same as the score for its core judicial innovation in 1976.)

It is important not to overstate the extent of renovation. As Table 5.8 shows, the mean gain in scores over the diffusion period was a mere .26 points. Table 5.6 also indicates that the year of adoption does not appear to be a major contributor to the level of facility of a state court's policy. The first innovators produced fairly permissive rulings, but this trend was partially arrested when other state courts adopted much more restrictive standards early in the diffusion cycle. Once the "take-off" phase was underway, a surfeit of different policies was produced in a sporadic manner. In fact, facility scores were regressed on date of adoption using an ordered probit estimation technique, and the results from this analysis support the view that innovations did not become significantly more permissive over time.[6]

To examine some of the ways in which the judicial policies varied across states (and over time), each of the three components comprising the judicial facility scores are discussed below.

Constitutional, Common Law, and Statutory Rights.
In creating a surrogate policy, state justices had to begin by identifying the legal basis for the individual's right to decline unwanted medical treatment. The first courts to take up the issue found constitutional (U.S. and state) guarantees of patient self-determination. Usually relying upon the right to privacy, these affirmations contribute to the highest levels of policy facility, because they guard against legislative and statutory encroachment on the judicial policies.

Table 5.8
Initial and Amended Judicial Surrogate Policy Facility Scores

State	Adopt Year	First Score	Final Score	Gain
AZ	1987	9	9	0
CA	1983	7	8	+1
CT	1989	5	5	0
DE	1980	8	8	0
FL	1984	8	8	0
GA	1984	8	6	-2
IL	1989	5	8	+3
IN	1991	9	9	0
IA	1987	7	7	0
KY	1993	6	6	0
LA	1982	7	7	0
ME	1987	4	4	0
MD	1993	5	5	0
MA	1977	6	9	+3
MI	1992	8	8	0
MN	1984	9	9	0
MO	1988	3	3	0
NJ	1976	8	8	0
NY	1981	3	3	0
OH	1984	6	4	-2
TN	1977	0	0	0
WA	1983	6	9	+3
WI	1992	9	9	0

First Score: $\mu = 6.35$ $\sigma = 2.31$
Final Score: $\mu = 6.61$ $\sigma = 2.48$
Gain Score: $\mu = +.26$ $\sigma = 1.25$

Figure 5.3
Sources of the Right to Refuse Treatment

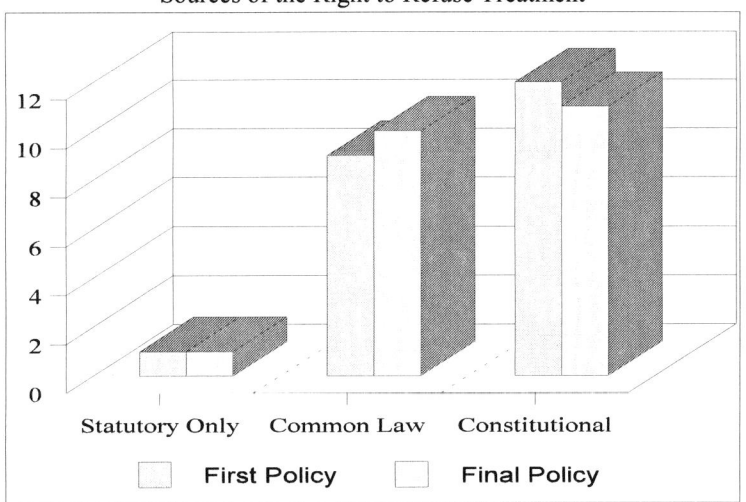

As shown in Figure 5.3, a slim majority of state courts followed the lead of early innovators, particularly New Jersey and Massachusetts, in finding such protections. However, a number of other high courts opted to restrict their analyses to common law principles, and, in so doing, allowed for the possibility of legislative alteration. Only one tribunal, the Supreme Court of Connecticut, restricted its analysis to extant statutes.[7]

Evidentiary Standards.
In specifying the decisional standards to be plied by family members, friends, and guardians of incompetent patients, the courts produced even more varied policies. The most restrictive standard is that of "clear and convincing" evidence of a patient's treatment preferences, whereby a decision maker must produce unequivocal proof that the patient possessed a deep-seated opposition to the continuance of the specific type of care under consideration. As Figure 5.4 shows, only three states have produced such a policy. However, four additional innovators have adopted a requirement of clear and convincing evidence, but the language in these opinions is a bit "softer," allowing for "character" testimony and the

Figure 5.4
Evidentiary Standards

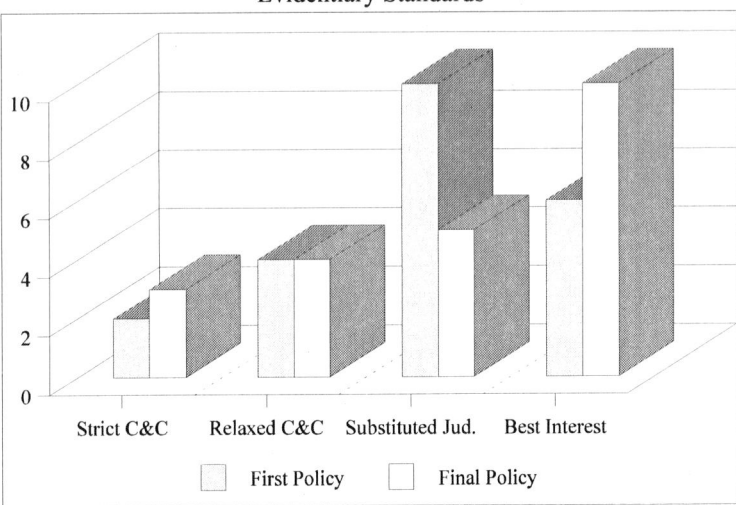

consideration of views expressed by the patient in informal settings and in casual conversations. (The distinction between these two types is clarified later in the chapter, when the policies of New York and Maine are contrasted.) Far more facilitative, and more frequently adopted, were substituted judgment and best interest standards. The former requires the decision maker to attempt to "stand in the shoes" of the incompetent patient and determine the decision that the patient would likely have made; the latter standard affords surrogates the greatest discretion by allowing them to reach that decision that they believe best serves the patients' needs and interests.

Judicial (De)Regulation.
The third major factor contributing to expedient implementation of judicial policies involves the level to which the decision making process is insulated from judicial intervention. As Figure 5.5 shows, while a majority of courts specified that prior judicial approval of a nontreatment decision was unnecessary in routine and nonconflictual settings (i.e., those in which family members and patients were in agreement as to the

Judicial Innovation and Reinvention

propriety of the decision), a number of other courts were either ambiguous as to the role of the courts or explicitly required judicial proceedings (replete with testimony from witnesses and an investigation by a guardian *ad litem* or similar patient ombudsman) in order for treatment to be ended. While all of the policies allowed for judicial intervention in the event of conflicts between families and providers or in instances of disagreement between potential surrogates, the absence of a "mandatory" judicial clearance clearly contributes to ease of use in the clinical setting.

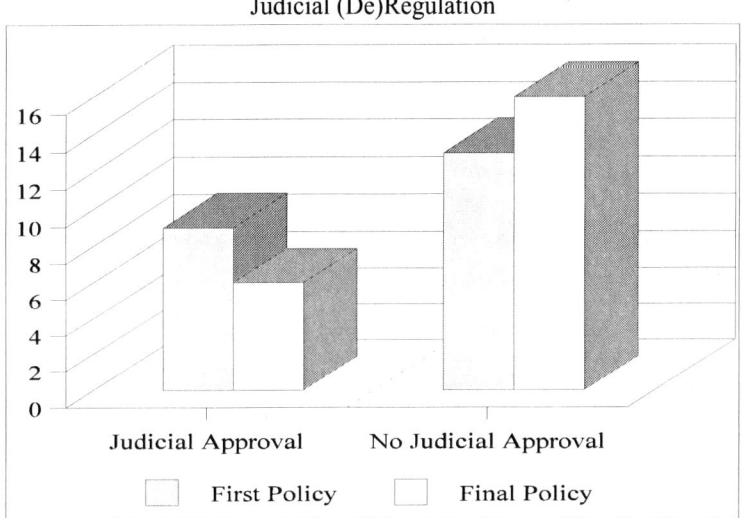

Figure 5.5
Judicial (De)Regulation

Having considered the above nuances in surrogate policies, it is clear that the pattern of judicial policy reinvention differs considerably from the "liberal reinvention" trend which characterized legislative revisions by state legislators reviewing living will and DPA statutes. However, it should be stressed that (as discussed in Chapter 3), the judicial facility scores are limited to three criteria, and a simple descriptive analysis of these scores may obscure some important aspects of how policies differ and how courts modified their decisions over time. In order to provide a more complete sketch of the renovation process and to describe in greater detail the various approaches advocated by state judiciaries, the next section examines the evolution of case law in six states which saw the right to die meet with different fates in their court systems.

REINVENTION AND RENOVATION: SIX STATES, SIX POLICIES

Each of the states to adopt a judicial surrogate policy has its own, unique right to die story; in the interests of parsimony I have confined my case studies to six states whose chronologies of events, when compared and contrasted, capture a tremendous amount of the diversity in the diffusion and reinvention process. Indeed, the courts in each of these states pioneered the six most common types of surrogate policies. New Jersey and Massachusetts produced substitute judgment policies, with a prominent role for trial courts in the former, but not in the latter. The New York Court of Appeals adopted the most restrictive and cumbersome bundle of procedures of any bench to ponder the refusal of treatment question, but this rigid "clear and convincing" policy was reinvented and "relaxed," first by the Maine Supreme Judicial Court, and later, and more "liberally," by the Supreme Court of Connecticut. Minnesota is examined because it produced the most permissive type of policy (judicial deregulation coupled with a best interests standard) and clearly influenced the decisions of courts in several other jurisdictions.

New Jersey: Core Innovation, Extensive Policy Refinement

As discussed in the beginning of this chapter, the Supreme Court of New Jersey crafted the core surrogate decision making policy in 1976. This seminal ruling established a series of relatively simple procedures to be followed when exercising surrogate decisionmaking in the clinical setting. Because the *Quinlan* court made clear the fact that prior judicial approval of a nontreatment decision was unnecessary, a reasonable political analyst might have concluded that a clear policy mechanism was in place, thereby obviating the need for subsequent reinvention. In fact, however, this was not the case. On several occasions, the high court confronted new

Judicial Innovation and Reinvention

circumstances, and this resulted in the creation of safeguards and the revision of the *Quinlan* doctrine.

Nursing Homes and the Potential for Elder Abuse.
Karen Quinlan was a young woman in the prime of life when she was rendered permanently vegetative. It seems clear from the record that no parties to the case questioned the sincerity of Joseph Quinlan's testimony regarding his daughter's wishes. However, most persons who are rendered medically incompetent are elderly residents of nursing homes, and this population is particularly vulnerable to abuse or neglect by caregivers and family members (Hilfiker 1983; Howell 1984). Some observers cautioned that the potential for acting contrary to geriatric patients' wishes was exacerbated by the lack of evidentiary requirements in *Quinlan*.

In a 1985 decision, *Matter of Conroy* (486 A.2d 1209), the New Jersey Supreme Court modified the procedures for withdrawing treatment from incompetent geriatric patients residing in residential nursing homes. The justices delineated a number of precautions to be taken in long-term geriatric health care facilities (in addition to those specified in *Quinlan*). Under the *Conroy* rules, no nontreatment decision can be implemented until (1) medical evidence indicates that the patient's death will occur in one year; (2) a trial court appoints a guardian or confers power upon an existing guardian to direct the course of end-of-life care for the patient; (3) new evidentiary tests (more strict than those in *Quinlan*) are satisfied; and (4) the state ombudsman for the elderly approves the decision after obtaining the diagnostic concurrence of two independent neurologists.

The *Conroy* ruling is significant for two reasons. First, the Court explicitly endorsed the use of living wills and noted that these directives are to be accorded legal validity in establishing a patient's wishes. Secondly, the Court also held that artificial feeding and hydration are not to be distinguished from other forms of invasive treatment. These two findings constitute significant reinventions of the evolving right-to-die case law in the state.

Further Clarification and Renovation.
Given the absence of any legislative guidelines governing decision making by surrogates, additional questions, often quite narrow in scope, arose. The

Supreme Court of New Jersey, which never denied *certiorari* when a case presented new material issues, created detailed procedures covering decision making in private (i.e., non-clinical) homes, created a mechanism for resolving disputes in instances of institutional noncompliance with a nontreatment decision (*Matter of Farrell*, 529 A.2d 404, 1987) and modified its policy for dealing with nursing home residents in PVS (*Matter of Jobes*, 529 A.2d 434, 1987; *Matter of Peter by Johanning*, 529 A.2d 419, 1987). In each instance, the court acted decisively by creating comprehensive and unambiguous guidelines to be followed by providers and patients alike.

Building upon the legal foundations articulated in *Quinlan* and *Conroy*, the three 1987 opinions effectively established a constitutional foundation for refusing treatment as well as provided decisive guidelines for health care providers to follow in considering requests for nontreatment. Not surprisingly, the number of cases before both trial and appellate courts subsided in the years following 1987.

At what appears to be the end of the judicial renovation process in New Jersey, multiple policies now cover a number of different end-of-life settings. The high Court has taken up the policy making slack left by a cautious state legislature. The New Jersey judges produced and refined a very permissive substitute judgment policy that deemphaizes the role of the courts while stressing institutional responsibility and leaving intact the intimacy of the patient-family-physician relationship. As an early adopter, the New Jersey Supreme Court would naturally influence the content of subsequent adoptions in other jurisdictions; however, as revealed in the next sections, *Quinlan* and its progeny would have only limited sway over the appellate judicial policies created in other states. While almost all courts to consider the right to die reviewed, cited and were otherwise deferential to the core innovation, the courts in the other 22 states which took up the surrogate issue engaged in various degrees of independent reinvention when they produced their own core tangential innovations.

Massachusetts: Second Adoption, Cautious Refinement

In 1977, the Massachusetts Supreme Judicial Court (SJC) became the second tribunal in the nation to hear a right-to-die case. In *Superintendent*

Judicial Innovation and Reinvention 167

of *Belchertown State School* v. *Saikewicz* (370 N.E.2d 417) the court produced an innovative opinion that both followed and departed from the logic employed by the New Jersey Supreme court in *Quinlan*. The *Saikewicz* judges endorsed the individual right to privacy encompassed in the "penumbra of specific guarantees of the Bill of Rights," and held that in "appropriate circumstances" a patient has the right to refuse "unwanted infringements of bodily integrity" (424). Moreover, the opinion makes clear that in Massachusetts, incompetent patients have the same privacy rights as competent ones. However, and in stark contrast to *Quinlan*, in order for incompetent persons to assert these rights, probate judges are required to apply a "substituted judgement" standard in order to "ascertain the incompetent person's actual interests and preferences" (431). These individual concerns must be balanced against countervailing state interests in: (1) the preservation of life; (2) the protection of innocent third parties; (3) the prevention of suicide; and (4) maintaining the ethical integrity of the medical profession (425). The Massachusetts court explicitly rejected the view that decisions to forgo treatment should be made by an incompetent patient's family, physicians and guardian; instead the court articulated procedures for the appointment of a guardian, the preparation of a case history and the criteria to be employed by probate judges in making a substitute judgement on a patient's behalf.

> Questions of life and death seem to us to require the process of detached but passionate investigation and decision that forms the ideals on which the judicial branch of government was created. (435)

Direction From Below: An Intermediate Appellate Court Takes the Lead. The 1977 decision generated considerable confusion and uncertainty in the Massachusetts medical community, and litigation was sure to follow. For example, medical practitioners and hospital administrators questioned the legality of institutional policies designating "no-code" or "do-not-resuscitate" orders in patients' medical records and charts. In *Matter of Dinnerstein* (380 N.E.2d 134, 1978) an intermediate appellate court ruled that, when no parties object to a DNR order, no prior judicial approval is required.[8] The *Dinnerstein* judge also clarified the SJC's holding in *Saikewicz* by establishing that judicial approval needs to be obtained for refusal of treatment only when there is the potential for "effecting a permanent or temporary relief from the illness or condition being treated" (138). Courts do not have automatic jurisdiction over termination of treatment cases when a patient is in the final stages of a terminal disease.

The SJC, in *Matter of Spring* (405 N.E.2d 115, 1980), affirmed the *Dinnerstein* view that prior judicial approval is not always required before withholding treatment from an incompetent patient. In determining whether or not a court order is required, the SJC advised health care providers to consider a number of factors, such as the prognosis for recovery, clarity of professional opinion, and familial consent. However, the *Spring* justices declined to specify any balancing formula or minimal requirements to be adopted by practitioners, thereby leaving considerable ambiguity as to what types of decisions must be approved by probate courts. Indeed, the SJC noted that judicial approval may reduce liability, but never confers full immunity. The *Spring* court also opined that once a probate court is faced with a decision, it cannot delegate the responsibility to a patient's family members and/or physicians, but must apply the substituted judgement standard itself. In the wake of the *Spring* decision, it seems reasonable to expect that the most risk-averse providers are the most likely to seek court approval for nontreatment decisions.

Three observations should be taken from the sequence of events discussed above. First, an intermediate appellate court demonstrated a willingness and ability to break ranks with its Supreme Court by engaging in policy liberalization. Secondly, the high Court allowed (and even embraced) the lower court's modifications, but not in their entirety. The Supreme Court justices were unwilling to approve the "full scale" judicial deregulation called for in *Dinnerstein*. Finally, the SJC judges were not nearly as decisive as their New Jersey brethren; where the latter produced detailed and extensive instructions for practitioners, the former opted to specify a list of suggestions and declined to confer wholesale immunity on providers attempting to apply the court's advice.

Artificial Sustenance: *Conroy* and *Jobes* Revisited.
Prior to 1986, no cases before the Massachusetts appellate courts concerned the withdrawal of artificial nutrition and hydration; in that year, however, the SJC considered the case of a living patient in PVS who was

sustained by a gastrostomy tube. In *Brophy* v. *New England Sinai Hospital, Inc.* (497 N.E.2d 626), the Massachusetts SJC, relying extensively upon the precedent set in New Jersey's *Conroy*, held that patients have a right to refuse artificial feeding like any other form of medical treatment. Rejecting the view that persons in PVS feel pain, the court further concluded that when a feeding tube is removed, the cause of death is the underlying condition that prevents swallowing, not the tube removal. Although the Massachusetts justices fully endorsed the legal reasoning in *Conroy*, they departed from the New Jersey "hard line" on provider compliance. *Brophy*, like *Jobes*, compels institutions with policies against refusal of treatment to facilitate transfer of the patient to a provider that will honor the nontreatment decision; however, the former strongly implies that health care facilities should never be compelled to act in a manner contrary to their institutional philosophy, and the *Brophy* opinion avoids the (all too common) problem of securing a transfer in the clinical setting. The SJC of Massachusetts had once again avoided formulating a complete policy, and the failure of the justices' policies to anticipate future contingencies would mean that further reinvention and clarification was necessary.

Ambiguities Beget Further Litigation.
The requirement of judicial determination (specified in *Saikewicz* but vaguely adumbrated in *Spring*) precipitated a number of cases in which appellate courts were required to resolve issues on behalf of incompetents and minors. In a case-by-case approach, judges applied the substituted judgement standard and produced varied decisions on the refusal of treatment.[9] In each such case that it heard, the SJC limited its holding to the specific facts at bar in a given case and crafted opinions that provided health care professionals with little-to-no general guidance.

Reinvention was neither as decisive in Massachusetts as it was in New Jersey, nor did renovation proceed as smoothly in the former as it did in the latter. As a result, judicial reinvention is likely to continue in Massachusetts.

New York: Early Adoption, Restrictive Policy, Intrastate Judicial Rivalry

Whereas the SJC of Massachusetts borrowed heavily from the New Jersey precedents (e.g., finding a constitutional right to privacy and adopting a substituted judgment standard) while only moderately reinventing the core innovation (i.e., requiring prior judicial approval of nontreatment decisions), the high Court in New York produced a restrictive innovation that departed dramatically from the approaches opted for by each of the above courts.

On March 31, 1981, the New York Court of Appeals (the court of last resort) issued two rulings which addressed the legality of refusal-of-treatment in the state. *Matter of Eichner* (438 N.Y.S.2d 266) concerned the fate of "Brother Fox," an eighty-three year-old member of a Roman Catholic Marianist order, who was in a persistent vegetative state and being maintained by a respirator. The evidence established that, prior to being hospitalized, the patient had expressed his wishes not to be maintained by any artificial means if there was no hope that his condition would improve. While it explicitly declined to consider a constitutional right to privacy, the high court did find that, under common law, all mentally competent adults have the right to bodily self-determination, including refusal of potentially life-saving treatment. In order for this right to be exercised upon behalf of an incompetent patient, the "highest standard applicable to civil cases" was adopted: there must be "clear and convincing" proof of the patient's intentions (274). Because Brother Fox, during a public discussion of the *Quinlan* case, had specifically stated his desire not to be hooked up to a respirator if he were in an irreversible vegetative coma, the court found that the standard of proof was satisfied and approved cessation of the treatment. However, for future patients who had not left such incontrovertible evidence of their wishes, the ruling established a requirement that would prove difficult to satisfy.

The cautious, conservative tenor of *Eichner* is more pronounced in its companion case. In *Matter of Storar* (438 N.Y.S.2d 266) the Court of Appeals refused to allow the discontinuation of life-prolonging blood transfusions to a fifty-two year-old profoundly retarded patient suffering from terminal bladder cancer. Because the patient was never competent, the court, likening the patient to an infant, found that it would be "unrealistic" to attempt to determine his wishes (275), but, unlike courts in other states, the justices rejected a substituted judgement standard that would allow a parent or close family member to make decisions on the "child's" behalf. Although the patient's mother refused to consent to the transfusions, the Court of Appeals held that a parent "may not deprive a child of life saving treatment, however well intentioned" (275). The court found that the state's interest, as *parens patriae*, in protecting the health and welfare of the child, was of paramount importance. Also of concern to right-to-die proponents is language in the opinion which could be construed to forbid or limit the right to refuse artificial nutrition and hydration; the *Storar* court specifically analogized the blood transfusions to food -- "they would not cure the cancer, but they could eliminate the risk of death from another treatable cause" (275).

Taken together, the *Eichner* and *Storar* decisions created a very limited right-to-die policy. While competent individuals have the right to refuse treatment, in order for incompetent patients and their families to avail themselves to that right, "clear and convincing" evidence of the patient's wishes must be produced. The Court of Appeals effectively banned the future adoption of a substitute/surrogate judgement or "best interest" standard. Moreover, the court declined to outline procedures to be followed by health care providers and was ambiguous as to when court approval was required in order to terminate treatment.

Restrictive Policies Breed Litigation:
Applying the Strict Evidentiary Standard.
In the wake of these two 1981 precedents, lower courts in the state produced varied rulings; some requests to discontinue treatment were approved (e.g., *Application of Lydia E. Hall Hospital*, 455 N.Y.S.2d 706, 1982), while many others were denied based on a lack of indisputable evidence (e.g., *Matter of O'Brien*, 517 N.Y.S.2d 346, 1986). One trial court even rejected the clear and connvincing standard, opting instead for a best interests rule (*Matter of Beth Israel Medical Center*, 519 N.Y.S.2d 511, 1987).

Artificial Nutrition and Hydration: Policy Expansion at Mid-Level.

Perhaps the most controversial cases concerned the provision of sustenance. New York trial courts repeatedly held that incompetent patients could not forgo artificial nutrition and hydration (*Vogel v. Forman*, 512 N.Y.S.2d 622, 1986), even in instances where patients had clearly expressed their preferences to decline such treatment (*Workmen's Circle Home v. Fink*, 514 N.Y.S.2d 893, 1987). In 1987, an intermediate appellate court produced an innovative opinion that attempted to clarify the apparent sustenance prohibition in *Storar*. In a unanimous opinion (*Delio v. Westchester County Medical Center*, 516 N.Y.S.2d 677, 1987) the court concluded that no distinction should be made between refusing sustenance and other forms of life-prolonging treatment:

> ...the withdrawal or withholding of feeding by artificial means should be evaluated in the same manner as any other medical procedure. In this respect, we view nutrition and hydration by artificial means as being the same as the use of a respirator or other forms of life support equipment. (689)

The *Delio* justices opined that the *Storar* holding is limited only to cases in which the patient was never competent or there is otherwise no evidence of a patient's wishes. Because the patient in the *Delio* case had left explicit instructions (i.e., clear and convincing evidence) directing that he not receive artificial nutrition and hydration if he became irreversibly comatose, the court required the hospital to comply with his wishes or facilitate his transfer to another institution.[10]

Evidentiary Standard Tightened from on High.

In order to anticipate medical contingencies and satisfy the "clear and convincing" evidence requirement set forth by the Court of Appeals, many practitioners and policy advocates supported the drafting of advance directives. In 1988, advance directives received a clear endorsement from the New York Court of Appeals. In *Matter of Westchester County Medical Center on Behalf of O'Connor* (534 N.Y.S.2d 886, 1988) the majority held that living wills and power of attorney directives are a viable and persuasive means of expressing one's future wishes regarding medical treatment. Although it approved the use of advance directives, there is

Judicial Innovation and Reinvention

little reason to believe the *O'Connor* ruling was warmly received by right-to-die advocates. Indeed, the majority opinion effectively made more rigorous the "clear and convincing" evidentiary standard:

> [the standard] requires proof sufficient to persuade the trier of fact that the patient held a *firm and settled commitment* to the termination of life supports under the circumstances like those presented. As a threshold matter, the trier of fact must be convinced, as far as is humanly possible, that the strength of the individual's beliefs and the durability of the individual's commitment to those beliefs makes a recent change of heart unlikely. (892) (italics added)

Applying this heightened litmus test to the facts in the case, the (slim) majority found that, despite the patient's repeated oral expressions of intent to decline artificial treatment, the evidence did not demonstrate that she possessed a sustained and enduring dedication to refusing sustenance. Specifically, the court noted that most of the oral statements were made following the deaths of the patient's family members, and that the statements did not specifically address the unique circumstances that characterized the patient's medical situation. In a scathing dissent, Judge Simons (joined by Judge Alexander) blasted the majority's rule as "unworkable" and requiring "humans to exercise foresight they do not possess" (904). Concurring in result only, Judge Hancock also attacked the standard and made clear his belief that the state of New York should join the majority of jurisdictions which have adopted a substitute judgement standard.

Limited Judicial Discretion in the Post-*O'Connor* Era.

Despite the division in the high court, the *O'Connor* rule became (and remains) binding authority in the state. In the wake of this decision, courts have often found evidence in the form of a patient's past oral expressions to be lacking in specificity and durability (e.g., *Wicker* v. *Spellman*, 552 N.Y.S.2d 437, 1990). New York courts have been called upon to settle over fifty suits dealing with the termination of treatment. In many instances, courts have had to deny such requests. The "specific subjective intent" rule, as reiterated in *O'Connor*, requires health care providers to obtain evidence capable of satisfying a rigorous standard.

The New York Experience Explicated.
The New York Court of Appeals, in 1981, took a bold and controversial step when it explicitly rejected the two most important components of the extant case law that existed in the nation at the time: substituted judgment and the constitutional right to decline treatment. In so doing, the New York justices produced an extremely restrictive opinion that presented a profound challenge to the status quo in their state. The requirement of judicial review of nontreatment decisions, coupled with the fact that long-standing informal medical practices no longer appeared to enjoy any immunity from civil or criminal actions, generated a slew of case activity in the state. Debate over common law principles gave way to an intrastate "battle of wills."

In the wake of *Storar*, lower courts produced extremely varied findings. Some trial courts applied the clear and convincing rule strictly, while others attempted to circumnavigate the policy or ignore it altogether. As in Massachusetts, an intermediate appellate court eventually asserted itself by attempting to clarify and limit the prohibition on discontinuing artificial sustenance. The Court of Appeals essentially allowed this discretionary reinvention when it declined *certiorari* in the *Delio* case. However, as lower benches increasingly began to produce facilitative opinions that violated the explicit rule of evidence promulgated in *Storar*, the Court of Appeals eventually reasserted its authority when it reinforced its clear and convincing rule in *O'Connor*. The high Court's decisive stance has effectively truncated the range of endogeneity to which lower courts can avail themselves, and judicial policy reinvention appears to have come to a standstill.

Minnesota: One-Time Facilitative Innovation Ensures Judicial Deregulation

Two years after the New York Court of Appeals produced the extremely restrictive policy that opened up a Pandora's box of subsequent litigation, the Supreme Court of Minnesota opted for a completely opposite policy which effectively precluded the need for future judicial renovation.

The Supreme Court of Minnesota has ruled only once on the right-to-die. Although *Matter of Conservatorship of Torres* (357 N.W.2d 332, 1984) was a case of first impression in the state, the justices, looking to *Quinlan* and other early precedents, held that the right to refuse life-prolonging treatment is guaranteed by the U.S. Constitution and is embedded in Minnesota's common law principles. This right, the court held, may only be overridden if the state's interest is "compelling" (333).

The primary question at bar concerned the authority of a probate court to order withdrawal of life-supports. Although no statute explicitly conferred such a right upon the courts (or conservators), the *Torres* justices, relying upon the state's general guardianship statute, the Minnesota Constitution and the Minnesota Patients' Bill of Rights, ruled that courts could approve nontreatment requests.

Having established that courts have the power to approve withdrawal of treatment, the Supreme Court briefly considered the proper decisional standard to be employed by conservators. Curiously, the court endorsed both a substituted judgement standard and a best interest standard. The justices adamantly rejected the contention that allowing a patient to die is inconsistent with the patient's best interests:

> Simply equating the continued physical existence of a conservatee, who has no chance for recovery, with the conservatee's "best interests" appears contrary not only to the weight of medical authority, but also to those indications of legislative opinion which exist. (339)

Breaking ranks with the New York Court of Appeals, the Minnesota bench ruled that "character" testimony (descriptions of a patient's personality and beliefs) provides some indication of a patient's desires and should, therefore, be considered by probate judges: "At a minimum, any determination of a conservatee's 'best interests' must involve some consideration of the conservatee's wishes" (339).

The high court found that, because the patient had no available family members, judicial proceedings were appropriate in the *Torres* case. However, the court majority (over the objections of three dissenters) made clear the fact that judicial approval is not mandatory when family members are available to make treatment decisions. Consider the comments contained in a footnote to the opinion:

> At oral arguments it was disclosed that on an average about 10 life support systems are disconnected weekly in Minnesota. This follows consultation between the attending doctor and the family with the approval of the hospital ethics committee. It is not intended by this opinion that a court order is required in such situations. (341)

By declining to prescribe institutional safeguards or strict evidentiary standards to be satisfied by surrogates, the Supreme Court produced a limited, yet highly facilitative, opinion that preserved the autonomy of the patient-family-doctor relationship.

Maine: Contentious Innovation Gives Way to Judicial Unity

The Maine Supreme Judicial Court first addressed the right-to-die issue in 1987. *In Re Gardner* (534 A.2d 947) concerned the fate of a twenty-three year-old man in a persistent vegetative state with no hope of recovery. The patient was receiving artificial nutrition and hydration through a nasogastric tube. In this case of first impression in the state, the court was required to address two important issues: the right of individuals to decline unwanted treatment and the legality of withholding artificial sustenance.

The high court issued a facilitative, yet very limited, opinion. Upon reviewing the voluminous case law in other jurisdictions, the Maine justices, departing from the logic embraced by the vast majority of state courts, declined to identify a constitutional right to privacy as the basis for refusing treatment. Instead, the court majority (relying heavily upon the rationale advanced by the New York Court of Appeals) recognized the individual's common law right of informed consent as justification for refusing or discontinuing futile or invasive medical care. On the sustenance issue, the court majority refused to draw any distinction between artificial nutrition and hydration and other forms of extraordinary care.

The court ruled that "clear and convincing" evidence of an incompetent patient's wishes must be established before a trial court can grant a guardian's request for discontinuance of life-prolonging procedures (953). Although it adopted the most rigorous evidentiary standard applicable to civil cases, the court ruled that informal statements made by the patient to his family members and friends were sufficient to establish the patient's decision to forgo artificial feedings. The court also recognized PVS as an appropriate triggering condition for considering a course of nontreatment (as long as a patient has made clear her or his wishes about treatment options under this particular circumstance). The opinion establishes that the withdrawal of treatment in accordance with a patient's previously declared intentions is not suicide, nor is it grounds for criminal or civil action against providers or any other parties to the treatment decision.

Limiting their analysis to the specific facts at bar, the majority judges refused to consider the legality of substitute judgement or best interest decisions made by surrogates in the absence of appropriate evidence as to patients' medical treatment preferences. Moreover, the court was silent on the procedural requirements to be satisfied before rendering a nontreatment decision; the opinion leaves unanswered questions as to whether or not guardianship proceedings and trial court approval are prerequisites to deescalating an incompetent patient's medical care. Also of concern to practitioners and policy advocates was the narrow court majority; three of the seven justices dissented. In a scathing opinion, Justice J.J. Clifford (joined by the other two dissenters) blasted the majority for failing to accord appropriate weight to "the state's legitimate interest in preserving life and preventing suicide" (956). *Gardner* effectively legalized surrogate decision-making, but only under a limited and incompletely specified set of circumstances. Policy proponents likely hoped for future judicial reinvention and expansion, but were undoubtedly concerned by the deep division in the high court.

<u>Reaffirmation and Homogenization.</u>
In 1990 the Supreme Judicial Court heard a case with facts nearly identical to those in *Gardner*. The patient in *In Re Swan* (569 A.2d 1202) was an irreversibly vegetative eighteen year-old man whose life was being

sustained by feedings delivered through a gastrostomy tube. Clear and convincing evidence existed to support the guardians' contention that the patient had previously expressed a desire to forgo the treatment in question. The only factor differentiating *Swan* from *Gardner* is the age of the patients. The patient in the former case was injured shortly after his eighteenth birthday; of concern to the District Attorney (the only party to object to the nontreatment decision) was the fact that the patient in *Swan* had expressed his treatment preferences while only seventeen years of age (i.e., he was technically a minor at the time). In a unanimous opinion, the high court ruled that age is "at most a factor to be considered by the factfinder in assessing the seriousness and deliberativeness" with which a patient's declarations were made (1205). The Court found that the declarations made by the seventeen year-old patient reflected an understanding and legitimate commitment to refusing the type of treatment at issue in the case.

The *Swan* justices extended the right-to-refuse treatment to minors (subject to findings of fact made by a trial court). This decision reaffirmed and buttressed *Gardner*. It also put to rest the possibility of a judicial reversal in the near future; indeed, two of the justices who dissented in the 1987 case signed a concurring opinion stating that the result in *Swan* was compelled by *Gardner*'s controlling authority. However, still left unresolved by the court were the procedural issues implicated in *Gardner*.

Increased Clarity Brings Closure.
The Maine SJC produced a policy that reflects a compromise between facilitation and restriction. The justices found only a common law basis for the right to decline treatment, and they required that surrogates demonstrate clear and convincing evidence of an incompetent patient's wishes prior to the implementation of a nontreatment decision. However, this was the first state court to advocate a "relaxed" approach to the evidentiary standard; the requirement in *Gardner* is not nearly as rigorous as the New York Court of Appeals' rulings in *Storar* and *O'Connor*. Moreover, the Maine precedent creates one policy governing both the use of sustenance and other "standard" forms of life-prolonging treatment. The ruling in *Swan* effectively clarified the "flexible" nature of the evidence rule, and it undoubtedly signaled to practitioners that the Court had

Judicial Innovation and Reinvention

reached a settled and clear position on the legality of surrogate decision making. No additional cases have reached the appellate judicial agenda in Maine.

The SJC of Maine pioneered the first "relaxed" clear and convincing evidentiary standard, and the *Gardner* and *Swan* opinions informed judicial innovation in at least four other states which adopted similar policies. The Supreme Court of Connecticut was one such tribunal, and, in 1989, it liberally (and creatively) reinvented the policy by strictly limiting the situations under which judicial intervention was necessary.

Connecticut: Statutory Construction, Moderate Policy Facility

In *McConnell* v. *Beverly Enterprises--Conn* (553 A.2d 596, 1989) the question centered on the legality of withdrawing artificial nutrition and hydration. State legislators had adopted rules governing decision-making by surrogates in 1985; however, that statute expressly forbid discontinuance of sustenance. In the majority opinion, the high court justices recognized, in *dicta*, a common law right to self-determination and a constitutional right to privacy. However, unlike courts in other states, the Connecticut court declined to invoke those rights and did not declare the statute a nonexclusive means of withdrawing treatment. Instead, the justices attempted to reconcile the statute with the patient's right to discontinue intubated feedings:

> The plaintiffs in this case have indeed raised ... a constitutional claim. We need not, however, address this claim on its merits when we can instead find redress for the plaintiffs by an appropriate construction of the applicable statutes. (603)

The court ruled that despite specific statutory language banning the removal of any device or system designed to deliver food, water and nutrients to a patient, the statute was "intended to recognize distinction between artificial technology to assist nutrition and hydration and normal procedures to assist in feeding" (597). The court further held that the removal of a patient's gastrostomy tube was not suicide or homicide, as such an action merely frees the patient of "extraordinary mechanical devices" and allows "nature to takes its course" (605).

McConnell left intact the procedures and requirements of the surrogate decision-making statute (meaning that no judicial intervention was necessary except in cases of conflict between parties to the decision) while expanding the act's coverage to include an additional, and extremely controversial, type of treatment. The court simultaneously engaged in judicial restraint (by not supplementing extant statutory law with a new judicial policy) and judicial activism (by liberally constructing and expanding the statute).

Judicial Innovation and Legislative Innovation: Preemptive Signaling.
The *McConnell* court's "middle ground" (600) approach of "reconstructing" statutory semantics and language to allow vegetative patients to forego artificial sustenance all but demanded a legislative response. Moreover, in *dicta*, the court endorsed the rulings of tribunals in other states which found both constitutional and common law rights to refuse treatment. In essence, the Connecticut high court was sending a message to legislators: any attempt to alter the statute to disallow refusal of intravenous feedings would be invalidated or eclipsed in subsequent legal action(s). Elected lawmakers received this message and, in 1991, overhauled the refusal of treatment statute to allow surrogates to end all types of life-prolonging therapies.

General Observations and Conclusions

Six general lessons can be taken from the preceding six examples. First, when addressing cases of first impression in their respective jurisdictions, state appellate courts pride themselves on independence from other courts and precedents. All of the opinions discussed above contain thorough and voluminous reviews of past decisions; however, in each new state to consider an issue, justices managed to renovate and alter past policies, and this process resulted in the creation of six distinctive policies. In some instances (e.g., the New York adoptions), justices, upon paying homage to the various precedents, departed from almost all of the substantive conclusions reached by other courts, a process Glick (1992, 147) terms "citation without impact." Other states made more subtle refinements to earlier policies and approaches, such as requiring review by a medical

Judicial Innovation and Reinvention

review board as opposed to a hospital ethics committee, and requiring confirmation of a diagnosis by different types (and numbers) of specialists. In the end, however, judicial policies are like snowflakes: they are made up of the same elements, resemble one another in many ways, and may appear indistinguishable to the untrained eye, but no two are ever exactly alike.

Unlike legislatures, courts do not control the scope or nature of the questions that they must resolve. As a result, judicial policies must be tailored to the specific facts at bar in a given case. The idiosyncratic details of these cases often condition justices' approach to the right to die. For example, New York's restrictive policy was created in response to a particularly controversial situation involving a conscious but incompetent adult who appeared to derive at least some minimal pleasure from his day-to-day life in a nursing home. The New York Court of Appeals, concerned by the thorny quality of life issues implicated in this case, produced a policy designed to protect helpless individuals from potential abuse and the rash judgments of others. Had the situation involved a less controversial set of circumstances (e.g., an unconscious patient whose family and physicians all agreed to the nontreatment decision), it is possible that the New York court might have engineered a somewhat different standard. Nevertheless, once a court has produced a policy, it is very likely that it will cling to this precedent in the future, acting as a jealous guardian against encroachments on its innovation. While justices have made minor procedural changes in response to new facts and concerns (e.g., adding safeguards against elder abuse, extending procedures to cover patient's being cared for at home by family members, and clarifying ambiguities in previous decisions), few courts ever abandoned or supplanted the central components of their first policies (i.e., legal basis of patient's rights, decisional standard to be donned, and requirement of judicial approval).

The third point flows from the observation that different courts are willing to engage in various levels of judicial activism and restraint. Some bodies are willing to promulgate a broad set of guidelines that anticipate a wide range of future contingencies, while others limit themselves to a small number of narrow issues at bar in a given case. "Limited" policies are more difficult to implement than are comprehensive ones, and judicial ambiguity is an open invitation to future litigation.

Fourthly, all other factors held constant, restrictive policies are much more difficult to implement than are permissive ones, and judicial proceedings are often necessary. Trial courts may apply and interpret restrictive policies in varied ways, and ultimately these lower court judges may seek to reinvent or "stretch" existing judicial policies; eventually, intrastate judicial policy rivalries can be expected to develop. In the event that a penultimate appellate court produces a modified or expanded ruling (provided it is not reviewed by the higher court), many subordinate courts will interpret this decision as controlling authority and alter their practices in keeping with the new policy. Ultimately, the court of last resort in a state must assert its preeminence by rendering a decisive ruling that resolves the ambiguities and clearly outlines the policy procedures to be followed and the standards to be employed by practitioners and judges alike.

The fifth point is a corollary to the fourth. Permissive policies which vest discretion in the hands of field administrators (e.g., doctors, social workers, and hospital ethics committees) are characterized by ease of implementation. A ruling which deregulates decision making may effectively "close the door" on later policy renovation. This was the case when the Minnesota judges adopted the best interest standard and truncated the role of the courts in the approval process; no later cases reached the appellate level in this state. Moreover, as Table 5.5 shows, a similar pattern was found in the majority of states which produced these facilitative policies.

Finally, judicial policy making does not take place within a vacuum. Issues often reach judicial agendas as a result of legislative inactivity. Right to die opinions are rife with admonitions to elected legislators and with calls for statutory guidelines. As the Connecticut example illustrates, legislative and judicial policies are often juxtaposed, and no analysis of the right to die can be complete without a careful look at the interplay between these two branches of government. Accordingly, this is the task to which the next chapter addresses itself.

CHAPTER 6
Judicial and Legislative Interaction

THE COMPLEX WEB OF RELATIONSHIPS

There are numerous ways in which the actions of legislative officials influence the decisions made by judges, and the reverse holds true as well. Traditional political science research, particularly of politics at the national level, has stressed the formal, constitutional mechanisms designed to juxtapose the two branches of government through "checks and balances" (e.g., judicial review of statutes, legislative confirmation of judicial appointments, etc.). However, the fifty states have developed varied constitutional arrangements, and the formal avenues of influence may not be of great importance in the study of interstate policy diffusion and reinvention for a number of reasons. First, with many types of potentially controversial public policies, legislators and judges alike may not be terribly inclined to place an issue on their decisional agendas, and the preferred course of action for policy makers may be to defer to the decisions made in the other institution. Institutional restraint, inaction and propensity for nondecision-making can delay or block the creation of meaningful policy for years. Furthermore, once a first innovation is adopted, the result is often a limited policy, rife with restrictions, vague provisions, and other ambiguities; this type of tentative policy making may well reflect a conscious effort to shift the locus of conflict to a different institutional venue for clarification or policy refinement. Potential policy makers have an arsenal of strategic options to which they can avail themselves, and many of these "choices" or alternate strategic paths are discussed below.

Judicial Innovation, Legislative Response

Let us assume, for the sake of argument, that a case of first impression involving surrogate decision making has been appealed to a state's court of last resort and that no refusal of treatment legislation is on the books. Justices may take any number of actions. First, courts always have the option of simply denying *certiorari* to a given case, and, even if review is granted, the most substantive right to die issues may not be addressed. Because the "real" parties (i.e., incompetent patients) to many refusal of treatment cases have died as the litigation unfolds, justices may declare the case technically moot, even if a question of law is presented that is capable of repetition and likely to evade future scrutiny. Similarly, appellate justices usually attempt to dispose of a case on "technical" or "narrow" grounds, and they may "pass" on addressing broad constitutional issues or legal doctrines if this can be avoided; in this instance, justices may indicate (in *dicta*) how they would handle similar conflicts in the future, or they might call on the state legislature to erect policy guidelines to guide practitioners and obviate the need for future litigation.

In the event that a state court does "tackle" the surrogate decision making question "head on," justices still have a full range of decisional endogeneity when crafting the opinion. At one extreme, an "aggressive" policy can be adopted; for example, the opinion could find a constitutional right to refuse treatment and detail a specific set of procedures to be followed in all future cases, including the specification of an evidentiary standard and the requirements needed to satisfy this standard. At the other extreme, a judicial policy can be extremely limited in scope; for example, if the case involved an incompetent and terminally ill patient sustained by a ventilator, and the patient had previously instructed her adult children that she did not wish to receive artificial respiration once a terminal diagnosis was made, and all her children agreed that such treatment should be discontinued, then a court might explicitly limit its holding to "only those cases involving discontinuance of artificial respiration therapy for terminally ill patients who have expressed a previous desire to avoid such treatment, given that all adult children are in agreement as to the propriety of the decision." This type of restrained holding obviously does not cover many future contingencies nor does it preclude the need for subsequent policy making on the right to die. Rather than choosing one of these extreme approaches, judges may also take a "middle road," whereby they rely on common law principles and articulate a surrogate policy and procedures, but make clear the fact that the opinion is merely an interim policy, to be replaced by a comprehensive statutory right to die package.

Once any of these types of judicial surrogate policies is created, elected legislators can respond in at least five different ways. First, they can do nothing. Indeed, as theorized in Chapter 2, this is probably the most palatable choice for risk averse lawmakers who may be content to allow the state judiciary to handle this controversial policy matter. Even if an appellate innovation is extremely limited in scope, lawmakers may hope that the judicial policy will be renovated in subsequent cases. For legislators, it is convenient (even if unrealistic) to assume that the state courts have "taken care of the problem."

However, because these high profile surrogate cases are often accompanied by publicity and public and professional calls for action, legislators may choose to adopt a surrogate decision making policy. Ostensibly, policy sponsors and supporters can argue that they need to create a surrogate statute in order to make legislative law consistent with judicial law; in the event of a highly facilitative judicial policy, particularly one that finds a constitutional right to refuse treatment, assembly members can make the case that "the court has already ruled, and there is nothing we can do but follow suit." On the other hand, if the judicial policy is limited or contains tough restrictions (e.g., a clear and convincing evidentiary standard with formal approval by a probate judge), lawmakers may, by adopting a more permissive surrogate innovation, "trump" the judicial policy while capitalizing on a favorable tide of public opinion. Conversely, when a judicial policy is not (or is no longer) highly salient, legislators may produce a "weakened" surrogate statute designed to satisfy the demands of right to die opponents.

Still another legislative option exists, and this one is perhaps the most pragmatic: adopt a living will and/or proxy law, as opposed to a surrogate law, in the wake of a judicial innovation. This approach allows lawmakers to "respond" rather than "doing nothing," and advance directives laws are likely to be accompanied by considerably less opposition and "heat" than would a surrogate adoption.

Of course, the preceding discussion presumes that a justiciable controversy is available for appellate resolution. Often, this is not the case, and few state legislatures are capable of ignoring the refusal of treatment question forever, particularly as interstate innovation increases and model laws are produced. The next section considers the options available to policymakers when legislative innovation precedes judicial innovation.

Legislative Innovation, Judicial Response

As revealed in Chapter 4, the majority of state legislatures adopted advance directives laws prior to (or in lieu of) approving a surrogate policy. The present discussion assumes that a state has already passed a living will and/or DPA law. Once such a statutory mechanism is in place, instances are likely to arise when the statute fails to confer legality upon a particular request for nontreatment; individuals may bring suit either challenging the restrictions contained in the legislative policy, asking courts to interpret vagaries in the law, or requesting that the provisions governing advance directives be extended to incompetent patients who have not drafted such a document. Ultimately, these cases will present questions inviting courts to rule on the legality of decision-making by surrogates.

State appellate courts have a number of choices when confronted with a surrogate case. The theoretical assumption, presented in Chapter 2, is that, all thing being equal, the presence of a statute will increase the likelihood of *certiorari*. Even if appellants are successful in having their case heard at the appellate level, justices might dismiss the case on grounds of mootness or address only minute technicalities of the case. However, once justices are willing to rule on the substantive policy issue at bar in a case, they can do at least four different things. An "activist" court might simply rule that the state's statutes are a nonexclusive means of the exercise of patient self-determination, and then create a constitutionally-based policy without regard to the statutes. Similarly, a court majority might carefully review the extant statutes and conclude that the laws evince legislative support for the right to die, and then craft an expansive judicial surrogate policy. Another, slightly more "restrained" option is to conclude that the advance directives guidelines should also cover incompetent persons without a document, but to "strictly" apply the conditions of the statute (e.g., disallow withdrawal of sustenance if the statute forbids the discontinuance of artificial nutrition and hydration, allow surrogate decisionmaking only when the statutory triggering conditions have been satisfied, etc.). A final option is for the judiciary to conclude that the right to die is an issue for legislative resolution, with the opinion indicating that surrogate decision making is not permissible unless a legislative policy is created to allow the practice. These latter two paths place the right to die firmly in the legislative court, whereas the first two would seem to decrease the likelihood of legislative renovation.

When a state's legislative body has previously adopted a surrogate law, appellate courts face similar choices to the ones discussed above, but, once a statutory surrogate device is in place, courts are seemingly forced to explicitly exercise some type of judicial review if they are, in fact, willing to hear such a case. (The relationship between surrogate statutes and judicial surrogate policies is given a detailed treatment later in this chapter.)

The adoption of judicial and legislative policies does not, of course, mark the end of the policy making process. Calls and opportunities for judicial and legislative renovation are likely to occur, and more strategic choices will have to be made by actors in both branches of government.

The purpose of the above discussion is to make clear the fact that there are numerous ways in which courts and legislatures can respond to the policy decisions (and nondecisions) of actors in other branches of government. The theory in Chapter 2 predicts that judicial innovation will decrease the likelihood of legislative innovation, while legislative policy adoptions will increase the opportunities for judicial innovation. These are certainly reasonable expectations, but it is important to stress that these are not the only possible options. Indeed, as discussed in subsequent sections, most of the possibilities listed in this section have been realized in one or more states.

Chapter Overview

This chapter is an attempt to untangle the complex web of legislative-judicial relationships. First, the results from Chapters 4 and 5 are reviewed, and patterns of legislative and judicial policy making on the right to die are compared and contrasted. Next, empirical models of adoption and renovation are estimated in order to determine how policy decisions in one institution influence actions by actors in the other branch of government. Next, case studies of the policy process in six states are presented, and the differences and similarities in policy formation are considered. The chapter concludes with a number of observations and generalizations regarding judicial and legislative behavior.

LEGISLATIVE AND JUDICIAL INNOVATION CONTRASTED

The results from the previous chapters reveal that there are pronounced differences in the ways that actors in the two branches of government have made right to die policy. Different temporal patterns of adoption and renovation are the function of different political dynamics, as discussed below.

Diffusion of Innovations

Clear patterns emerge when tracking the diffusion curves of all three legislative policies, whereas judicial surrogate innovations were adopted in an uneven and disjointed fashion. The diffusion of living will laws closely approximates social learning theory: following California's core innovation, a number of states immediately followed suit; after a short period in which potential adopters monitored the success of these first policies, there was a clear "take-off" phase followed by rapid adoption and then a gradual "mopping up" of laggard adopters. Durable power of attorney statutes diffused at a much quicker rate: the rapid take-off phase and quick pace of adoption reflects a truncated learning curve, as these tangential proxy innovations were not as controversial as their living will predecessors. While not as "neatly" diffused as their advance directives cousins, the legislative surrogate decision making policies also spread through the states in a patterned manner; there are three clear periods or "clusters" of activity: 1977 (the year of the two core tangential innovations), 1983-1985 (a point in which surrogate adoptions enjoyed some "fallout" from the living will take-off phase), and 1989-94 (fairly rapid adoption in the wake of the two NCCUSL resolutions). The diffusion curves of all three legislative policies suggest that states learned from, and were inspired by, one another when making public policy on the right to die.

No such pattern characterizes the diffusion of judicial surrogate policies. The meandering and episodic ordering of innovations, lack of a take-off phase, and absence of any clear interstate grouping suggest that state appellate courts are not nearly as influenced by regional and national trends as are their legislative counterparts; the former are reactive policy making institutions, and judges, who must await the emergence of real, justiciable controversies before deciding policy questions, are largely insulated from "bandwagon" trends and mass demands for policy action.

Determinants of Policy Adoption and Renovation

All four of the event history models were successful in accounting for variation in their respective patterns of policy adoption. However, very different dynamics were at work in influencing legislatures and judiciaries; variables that were of primary importance in the former did not play a major role in the latter, and vice versa. Factors for which the differential effects are most pronounced include the extent of interest group and issue public influence, institutional professionalism and prestige, response to electoral threat, and the impact of horizontal and vertical developments.

Extent of Opposition and Support.
For legislative policies, opposition to policy adoption was of crucial importance. State Catholic Conferences were extremely effective in blocking, stalling and "watering down" the content of living will laws; the

size of a state's Catholic population had a strong and negative impact on the likelihood of legislative innovation, suggesting that, once a sizable interest group registers its opposition to a policy, risk averse lawmakers immediately see "red flags" and the possibility of electoral or other retribution. The extent of organized support for a policy does not appear to be nearly as important, as evidenced by the relatively weak effects exerted by variables tapping the size of state medical and geriatric lobbies. The amount of opposition to, not support for, policy adoption looms heavy in the calculus of the elected legislator.

Interest group participation in the judicial arena, by contrast, takes place on a much more level playing field. Despite the lopsided ratios (i.e., right-to-life groups grossly outnumber right-to-die supporters), policy proponents from both camps participated in roughly equal numbers in the filing of *amicus curiae* briefs. Courts seemed to accord the most substantive weight to the advisory briefs issued by organized medicine (which usually staked out positions in support of deregulating and facilitating the right to discontinue treatment), and it is important to stress the fact that state Catholic conferences, unlike in the legislative domain, do not appear to have been successful in precluding or deterring judicial adoptions. Regardless of the size of their respective organizations and population segments, interest groups are accorded nearly equal voice in the judicial process; moreover, the presence of organized opposition to policy adoption does not inhibit judicial innovation like it does legislative innovation.

Similar observations on the role of interest groups can be made with respect to policy renovation by the two branches of government. The Catholic lobby was tremendously effective in limiting the amount of legislative renovation. This effect is most pronounced for living will laws; recall that once the Catholic Conferences modified their strategic positions in the early 1980s, the size of a state's Catholic population was the second strongest variable in the renovation regression model, indicating that once legislators approved a "compromised" policy, future policy liberalization through amendment was curtailed to a large extent. Extent of support for policy renovation did not prove to be nearly as important as did the extent of opposition to such changes.

In accounting for the pattern of judicial renovation, organized interests again seemed to have relatively "equal" (i.e. "no") voice in the process, as both the "opposition" and "support" variables proved to be unimportant in predicting renovation of judicial surrogate policies. Where justices appear to have been only modestly influenced by interest group efforts in adopting surrogate policies, they do not appear to have responded to these factors at all in determining whether or not to alter their existing precedents and policies.

Institutional Determinants: Professionalism, Prestige, and Electoral Threat.

The results from the legislative EHA analyses suggest an important finding that runs counter to the extant body of state politics research: part-time, "citizen" legislatures are more likely to approve controversial, permissive policies than are full-time "professionalized" assemblies. This is consistent with the assumption that lawmakers in the former bodies have "less to lose" than do the more reelection-minded politicians in the more prestigious and full-time institutions. Legislative salary was an important inverse determinant of innovation in both the living will and legislative surrogate models.

Similarly, legislative adoption was considerably less likely in periods when lawmakers had to stand for re-election than it was in "off years." The election index was a strong and negative correlate of innovation in both the legislative surrogate and living will models. All things being equal, controversial policy adoptions are more likely to occur the further off elections (and their attendant publicity) loom on the horizon.

State appellate justices do not appear to be influenced to the same extent by the threat of electoral retribution. Indeed, judicial selection did not emerge as a significant predictor of judicial policy adoption; judiciaries with justices whose tenure in office is determined by popular election were no more likely to produce innovations than were courts comprised of judges who are effectively insulated from electoral retribution. This may reflect a number of factors: the low saliency of judicial elections, the limited campaign resources needed in judicial (as opposed to legislative) elections, and the generally high public support for the right to die in most state electorates.

Also important is the finding that judicial reputation had a positive and strong effect on likelihood of surrogate adoption. Courts with the highest reputation ratings also tend to be the most prestigious and "professionalized" (Caldeira 1987). The opinions issued by the most reputed tribunals are accorded tremendous weight by justices in the courts of other states; and such professionalized judiciaries boast high rates of case disposition, the highest paid and best-educated judges, and are often "recruiting grounds" for more prestigious federal judicial appointments. It would seem that officials in these high profile courts pride themselves on tackling tough policy questions, a finding that contrasts markedly with the conclusion that permissive innovation is less likely in professionalized assemblies than in part-time, citizen legislatures.

Horizontal and Vertical Influences.
Regional policy influences claimed the lion's share of explanatory power in the legislative models. By far the most important factor in accounting for the adoption of both living will and DPA policies by state legislatures was the extent of policy development in neighboring jurisdictions. As more policies were adopted in a region and as those policies grew more comprehensive and facilitative in nature, so too did the pressure on nonadopting states to keep pace with regional trends. The exact opposite pattern characterized adoption by state appellate courts. The negative direction and modest size of the coefficient of the lagged regional judicial facility score suggests that judges are not nearly as influenced by regional trends as are legislators. To be certain, this finding reflects the fact that courts are reactive actors and that state justices rarely have the option of hearing a right to die case simply because several nearby state courts have innovated. However, the varied patterns described in the case studies in Chapter 5 also point to the fact that state justices, while cognizant of regional developments when hearing cases of first impression, also pride themselves on a certain degree of independence from other tribunals (i.e., "citation without impact"). Whatever the reasons, it is clear that regional patterns of permissive policy adoption exert tremendous influence over legislatures, but not over judiciaries.

Horizontal and vertical policy "directives" also had differing impacts on judicial and legislative policy adoption. The approval of each of the

Judicial and Legislative Interaction

three NCCUSL model laws stimulated an almost immediate surge of legislative adoptions. Legislators in many states were able to successfully characterize the NCCUSL recommendations as "mandates" for policy innovation, and bill sponsors likely marketed policy proposals as necessary and compulsory changes designed to bring their state laws into compliance with national trends and standards.

The judicial analogue to the Commissioner's model laws, the U.S. Supreme Court's 1999 *Cruzan* ruling, did little to stimulate judicial surrogate innovation. In fact, policy adoption was less likely in the post-*Cruzan* era than it was in the previous period. This result is probably owing to the innocuous nature of the Supreme Court's ruling. As discussed previously, the high justices issued an opinion which essentially validated the creation of state-level evidentiary and implementation restrictions. Prior to 1990, many state courts produced policies consistent with the "new" judicial federalism, whereby constitutional rights to patient self-determination served as the foundation for the creation of a set of procedures designed to guarantee the exercise of those rights. *Cruzan* may have, to some extent, supplanted this judicial liberalization trend with a doctrine that essentially affirmed the right of state lawmakers to place statutory restrictions and limitations upon the exercise of surrogate decision making. *Cruzan* was clearly not as important to judiciaries as the NCCUSL adoptions were to legislatures.

Horizontal influences also contributed to legislative renovation efforts, but did not similarly affect the revision of judicial policies. Renovation of all three legislative policies was conditioned by regional factors. The further a state's existing living will policy was from its regional average, the more likely legislators were to amend the policy to bring it in to line with standards in nearby states. Similarly, proxy and surrogate statutes were more likely to be renovated with the passage of time, reflecting the fact that earlier policies were more restrictive than later ones and that lawmakers endeavored to update their policies in a manner consistent with regional and national trends. Judicial renovation, by contrast, was rare, driven by idiosyncratic developments, and appears to have occurred independently of developments in other state courts. Once justices articulated a policy, they were usually very reluctant to depart from the fundamental tenets set down in their original opinion, regardless of any interstate policy changes or intrastate political developments.

Intrastate Policy Influences.
Contrary to theoretical expectations, the adoption of legislative policies was not substantially facilitated by prior right to die statutory adoptions in the state. As discussed in Chapter 4, many states chose a strategy of "dual" or "combined" adoptions and approved two or more policy types in the same session (often as part of a single piece of legislation). Legislators in other states, having previously expended political capital on controversial advance directives laws, may have been unwilling to revisit the "tough turf" on which the battle for surrogate statutes would have to be waged. Whatever the particular process at work, intrastate policy variables played only a minor role in the diffusion of tangential legislative innovations.

Once again, a completely different pattern emerges in the diffusion of judicial surrogate innovations. The single most important determinant of judicial adoption was the amount of prior case activity in the state. As state courts increasingly issued more and more right to die opinions, often creating policies to govern decision making by competent patients and/or indicating in *dicta* how a surrogate decision making question might be resolved in a future case, a canon of case law began to develop, signaling to appellate justices the need for judicial policy making. The number of prior right to die cases, even cases dismissed due to mootness, undoubtedly increased the likelihood of appellate *certiorari* once a real controversy involving surrogates arose (and was appealed); and cases that were granted review almost invariably resulted in the creation of some type of surrogate decision making policy.

Facilitative Renovation Over Time

Legislative policies were renovated on many more occasions than were judicial policies. Changes in the former laws are characterized by marked patterns and were conditioned by temporal and regional influences; judicial policies were less likely to be renovated, and, when they were, the

Judicial and Legislative Interaction

particular (often idiosyncratic) facts of the particular cases seemed to exert the most influence over policy outcomes.

It is important to note that legislative policies grew increasingly facilitative over time. Statutory renovation was exclusively a "positive" phenomenon; not one single legislative policy was amended in a manner which resulted in a lowered facility score; legislative facility scores increased "across the board" whenever renovation efforts were approved. Date of adoption was an important correlate of statutory policy facility, with early adoptions containing substantially more restrictions than later, revamped ones.

This "liberal" renovation trend is decidedly less pronounced for judicial policies. Few courts either had the opportunity to renovate their policies or were willing to alter their previous precedents. While the judiciaries in four states renovated their policies in a facilitative direction, there was also a "contrary substream" of renovation: two state courts imposed greater restrictions on their policies or otherwise limited the scope of their prior holdings. It should also be stressed that date of adoption did not prove to be an important determinant of judicial facility scores. Courts simply innovated less often and less consistently than did legislatures.

Having identified the various differences that distinguish policy making in these two branches of state government, it is now appropriate to examine the ways in which legislative and judicial policy developments influence one another. The next section presents the results from "integrated" or "updated" regression analyses; the models from Chapters 5 and 6 have been re-estimated to include policy variables from the "other" branch of government.

ADOPTION AND RENOVATION: INTEGRATED MODELS

First, the impact of judicial policy making on legislative innovation and renovation is considered, then the results of models exploring legislative influences on judicial policy production are considered. The reader should note that, for the sake of parsimony (and to combat a small multicollinearity problem), the regression models below were estimated by including, as independent variables, the predicted probabilities from the respective models estimated in the previous two chapters. The predicted probability variables serve as a proxies for all of the political, horizontal and vertical, opposition and support, and intrastate policy variables previously utilized[1]. The focus in this section is on the "new" institutional variables.

Legislative Policy Models

Table 6.1 reports the results of the living will, proxy, and surrogate decision-making event history models. A brief perusal of the results reveals that the judicial variables contribute very little towards explaining the decisions of state legislatures to adopt right to die policies. Although each of the overall models is statistically significant, this is simply due to the inclusion of the predicted probabilities in the set of regressors. Not one of the coefficients of the substantive judicial variables is statistically significant or in the hypothesized direction.

The number of cumulative intrastate cases, which proved to be the most important determinant of judicial innovation, did not appreciably affect legislative innovation. The expectation was that this variable would have a negative effect on the likelihood of adoption, as a growing case load in a state may have signaled to lawmakers that judicial innovation was likely in the near future and that legislative policy might, therefore, be unnecessary. Two of the three coefficients are negative; although they are in the hypothesized direction, they are statistically insignificant with calculated impact scores lower than 2 percent. Little support exists for this hypothesis.

Similarly, a state's lagged judicial surrogate facility score did not prove to be an important predictor of legislative adoption. The theoretical expectation was that legislatures in states governed by permissive judicial surrogate policies would be more inclined to nondecision-making on the right to die than would states lacking a strong judicial policy. However, all three coefficients are positive in direction and statistically insignificant.

A state's mean regional judicial facility score was also expected to deter legislative policy action, as a growing tide of adoptions in neighboring states could have been interpreted by legislators as being a precursor to inevitable judicial policy making in their state. Two of the coefficients are negative in direction but are insignificant, while the coefficient for the living will model is positive and significant at just better than 90 percent confidence. This latter finding runs counter to theoretical expectations and should not be accorded much weight given the small impact it had on the decision to adopt; indeed, the impact score is a mere .0122, meaning that a one standard deviation shift in a state's lagged regional facility score only resulted in a 1.22 percent increase in the likelihood of adopting a living will law.

The lack of judicial influence over legislative policy making

Table 6.1
Judicial Influences on Legislative Adoptions: Event History Analyses

Variable	LW EHA[a]	DPA EHA[b]	Surg. EHA[c]
Predicted Probabilities[d]	7.6456***	6.4997***	13.6606***
	(31.8153)	(32.946)	(8.5075)
Cumulative Intrastate Cases$_{t-1}$	-.0509	.0153	-.0923
	(.2027)	(.0177)	(.2724)
Mean Regional Jud. F. Score $_{t-1}$	.1902*	-.0170	-.1306
	(3.2247)	(.0197)	(.6249)
Judicial Facility Score$_{t-1}$	.0297	.0625	.0642
	(.1045)	(.6729)	(.4386)
Constant	-3.3523	-3.0717	-3.8071
	(128.4643)	(92.1319)	(134.2619)
Initial Log Likelihood	-150.166	-142.982	-105.224
Final Log Likelihood	-131.587	-122.872	-99.295
Model χ^2 (4 d.f.)	37.159***	40.222***	11.859**
Number of Cases	466	386	720
Cases Scored as Adoption	46 (9.9%)	47 (12.2%)	24 (3.3%)

Maximum likelihood estimation of logit models of legislative adoptions. Regression coefficients above the Wald values, with the latter in parentheses.
[a] Logit model of the probability of a state adopting a living will law.
[b] Logit model of the probability of a state adopting a proxy/DPA law.
[c] Logit model of the probability of a state adopting a surrogate statute.
[d] The predicted probabilities from the EHA models estimated in Chapter 4 serve as proxies for all of the "legislative" independent variables previously used to predict these legislative adoptions.
* Significant at .10 α-level in a two-tailed test; **.05; ***.01.

suggested by the results of the three event history models is further reinforced by the results from the three legislative renovation models. Table 6.2 reports the results from these regressions. Only the predicted probabilities are statistically significant, with none of the judicial variables having an appreciable effect on the likelihood of reinvention through renovation.

Many alternate model specifications were attempted[2], with the end result being essentially the same: judicial innovation did not impact legislative innovation in any discernible manner. The reverse seemed to hold true as well, as indicated in the next section.

Table 6.2
Judicial Influences on Legislative Renovations

Variable	LW logit[a]	DPA logit[b]	Surg. logit[c]
Predicted Probabilities[d]	8.3451***	6.5111***	9.6557**
	(30.9607)	(11.3446)	(6.0157)
Cumulative Intrastate Cases$_{t-1}$	-.0076	.0530	-.2766
	(.0051)	(.4295)	(1.1522)
Mean Regional Jud. F. Score $_{t-1}$	.0154	-.0354	.2719
	(.0223)	(.0733)	(1.8906)
Judicial Facility Score$_{t-1}$	.0713	-.0274	.1498
	(1.3441)	(.1595)	(1.2240)
Constant	-3.4243***	-2.8520***	-4.4446***
	(90.4396)	(36.1361)	(32.4591)
Initial Log Likelihood	-158.824	-89.843	-34.644
Final Log Likelihood	-141.389	-84.279	-28.958
Model χ^2 (4 d.f.)	34.872***	11.127**	11.372**
Number of Cases	466	251	160
Cases Scored as Renovation	50 (10.7%)	29 (11.6%)	9 (5.6%)

Maximum likelihood estimation of logit models of legislative renovations. Regression coefficients above Wald values, with the latter in parentheses.
[a] Logit model of the probability of a state renovating its living will law.
[b] Logit model of the probability of a state renovating its proxy/DPA law.
[c] Logit model of the probability of a state renovating its surrogate statute.
[d] The predicted probabilities from the renovation models estimated in Chapter 4 are proxies for the prior "legislative" independent variables.
* Significant at .10 α-level in a two-tailed test; **.05; ***.01.

Judicial Surrogate Policy Models

Table 6.3 displays the results from the event history analysis of judicial surrogate innovations and from the judicial renovation model. The innovation model was statistically significant owing only to the inclusion of the predicted probabilities from the model in Chapter 5, while the overall renovation model was not even significant and failed to predict a single renovation. Without exception, none of the substantive legislative variables appreciably influenced the likelihood of judicial policy adoption or renovation. Each of these six variables was hypothesized to have a positive impact on the likelihood of judicial surrogate policy making, as legislative action always presents opportunities for statutory challenges and judicial review. Nevertheless, the null results from the models suggest that there is no such causal dynamic at work[3].

The lack of findings in the above models is puzzling; nevertheless, as discussed in the next sections, these null results may simply be indicative of the fact that different legislative-judicial processes were at work in different states. It hardly seems reasonable to simply conclude that legislative and judicial innovation on the right to die took place independently of one another. The next section examines legislative and judicial surrogate policy adoptions in an attempt to "sort out" and identify different patterns of interaction. And this effort is followed by a detailed case study of policy making in six states, all of which were selected due to the fact that there were pronounced, yet very different, interbranch relationships influencing policy making. While legislative and judicial interaction is not as simple as suggested in the theory, actors in each of these institutions are influenced by their counterparts in the other branches of state government.

Table 6.3
Legislative Influences on Judicial Policy-Making

Variable	Adoption EHA[a]	Renov. Logit[b]
Predicted Probabilities[c]	12.2982***	13.3222
	(34.3737)	(8.3465)
Living Will Facility Score$_{t-1}$	.0191	-.0665
	(.2611)	(1.7601)
Mean Regional LW F. Score$_{t-1}$	.0311	-.0255
	(.2872)	(.0978)
DPA/Proxy Facility Score$_{t-1}$	.0287	-.0053
	(.5147)	(.0086)
Mean Regional DPA F.Score$_{t-1}$	-.0325	.0462
	(.2132)	(.4319)
Surrogate Stat. Facility Score$_{t-1}$	-.0658	.0438
	(.9450)	(.3469)
Mean Regional Surg. F. Score$_{t-1}$	-.0299	.0687
	(.0636)	(.2270)
Constant	-4.4669***	-3.5878***
	(96.4408)	(20.6338)
Initial Log Likelihood	-102.820	-41.528
Final Log Likelihood	-82.0605	-35.543
Model χ^2 (7 d.f.)	41.519***	11.970
Number of Cases	751	182
Cases Scored as Adopt./Renv.	23 (3.1%)	11 (6.0%)

Maximum likelihood estimation of logit models of legislative adoptions and renovations.
Regression coefficients above Wald values, with the latter in parentheses.
[a] Logit model of the probability of a state appellate court adopting a surrogate decision-making policy.
[b] Logit model of the probability of a state appellate court renovating its existing surrogate decision-making policy.
[c] The predicted probabilities from the EHA and renovation models estimated in Chapter 5 serve as proxies for all of the "judicial" independent variables previously used to predict these judicial events.
* Significant at .10 α-level in a two-tailed test; **.05; ***.01.

Surrogate Decision-Making Policies: Timing of Legislative and Judicial Adoptions

Of the three types of legislative policies, surrogate decision making laws confer a set of rights that most closely approximate the rights created by judicial surrogate policies. Whether adopted by a state assembly or appellate court, surrogate policies permit a third party to direct the discontinuance of life-prolonging treatment to an incompetent patient in the absence of an advance directive. Clearly, these are the most controversial type of refusal of treatment law; they shift the locus of decision-making from the principal (patient) to an agent (family member). Whereas forty-eight states have adopted proxy laws and forty-seven have approved living will statutes, only twenty-three states have judicial surrogate policies, and only twenty-four are covered by statutory surrogate laws. Surrogate policy adoption has the potential to exact tremendous political costs from policy makers, and if strategic legislative-judicial behavior exists, it should probably be most apparent for this policy type.

Table 6.4 reports the order of surrogate adoptions in each state. The "first adoption" column indicates which branch of government was the first to approve a surrogate innovation, with the year of adoption indicated in parentheses; the "next adoption" column notes whether or not a surrogate policy was subsequently adopted by the "other" state institution, and "lag time" is the length of time, measured in years, between the two adoptions. Looking at the entries for both Alaska and Arizona, we see that neither of these states, as indicated by the recording of "none" in the first adoption column, is governed by either a judicial or legislative policy. Looking down to the third row, we see that in Arizona a judicial adoption occurred first in 1987, and this was followed by a legislative surrogate adoption in 1992, with a five year span between these two innovations. The state legislature innovated in 1977 Arkansas, but this effort has not been followed by a judicial adoption. A quick review of all fifty entries suggests that no single pattern of "adoption and response" was predominant; rather, a number of different patterns are evident.

Table 6.4
Judicial and Legislative Adoptions

State	First Adopt.[a]	Next Adopt.[b]	Lag Time[c]
AL	NONE	---	---
AK	NONE	---	---
AZ	Jud (87)	Leg (92)	5 years
AR	Leg (77)	NONE	---
CA	Jud (83)	NONE	---
CO	Leg (92)	NONE	---
CT	Leg (85)	Jud (89)	4 years
DE	Jud (80)	NONE	---
FL	Jud (84)	Leg (84)	0 years[d]
GA	Jud (84)	NONE	---
HI	NONE	---	---
ID	NONE	---	---
IL	Jud (89)	Leg (91)	2 years
IN	Leg (85)	Jud (89)	4 years
IA	Leg (85)	Jud (87)	2 years
KS	NONE	---	---
KY	Jud (93)	Leg (94)	1 year
LA	Jud (82)	Leg (84)	2 years
ME	Jud (87)	Leg (89)	2 years
MD	Jud (93)	Leg (93)	0 years[d]
MA	Jud (77)	NONE	---
MI	Jud (92)	NONE	---
MN	Jud (84)	NONE	---
MS	NONE	---	---
MO	Jud (88)	NONE	—
MT	Leg (91)	NONE	---
NE	NONE	---	---
NV	Leg (91)	NONE	---
NH	NONE	---	---
NJ	Jud (76)	NONE	---
NM	Leg (84)	NONE	---
NY	Jud (81)	NONE	---
NC	Leg (77)	NONE	---
ND	NONE	---	---
OH	Jud (84)	Leg (91)	7 years
OK	NONE	---	---
OR	Leg (83)	NONE	---
PA	NONE	---	---
RI	NONE	---	---

Table 6.4 (continued)
Judicial and Legislative Adoptions

State	First Adopt.[a]	Next Adopt.[b]	Lag Time[c]
SC	Leg (90)	NONE	---
SD	NONE	---	---
TN	Jud (77)	NONE	---
TX	Leg (85)	NONE	---
UT	Leg (85)	NONE	---
VT	NONE	---	---
VA	Leg (83)	NONE	---
WA	Jud (83)	NONE	---
WV	Jud (83)	NONE	---
WI	Jud (92)	NONE	---
WY	Leg (92)	NONE	---

[a] Indicates which branch of government was the first to adopt a surrogate decision making policy. "Leg" denotes a legislative adoption, and "Jud" indicates an adoption by a state appellate court. Year of adoption appears in parentheses.
[b] Indicates whether or not an innovation was subsequently adopted by the "other" branch of government.
[c] Length of time (in years) between judicial and legislative adoptions, or vice versa.
[d] Judicial and legislative policies adopted in the same year.

Nonadopting States

First, fourteen states lack either type of policy. This lack of adoption points to two possibilities. First, medical decision making at the end of life in these states, which, with the exception of Pennsylvania, have populations below the national average, may take place at the traditional and unregulated patient-family-doctor-level. Although, to be certain, there are instances in which nontreatment decisions by surrogates are allowed despite the absence of a statewide policy, it is also likely that there are times when health care providers refuse to honor such requests. Surrogate adoptions would help to resolve such conflicts and assuage practitioners' fears of liability, yet no policies have been adopted, suggesting the second possibility: judicial inactivity begets legislative inactivity, and vice versa. No controversial court cases were granted appellate review, thereby closing a potential window of opportunity for policy entrepreneurs wishing to place the issue on the mass and legislative agendas; conversely, no statutory adoptions were created that allowed parties to challenge the constitutionality of the provisions in court, thus limiting the opportunities for judicial scrutiny.

Judiciaries Strike First

In twenty states, judicial innovation preceded legislative innovation. Of these twenty states, twelve failed to adopt a legislative policy in the wake of the judicial adoption. This suggests that, in keeping with theoretical expectations, decisive judicial action helped to drive the issue off of legislative agendas. However, in eight of the states, judicial innovation was followed by legislative adoption, suggesting that legislatures were responding to these judicial policies. In all but two of these latter cases, legislative adoption occurred within two years of the publication of the judicial policies, implying that these policies were not adopted independently of their judicial predecessors. In Florida and in Maryland, legislative policies followed closely on the heels of these judicial adoptions. The Maryland General Assembly approved a surrogate law only thirteen short weeks after the state's high court approved a surrogate law (this is discussed in greater detail in the case study in the next section), and in Florida, lawmakers adopted in hopes of restricting a rising tide of facilitative case law.

Florida: Race to Control Policy.
In 1984 the surrogate question was before an appellate court in the Sunshine State. *In Re Guardianship of Barry* (445 So.2d 368) addressed the rights of a terminally ill infant in a persistent vegetative state. The Second District Court of Appeals ruled that the right to privacy extends to incompetent patients (including minors) and, under the doctrine of substituted judgment, can be exercised on their behalf by others (i.e., parents and guardians) without prior court approval once medical evidence (confirmed by two nonattending physicians) reveals that there

is little or no probability of the patient returning to a cognitive, sapient state.

Only four short months after *Barry*, the first surrogate innovation, the intermediate appellate court's holding had the potential to be endorsed by the Florida Supreme Court in another case implicating all incompetent patients in PVS (*John F. Kennedy Hospital* v. *Bludworth*, 452 So.2d 921, 1984). The high court had previously issued a facilitative ruling in a 1980 case involving a competent patient (*Satz* v. *Perlmutter*, 379 So.2d 359) in which the justices made clear that they would continue to hear cases if the Florida Legislature failed to adopt a policy in this area:

> It is this type of issue which is more suitably addressed in the legislative forum. Nevertheless, preferences for legislative treatment cannot shackle the courts when legally protected interests are at stake. (359)

Both the state Supreme Court's expected ruling in *Bludworth* and the *Barry* decision (issued four months earlier) galvanized policy proponents, particularly the Florida Catholic Conference, into action (Glick 1992, 111-113). By "beating the high court to the punch," right-to-die opponents hoped to create fairly restrictive legislation and retain control over the most controversial provisions of the state's surrogate decision-making policy. Just two days prior to the high court's announcement in the *Bludworth* case, the Legislature passed the Florida Life-Prolonging Procedures Act (Fla. Stat. Ann. §§ 765.101 to 765.401).

This legislation allowed family decisionmaking in the absence of an advance directive; however, with a facility score of only 10 points, the provisions governing surrogates were extremely prohibitive. Physicians were required to consent to all nontreatment decisions, and the statute did not cover persons in PVS nor did it permit the discontinuance of artificial nutrition and hydration. This limited policy stood in marked contrast to the Supreme Court's ruling, two days later, in *Bludworth*; the justices held that there is no distinction between PVS and other terminal diagnoses and also ruled that prior physician approval (as opposed to diagnosis) was not required in order for a patient's family members to direct discontinuance of treatment. Legislative and judicial policies directly contradicted one another.

The end result in Florida was a stalemate that, despite legislative and judicial renovations, continues to the present day. Statutory and case law conflict on a number of different provisions in a state in which legislators and judges have vied for control over right to die policy guidelines. The central point of this example is that, without prior judicial action, the Florida Legislature might have been content to ignore the issue; but once judicial innovation occurred, elected lawmakers in Tallahassee were quick to innovate and challenge their state's judicially prescribed policy.

It should be noted that, even though it is clear that judicial innovation precipitated legislative innovation in Florida, this relationship was not tapped by the event history model run earlier due to the fact that the judicial variable was lagged. Indeed, it can take a small amount of time (e.g., a few months in Florida and Maryland) or a much longer period of time for legislators to react to judicial innovation. Legislators in Ohio responded to their state's judicial policy a full seven years after it was originally adopted, yet it is clear that lawmakers were responding to judicial policymaking in their state (see the Ohio case study below). Such "delayed" effects are also lost in the event history models.

Legislatures Take the Lead

Although we have established that courts in twenty states innovated first, it would be premature to conclude that right to die policy making is characterized by judicial leadership across the United States. In fact, in sixteen states, legislatures adopted surrogate statutes first. Most interesting about these particular adoptions is that only three judicial policies followed statutory innovations. The opinions issued by the courts in Connecticut, Iowa and Indiana (the latter is discussed shortly in a case study) all involved challenges to their states' existing surrogate statutes, showing that legislative adoptions can, as previously theorized, inspire judicial responses. Nevertheless, such a pattern was not evident in the majority of states where legislatures produced first policies. Appellate courts in thirteen of these sixteen states have not adopted innovations, suggesting that, once a statutory mechanism is in place, litigation is less likely and that courts may be less inclined to hear a case once their state legislature has addressed the issue.

Surrogate Adoptions Summarized

The various combinations of surrogate outcomes and their relative frequencies are summarized in Table 6.5. These findings help to explain why the event history models in this chapter failed to evidence clear patterns of legislative-judicial interaction. Because, instead of one dominant trend, there are several countervailing patterns present, these varied dynamics essentially "cancel out" one another. Also important is the fact that most states adopted only one single type of policy, indicating that policy makers in both branches of government may be less inclined to take up an issue once it has been handled by other state leaders. In those cases when dual adoptions did occur, long and immediate lag times between policies may have also contributed to the null findings in the empirical models. Moreover, of states that did produce both types of policies, legislatures, contrary to expectations, were more likely to respond to judicial innovations than were courts to legislative adoptions.

Table 6.5
Temporal Ordering of Surrogate Innovations

Outcome	Number of States
No Judicial or Legislative Innovation	14 States
Judicial Adoption First	20 States
Subsequent Legislative Adoption	8 States
No Legislative Adoption	12 States
Legislative Adoption First	16 States
Subsequent Judicial Adoption	3 States
No Judicial Adoption	13 States
Judicial and Legislative Policies	11 States

In order to further "flush out" the various patterns of legislative and judicial interaction that took place in the states, the next section presents six case studies of right to die policymaking.

INNOVATION AND RENOVATION IN SIX STATES

This section presents policy histories for six states, all of which were selected because they were host to pronounced, yet diverse, processes of legislative and judicial interaction. Policy making in Indiana and Maryland was characterized by judicial leadership that served as the catalyst for legislative response. Courts in Ohio and Missouri exercised considerably more judicial restraint and deferred to legislative intent. Legislatures and courts in Washington state and Illinois created and renovated polices in a manner that allowed state law to grow increasingly facilitative over time.

Each of these case studies is organized in a deliberate fashion. Policy making in courts and legislatures is discussed chronologically in separate sections in order to allow for continuity in tracking intra-institutional policy renovation. Once the separate institutional histories have been described, a third section ties the two processes together and characterizes the nature of legislative-judicial interaction in the state. To help the reader "keep track" of the developments, each case study is accompanied by a table that orders the chronology of events in the state.

Maryland: Judicial Restraint Places Ball in Legislative Court

The right-to-die proved to be a political "hot potato" in Maryland, with officials in both branches of government disinclined to take up the issue. Legislative inaction was followed by years of judicial inaction on the surrogate decision-making question (see Table 6.6). This cycle was finally broken by a calculated, limited judicial innovation that prompted an immediate legislative response.

Statutory Law.
In 1985 Maryland legislators enacted the Maryland Health Care Decisions Act (Md. Health-Gen. Code Ann. §§5-601 to 5-618). This first living will policy was somewhat limited in scope. The law did not recognize PVS or similar conditions; no penalties were prescribed for noncompliance by physicians and/or providers, and the statute was ambiguous on the question of artificial sustenance. Although minor amendments to the

Judicial and Legislative Interaction

policy were offered in 1986 and 1987, it was not until May of 1993 that the General Assembly significantly altered the statute. In that session, lawmakers abandoned a number of restrictions, including the limited construction of triggering conditions and the sustenance restriction.

More importantly, the 1993 amendments also created proxy and surrogate policies. The provisions of the DPA law essentially mirror those of the living will policy. The surrogate decision-making policy affords families of incompetent patients tremendous freedom in directing the course of a patient's medical care. In fact, the law endorses a "best interests" standard.

Judicial Innovation/Case Law:
Maryland courts were first presented with the opportunity to consider surrogate decision-making in the late 1980s. In *In Re Riddlemoser* (564 A.2d 812, 1989) the Maryland Court of Special Appeals certified the question of law, and the case went to the state Court of Appeals (court of last resort).

Sixteen parties (the Society for the Right to Die and fifteen health care organizations) filed friend of the court briefs, all of which urged the high court to interpret the state's estates and trusts statute to allow guardians to order the withholding of health care from irreversibly ill patients. In a unanimous opinion, the appellate court held that it would not rule on the substantive matter of law, as the case was rendered moot by the patient's death. Conceding that the law was unclear, the court noted that "the 1990 session of the General Assembly will soon commence, thus allowing the legislature to eliminate the ambiguity" (817). The right-to-die was (at least temporarily) "processed off" of the Maryland judicial agenda.

However, by early 1993 the issue was again before the high court, and this time the case involved a living patient (in PVS being maintained by artificial nutrition and hydration) and a heated adversarial contest (between the patient's spouse/guardian and the patient's father and sister, with the former party requesting withdrawal and the latter pair demanding continuation of treatment). In *Mack* v. *Mack* (618 A.2d 744, 1993), a highly publicized case of first impression, the justices found that, by virtue of the common law doctrine of informed consent, guardians of incompetent patients may decline unwanted treatment, including artificial nutrition and hydration, on behalf of such patients. The high court ruled that guardians are required to apply a rule of "substitute judgement," whereby the inquiry focuses on "whether the ward had determined, or would determine, that treatment should be withdrawn under the circumstances of the case" (757). Although it adopted the most stringent evidentiary standard applicable to civil cases (clear and convincing evidence), the court majority tempered this portion of its holding with a somewhat relaxed view of the evidence needed to support such a decision. Citing the Supreme Court of New Jersey in *Jobes*, the Maryland court opined that surrogates should consider the patient's "philosophical, religious and moral views" in reaching a nontreatment decision (758).

The *Mack* court explicitly rejected a "best interests" standard, noting that, if adopted in Maryland, such a rule must be approved by the General Assembly:

> A legislative body is better equipped to determine, within constitutional limits, whether some lives are not worth living and, if so, how to determine which are the lives that are not worth living. (759-60)

The divided court's (4-3) ruling furnished the basis for the state's first surrogate decision-making policy; however, the controversial opinion raised as many questions as it answered. Rather than resolving the issue, the opinion elevated the right to die to a prominent place on both the mass and governmental agendas.

Judicial and Legislative Interaction:
Risk-averse lawmakers had numerous opportunities to enact a policy, but failed to do so for years. Indeed, individual legislators had sponsored and introduced some type of refusal of treatment proposal in every session since 1974 (Kronmiller 1988). It was not until 1985 that their efforts were successful. In that year, the NCCUSL model law provided a window of opportunity. However, in order to muster a critical mass of support for the living will law, bill sponsors had to offer a number of concessions to potential policy opponents.

Judicial and Legislative Interaction

The Court of Appeals of Maryland had an opportunity to place the issue on the governmental agenda in 1989, but the justices exercised judicial restraint by declaring the *Riddlemoser* appeal moot due to the patient's death. This "judicial nondecision" was accompanied by the unanimous court's call for legislation. Not surprisingly, this request appears to have fallen on deaf ears, as legislators did not change the law until the issue was placed squarely on the mass agenda several years later.

The highly visible and controversial ruling in *Mack* provided the vehicle for a major overhaul of the state's right-to-die policy. The high court, by refusing to extend its ruling to families and non-guardians, and by rejecting a best interests standard, produced a policy that likely satisfied few individuals and confused most providers. The justices, seemingly anticipating the professional and popular responses to its holding, placed the burden of policy expansion squarely on legislative shoulders:

> Unless and until current public policy, as we perceive it, is changed by the General Assembly, sustaining Ronald [the patient] and other persons like him, whose desires ... cannot clearly be determined, is the price paid for living in a society that highly values human life. (761)

After nearly eight years of legislative inaction, lawmakers mounted a rapid response to the Supreme Court's challenge. On May 11, 1993, just thirteen weeks after the opinion was issued, the General Assembly approved the landmark overhaul of the Health Care Decisions Act. The surrogate policy specifically addresses the two most controversial features of the *Mack* decision. The law does not require guardianship proceedings, and the statute clearly approves a "best interest" standard, something the court made clear it would never sanction without statutory authority.

The 1993 statute has not been substantively altered; unless another court case propels the issue back onto the mass and governmental agendas, future policy renovation is unlikely to occur in this state where policy makers would clearly prefer to avoid expending political capital on such a heated issue.

Table 6.6
Judicial and Legislative Policy Making in Maryland

Year	Legislative Action	Judicial Action
1985	Living will adoption. PVS not recognized and ambiguous sustenance provisions. (Facility score = 18 points)	
1986	Numerous amendments to living will law proposed, but only minor changes approved. Facility score goes unchanged.	
1987	Cosmetic changes approved to living will law. Facility score is not altered.	
1989		Surrogate before high court (*Riddlemoser*). Case declared moot, and justices urge legislative resolution.
1993	Living will law renovated: sustenance withdrawal allowed, PVS recognized, and drafting made easier. (Facility score = 28 points) DPA adoption. Provisions mirror those in living will law. (Facility score = 29 points) Surrogate adoption. Best interests standard and no prior court approval. Does not apply to minors. (Facility score = 26 points)	Judicial surrogate adoption (*Mack* decision). Common law rights, substituted judgment, prior judicial approval required. Limited to cases of intrafamilial conflict. (Facility score = 5 points)
1994	Minor amendments to policies approved. No score changes.	

Indiana: Court Takes Maximum-Feasible Liberties, Statutory Renovation Follows

Although Indiana approved a major right to die package in 1985, the result was a limited and ambiguous refusal of treatment policy. Legislative inactivity was interrupted by an innovative Supreme Court ruling which liberally interpreted the state's statute and essentially forced legislators to renovate their policy. A single "aggressive"court decision can completely reinvigorate the right to die policy making process in a state. (The chronology of events is depicted in Table 6.7.)

Statutory Law.
The NCCUSL's model living will adoption opened the door to legislative innovation in Indiana in 1985. In that year lawmakers scored the coveted "hat trick" when they simultaneously approved three refusal of treatment laws. The Indiana Living Wills and Life-Prolonging Procedures Act (Ind. Code Ann. §§16-36-4-1 to 16-36-4-21) and the Indiana Health Care Consent Act (Ind. Code Ann. §§16-36-1-1 to 16-36.1-14 and §§16-36-3-1 to 16-36-3-10, 1985) departed appreciably from the guidelines articulated by the Commissioners. These laws included restrictive definitions of "terminal" illness, thereby excluding vegetative and persistently comatose patients from coverage. This limitation was further exacerbated by the statutes' unilateral moratorium on the withdrawal of artificial nutrition and hydration. In addition, the surrogate law was worded in very general terms, referring only to the right to "consent" to health care; whether the right to refuse health care was also implied was open to some interpretation.

No substantive amendments were approved until the end of the 1991 legislative session, when the advance directives statute was altered to allow proxies to refuse treatment on behalf of vegetative patients. In addition, the statutory prescription against withdrawing artificial sustenance was rescinded; however, the new wording of the statute did not explicitly allow removal of feeding tubes, it was simply silent on the matter, reflecting a compromise through ambiguity.

1993 was host to a contentious legislative battle in which numerous proposals were offered. Although the issue progressed to the decisional agenda, the end result was the status quo. Undeterred, policy sponsors pressed the issue again in 1994, and they were finally successful in securing important changes to the policies. Most importantly, both statutes were amended to allow for the discontinuance of sustenance.

Judicial Innovation/Case Law.
The right to die did not reach the judicial agenda in Indiana until the early 1990's. In *Matter of Lawrance* (579 N.E.2d 32, 1991) the parents of a never-competent patient in a persistent vegetative state brought an action seeking court authorization for the withdrawal of artificially provided hydration and nutrition from their daughter. Although, while pending appeal, the case was rendered moot by the patient's death, the high court granted an exception to the mootness doctrine, citing the "great public interest at stake" (37). This display of judicial activism was followed by the justices' adoption of a very permissive surrogate decision making policy.

The high court issued a comprehensive ruling that addressed all of the issues central to decision making by surrogates: (1) patient's have a constitutional right to decline unwanted treatment, and the exercise of this right transfers to the next of kin in the event of incompetency; (2) surrogates are required to make decisions in the "best interests" of the patient; (3) no court approval of a nontreatment decision is required when all family members agree to the decision; and (4) artificial sustenance can be discontinued like any other type of medical treatment. As justification for this decision, the court looked to the state's recently enacted Health Care Consent Act (see above). Although the statute made no mention of withdrawing or denying life-sustaining care, the court, nevertheless, opined that this "right to consent to a course of treatment necessarily includes the right to refuse a course of treatment" (39).

This ruling effectively legalized surrogate decision-making, and it did so in a manner that placed few (if any) substantive restrictions on the rights of families to make treatment decisions on behalf of terminally ill, incompetent family members.

Table 6.7
Judicial and Legislative Policy Making in Indiana

Year	Legislative Action	Judicial Action
1985	"Hat Trick:" all three legislative policies adopted. Moratorium on artificial nutrition and hydration and narrow definition of terminal illness. (Living will score = 16 points) (DPA score = 14 points) (Surrogate score = 11 points) Language in surrogate statute ambiguous: allows "consent" but silent on "refusal."	
1991	DPA statute renovated. Sustenance and triggering conditions liberalized. (Facility score = 20 points)	Judicial surrogate policy adopted (*Lawrance*). Very permissive: best interests standard, constitutional rights, no prior court approval, and sustenance refusal allowed. Surrogate statute liberally interpreted.
1993	Cosmetic changes approved to each of the policies. All three facility scores go unchanged.	
1994	DPA enforcement procedures strengthened. (Facility score = 26 points) Sustenance and triggering provisions of living will law renovated. (Facility score = 21 points) Sustenance restriction stricken from surrogate policy. (Facility score = 16 points)	

Judicial and Legislative Interaction.

The 1985 adoptions are somewhat anomalous, given the combined approval of all three policy types and the restrictive nature of each of these policies. It is surprising that, given the level of opposition in the Indiana Legislature, lawmakers approved such a package. Indeed it seems reasonable to assert that policy opponents accepted "watered-down" versions of the right to die laws in order to retain strict control over what had become a bandwagon issue across the nation. The fact that legislators were unwilling to touch the issue for more than half a decade, despite an intervening NCCUSL adoption in 1989, is further evidence of just how contentious the refusal of treatment issue had become in the state.

Without the Supreme Court's permissive ruling in *Lawrance* it seems unlikely that the issue would ever have been able to once again permeate the mass and governmental agendas. The Indiana court took "maximum-feasible liberties" in interpreting the HCCA and applying it to surrogate decision-making. Indeed, a number of legislators jointly filed an *amicus* brief urging the court to avoid reading a right to refuse treatment into the 1985 statute. Nevertheless the court majority liberally explicated that statute, and their findings were further augmented by constitutional and common law doctrines. Had policy opponents endeavored to alter the HCCA to explicitly disallow the refusal of treatment, it is likely that the justices would have nullified the relevant portions of the statute through judicial review.

Despite the statutory restrictions on triggering conditions and sustenance, the *Lawrance* ruling created a means through which individuals and their surrogates could refuse a host of unwanted treatments with minimal procedural hurdles and no evidentiary requirements. Because the statutory law was in direct conflict with the 1991 decision, it is likely that providers and other parties urged their elected representatives to eliminate the discrepancies in the law. Eventually, in 1994, lawmakers approved sweeping changes to the statutes; but, without the judicial impetus, it is unlikely that the 1985 package would ever have been the subject of serious reconsideration by risk-averse lawmakers.

Judicial and Legislative Interaction 217

Ohio: Judicial Leadership Defers to Legislative Intent

An intermediate appellate court took the lead in Ohio by adopting a surrogate decision making policy, but the justices made clear their willingness to bow to legislative policy guidelines. A hesitant legislature soon approved a very limited DPA statute, and the next court to consider a surrogate case renovated the extant judicial policy to bring it in to line with the restrictive provisions of the DPA law. Once the General Assembly had innovated, appellate courts were unwilling to expand policy boundaries in the absence of a clear legislative mandate. Legislators were forced to deal with the issue, and statutory renovation resulted in modest and limited gains in policy facility.

Judicial Innovation/Case Law.
The right to die reached the appellate judicial agenda in Ohio in 1984. In *Leach* v. *Shapiro* (469 N.E.2d 1047, 1984), an intermediate appellate court created the state's first surrogate policy. The justices found that family members may exercise an incompetent patient's right to decline treatment by applying the substitute judgment standard; however, the opinion also made clear that prior court approval is always required to terminate life-supports. While the court drafted a permissive ruling, it was only controlling authority in one judicial circuit, leaving Ohio with no statewide policy.

In 1989, the legality of refusal of treatment was further obscured when an intermediate appellate court produced a ruling in partial conflict with *Leach*. The Court of Appeals for Montgomery County heard the first case involving the right of an incompetent patient to refuse artificial nutrition and hydration. In *Couture* v. *Couture* (549 N.E.2d 571) the justices looked to Ohio's recently enacted Durable Power of Attorney Statute for guidance and noted that the statute expressly forbid agents from withdrawing artificial sustenance from a principal unless a number of demanding requirements were met (see statutory law section below). Although the court held that the facts clearly indicated that the patient was in PVS with no hope of recovery, and that it was firmly established that the patient would refuse treatment under the circumstances present, the justices ruled that because the General Assembly of Ohio was opposed to discontinuance of sustenance, a "guardian may not act to withdraw nutrition or hydration and the court may not approve that withdrawal" (576).

Subsequent cases in the state did little to alter the *Couture* ruling or to clarify the legality of surrogate decision-making in Ohio.

Statutory Law.
Despite the fact that the right-to-die was present on the legislative agenda throughout the 1980's, Ohio was a laggard adopter. The General Assembly did not approve a policy until 1989. In that year, legislators finally agreed upon a durable power of attorney for health care as a viable alternative to a living will law (Ohio Power of Attorney for Health Care Act, Ohio Rev. Code Ann. §§1337.11 to 1337.17). Policy opponents were able to exact a number of concessions from bill supporters; indeed, the DPA statute was the second most restrictive law in the nation. The statute imposed cumbersome drafting requirements, specified few enforcement mechanisms, failed to recognize PVS, and explicitly disallowed refusal of sustenance.

In 1991 the General Assembly overhauled its right-to-die policy by amending the DPA statute and adopting both a living will policy and surrogate decision-making statute. The amendments to the DPA law did not alter the general triggering conditions required for implementation (i.e., the definition of "terminal condition" still excluded PVS); however, the nutrition and hydration restrictions were stricken. The Ohio Modified Rights of the Terminally Ill Act (Ohio Rev. Code Ann. §§2133.01 to 2133.15) governs living wills and decision-making by a surrogate in the absence of a directive. The living will section is reasonably facilitative; the surrogate provisions, by contrast, are very restrictive. Particularly troubling to policy advocates is the requirement stating that, in order for a surrogate to order withholding of sustenance, a probate court must determine that the patient has been terminally ill or vegetative for at least a period of twelve months.

Judicial Innovation and Legislative Innovation.
Neither Ohio's General Assembly nor the state's appellate courts appeared anxious to tackle the right-to-die issue. (A time line appears in Table 6.8.)

Judicial and Legislative Interaction

The first intermediate appellate court to hear a refusal of treatment case produced a permissive, yet cautious policy. The *Leach* court (1984) was unequivocal in its stance on informed consent, yet the justices declined to lay the foundation for a comprehensive surrogate policy. Like their robed counterparts in other states, the Ohio brethren placed responsibility for such policymaking squarely on the shoulders of elected legislators. The court's (restrained) policy was that treatment could only be withdrawn from incompetents after a probate court approved such a request by a patient's guardian:

> Until such time as the legislature provides some more efficient means of protecting the rights of patients in ... [vegetative] condition[s], we join those courts that require judicial authority for the termination of life-prolonging treatment of an incompetent patient. (1052-53)

Leach is silent on the evidentiary standard to be satisfied in such proceedings. Unlike appellate courts in other states, this Ohio Court of Appeals declined to fill the policy vacuum created by legislative inactivity.

Despite the court's fairly limited ruling, the case propelled the issue onto the mass and governmental agendas. In 1989, the Legislature finally adopted the (compromised) durable power of attorney policy described earlier; the bill was signed by the Governor on June 28. The next case to reach the appellate courts was decided on August 21, 1989, over one month before the DPA statute was to go into effect on September 27. The *Couture* court, while sympathizing with the plight of the patient and his family, made clear the fact that it would defer to legislative intent on matters of refusal of treatment. Despite the fact that incompetent patients without a directive were not covered by this statute which was not yet effective, the justices nevertheless found that allowing the withdrawal of sustenance would contradict the will of legislators:

> The public policy of Ohio, as determined by the General Assembly, is opposed to the withdrawal of nutrition or hydration ... notwithstanding the wishes of the patient or the surrogate. (576)

Where courts in other states (e.g., California, Washington), in order to expand the right-to-die, ruled that legislative statutes were nonexclusive means of exercising the right to decline treatment, the Ohio court exhibited the opposite tendency:

> We cannot ignore the prohibitions of R.C. 1337.13 [DPA statute] ... it is concerned with matters involving the ward's *express written direction*; a guardian's decision relying upon casual oral remarks of the ward is less compelling. If the ward's express written direction to withdraw nutrition or hydration is deemed not in his interest as a matter of law in R.C. 1337.13, so it must be in regard to oral statements of a ward to the same effect upon which a guardian ... would rely. The guardian may not act to withdraw nutrition or hydration and the court may not approve that withdrawal. (576) (italics original)

The *Couture* opinion placed policy-making responsibility squarely in the legislative domain. Both the appellate opinion and the DPA law were sharply criticized, and in 1991 legislators renovated the policy by adopting living will and surrogate rules, as well as amending the DPA law. Lawmakers were clearly responding to *Couture* when they included the following (apologetic) clarification in section 5 of the 1991 enrolled bill (Am.Sub.S.B. No. 13):

> The General Assembly declares that its several intents in enacting Amended Substitute Bill No. 13 of the 118th General Assembly [the 1989 DPA law] did not include any intent to affect the ability of competent adults or the guardians of incompetents or minors to make informed health care decisions for themselves or their wards.

The General Assembly then proceeded to liberalize the nutrition and hydration section of the DPA statute, as well as to establish an even more facilitative living will law. (Opponents were, however, able to secure the twelve-month waiting period in the surrogate statute.)

A number of observations can be offered regarding the interaction of appellate courts and the Ohio General Assembly. Neither branch of government was particularly ambitious in taking up the right-to-die issue.

Table 6.8
Judicial and Legislative Policy Making in Ohio

Year	Legislative Action	Judicial Action
1980		Probate court allows surrogate decision making (*Leach*). Appealed 4 years later.
1984		Judicial surrogate policy adopted (*Leach* v. *Shapiro*). Constitutional rights, substituted judgment, prior court approval. (Facility score = 6 points)
1987		Freedom of religion a basis for refusal of treatment (*Milton*).
1989	DPA adoption. Second most restrictive statute ever adopted. Narrow triggering conditions; sustenance restrictions; weak enforcement provisions. (Facility score = 13 points)	Judicial surrogate policy renovated. No constitutional or common law rights -- statutory only; clear and convincing evidence; prior court approval (*Couture*). (Facility score = 3 points).
1991	DPA renovated; sustenance restrictions lifted. (Facility score = 18 points) Living will law adopted. (Facility score = 23 points) Surrogate policy approved. 12-month waiting period and court approval. Restrictive. (Facility score = 13 points)	
1992		Judicial policy renovated (*Anderson*). Common law right to refuse treatment; other restrictions remain. (Facility Score = 4 points)

The judiciary ruled first, but produced a narrow holding that called upon legislators to fill in the substantive gaps in the evolving policy. After a considerable time lag, lawmakers responded by passing a very restrictive DPA statute. This statute was immediately constructed by the courts as providing the basis for future right-to-die decisions, even those which did not expressly fall within the purview of the statute. Public and professional dissatisfaction with the statute and the attendant *Couture* holding catalyzed the General Assembly into action, and the result was a move from a superficial policy to a somewhat "deeper" adoption.

In short, Ohio lawmakers engaged in conflict avoidance by "putting off" the controversial issue. However, unlike in other states, the appellate courts were unwilling to expand policy boundaries in the absence of legislative fiat. The legislature was forced to deal with the issue. The result is that current statutory law is considerable less facilitative than most other refusal of treatment laws in the United States. Intermediate appellate courts are unwilling to engage in judicial activism, and the Supreme Court of Ohio has all but extricated itself from the policy debate, meaning that future liberalization of Ohio law will probably require another highly salient court case capable of forcing the issue back on to the legislative agenda.

Missouri: Judicial Acquiescence, Limited Legislative Response

Missouri legislators approved an extremely restrictive living will law in 1985; as this was the only statutory guidance available to them, the justices of the Missouri Supreme Court, in crafting a surrogate decision making policy, strictly and literally adopted all of the restrictions contained in the living will statute. This deference to legislative intent was accompanied by judicial restraint, as the high court has refused to hear cases challenging the constitutionality of the state's statutory law. Unlike legislators in other jurisdictions, representatives in Missouri have not picked up the policy making slack left by the judiciary.

Statutory Law.
Shortly following the NCCUSL's model living will adoption, Missouri legislators joined a dozen other states in approving a similar law in 1985.

The Uniform Rights of the Terminally Ill Act (Mo. Ann. Stat. §§459.010 to 459.055) was, in both title and drafting provisions, modeled after the NCCUSL policy. However, the former departs appreciably from the latter, particularly in terms of implementation rules.

Lawmakers again took up the refusal of treatment issue in the 1991 legislative session. Although the NCCUSL had just adopted a model surrogate law earlier in the year, Missouri lawmakers were unwilling to approve such a controversial law. They were, however, amenable to the adoption of a permissive proxy law. The Missouri Durable Power of Attorney for Health Care Act (Mo. Ann. Stat. §§404.800 to 404.872) overcomes most of the limitations in its cousin living will policy. The DPA statute explicitly includes PVS in its definition of terminal illness, and declarants are permitted to instruct their proxies to discontinue artificial nutrition and hydration.

Judicial Innovation/Case Law.
Although Missouri courts were host to few cases during the 1970s and the better half of the 1980s, the right to die issue exploded onto the mass and appellate judicial agendas in 1988 when the state Supreme Court issued its ruling in the, now infamous, Nancy Cruzan case (*Cruzan, by Cruzan* v. *Harmon*, 760 S.W.2d 408). The plaintiffs were the parents of an adult woman who sustained numerous injuries in an automobile accident which left her in a persistent vegetative state. The diagnosis indicated that, with the continued delivery of artificial nutrition and hydration, the patient, whose condition was irreversible, could survive for an estimated thirty years. The patient's parents requested that the artificial feedings be discontinued, in order to permit their daughter to die a natural death. The rehabilitative center in charge of the patient's care refused to remove the feeding tube, and the parents brought an action seeking declaratory judgment. The trial court ruled in favor of the parents, but, in a landmark decision, the Supreme Court of Missouri reversed the trial court's ruling, and, in so doing, created what is, arguably, the nation's most restrictive surrogate decision making policy.

Although they acknowledged the individual right to refuse treatment, the justices were careful to note that this right is not absolute and that it must yield to countervailing state interests, particularly the preservation of life: "[T]he state's interest is not in quality of life. The state's interest is an unqualified interest in life" (422). The court ruled that, in the case of a PVS patient, the state's interest in preserving life is "particularly valid" given the fact that such a person is "not terminally ill" as "death is imminent only if she is denied food and water" (419). The court reviewed the arguments for and against the discontinuance of artificial sustenance, but declined to offer a definitive opinion as to whether or not artificial nutrition and hydration could be refused like any other type of life-prolonging therapy. Instead, the court reasoned as follows on the matter:

> The issue is not whether the continued feeding and hydration of Nancy [the patient] is medical treatment; it is whether feeding and providing liquid to Nancy is a burden to her ... We do not believe the care provided by artificial nutrition and hydration is oppressively burdensome in this case (424).

This is, perhaps, the most restrictive ruling ever issued by a state court of last resort. The *Cruzan* opinion embodies a number of distinctive views. First, the justices found that PVS is an inappropriate triggering condition for the refusal of treatment. In addition, the court's refusal to overturn the statutory sustenance restriction, coupled with its finding that the removal of feeding tubes produces "death by dehydration and starvation," implies that, even with appropriate evidence of a patient's desire to decline artificial nutrition and hydration, such a decision need not be honored (412). The opinion rejects substituted judgment and requires surrogates to support a nontreatment decision with a corpus of uncontrovertible evidence that would appear to be lacking in virtually any type of previous oral statement made by a patient.

The case was decided by a four-to-three vote, with an interim judge siding with the majority. The division within the high court mirrored the level of dissension in the general public, and the case attracted widespread media coverage. Activists on both sides of the issue anxiously anticipated the possibility of federal judicial review. The decision was appealed, and the United States Supreme Court granted *certiorari* the following year. In its only ruling on passive euthanasia (*Cruzan* v. *Director, Missouri Department of Health*, 497 U.S. 261, 1990), the high court of the land found a constitutional basis of the right to refuse treatment. The justices

Judicial and Legislative Interaction

did not rely on the right to privacy, but instead ruled that the liberty clause of the U.S. Constitution guarantees an individual the right to direct the course of her or his own treatment. Although it added this constitutional dimension, the court issued a very limited and, for right to die supporters, disappointing holding. The primary question addressed by the court was whether or not a state could require clear and convincing evidence before allowing a withdrawal decision. The majority ruled in the affirmative, finding that states have the right to erect appropriate safeguards in order to protect against the usurpation of an incompetent's right to life.

In the wake of the *Cruzan* decisions, the right to decline treatment was severely curtailed in the state of Missouri. Given the narrow division on the court, policy proponents likely hoped to promote a new case which would allow the justices (the composition of the court had changed) to reverse or modify their holding in *Cruzan*. Such an opportunity presented itself in early 1993. A trial court in *In Re Busalacchi* (No. 73677, January 26, 1993, discussed in Choice in Dying 1997) ruled that the clear and convincing evidentiary standard is not applicable to minor children, and that parents have the authority to make all life-sustaining treatment decisions, including the discontinuance of sustenance. The case was appealed to the Missouri Supreme Court, but it was dismissed. No subsequent cases have been heard by the state's high court.

Judicial Innovation and Legislative Innovation.
As indicated in Table 6.9, legislative innovation preceded judicial innovation, but the 1985 living will law was very restrictive in terms of its provisions, reflecting a legislative opposition to future adoptions and policy liberalization. The absence of a legislatively prescribed surrogate policy essentially "forced" the Supreme Court to promulgate guidelines, but the justices made clear that they would be guided be legislative intent, as reflected in the living will law. Upon noting the conservative definitions of "terminal illness" and "death-prolonging procedure" specified in the living will law, the court majority concluded that "the statute's import here is as an expression of the policy of this state with regard to the sanctity of life" (420). The court went on to rule that the statute could not be considered unconstitutional and that the court would

not extend the scope of its ruling beyond the legislatively constructed boundaries:

> We intend no judgment here as to whether the common law right to refuse medical treatment is broader than the Living Will statute. Beyond the broad policy statement it makes, the statute is not at issue in this case. (420)

The court made clear that the burden of developing a comprehensive right to die policy fell squarely upon legislative shoulders, and that the court would not substitute its judgment for that of an assembly of representatives elected directly by the citizens of the state:

> To the extent that courts continue to invent guidelines on an *ad hoc*, piecemeal basis, legislatures, which have the ability to address the issue comprehensively, will feel no compulsion to act and will avoid making the potentially unpopular choices which issues of this magnitude present. (426)

The dissenting justices fueled this call for legislative action using very sharp language. For example, Justice Welliver called the living will statute a "fraud on the people of Missouri from the beginning," and the judge indicated his willingness to rule it unconstitutional. Similar sentiments were echoed by the other two dissenters.

This type of negative commentary became increasing pervasive in the early 1990's. Indeed, it was the widespread media coverage generated by the *Cruzan* decisions that was responsible for issue maintenance on the mass and governmental agendas. When the litigation had ended in 1990, the Legislature reacted to the barrage of public criticism by approving a reasonably permissive DPA law. However, it is significant that lawmakers did not enact a surrogate policy. The DPA law was only a limited solution to a much broader problem.

Without a surrogate statute, in order for the provisions of *Cruzan* to be relaxed or otherwise modified, another court case will be required. It will ultimately be left to the Supreme Court justices to determine whether or not the liberalized DPA provisions evidence a legislative preference with regards to decision making by surrogates and close family members.

Judicial and Legislative Interaction

Recent evidence suggests that the high court is not anxious to reopen this issue. Four refusal of treatment cases have reached the trial courts since 1990 (Choice in Dying 1998), yet no *writ of certiorari* has been issued by the state Supreme Court. And judicial nondecisions beget legislative nondecisions in Missouri.

Table 6.9
Judicial and Legislative Policy Making in Missouri

Year	Legislative Action	Judicial Action
1985	Living will law adopted. Sustenance and triggering restrictions. (Facility score = 19 points)	
1988		*Cruzan* decision creates very limited judicial surrogate policy. Common law rights, strictest evidentiary standard, prior judicial approval required, and sustenance restriction. (Facility score = 3 points)
1990		U.S.S.C. essentially affirms state's holding in *Cruzan*.
1991	DPA adoption. Expansive sustenance and triggering provisions. (Facility score = 22 points)	
1993		State Supreme Court drops *Busalacchi* case (involving surrogate decision making) at request of newly-elected Attorney General, Jay Nixon.

Illinois: Mutually Reinforcing Reinvention

In hearing two controversial surrogate decision making cases, the justices of the Illinois Supreme Court took a "middle-of-the-road" approach with respect to existing statutory law. A "judicially active" agenda was tempered by a posture of deference to legislative intent, and the high court invited legislative revision of its judicial surrogate policy. Legislators responded to this call for action, and overhauled their right to die policy in order to overcome some of the restrictions imposed by their state's Supreme Court. Renovation grew increasingly facilitative over time.

Statutory Law.
Adopted in 1983, the Illinois Living Will Act (Ill. Comp. Stat. Ann. Ch. 755, §§35\1 to 35\10) was a restrictive first policy that limited implementation of nontreatment decisions. In 1987 policy proponents were successful in securing passage of a health care agent law. The Illinois Powers of Attorney for Health Care Act (Ill. Comp. Stat. Ann. Ch. 755, §§45\4-1 to 45\4-12) contained far more permissive implementation provisions than did its predecessor living will law; in 1988, many of the provisions of the former were brought into harmony with the later. In 1991, legislators adopted a very permissive surrogate policy (The Health Care Surrogate Act, Ill. Comp. Stat. Ann. Ch. 755, §§40/1 to 40/55) that allowed decision makers to employ a "best interests" standard.

Judicial Innovation/Case Law.
The right to die did not reach the appellate judicial agenda in Illinois until 1989. *In Re Estate of Longeway* (549 N.E.2d 292) was a detailed opinion that created a limited judicial surrogate policy. The justices of the high court, relying solely on common law principles, ruled that an incompetent patient's guardian could only direct the removal of life-supports after she or he provided clear and convincing evidence of the patient's intent to a probate judge.

In the following year, 1990, a similar case was again before the Supreme Court. In *In Re Estate of Greenspan* (558 N.E.2d 1194) the court reaffirmed and clarified its surrogate policy articulated in *Longeway*. The court also interpreted the Living Will Act's definition of "terminal illness"

Judicial and Legislative Interaction 229

to include PVS and similar diagnoses, regardless of whether or not death was imminent. The issue of surrogate decision making was again capturing headlines in 1992, when an intermediate appellate court renovated the existing policy and adopted a "best interests" evidentiary standard (*In Re C.A.*, 603 N.E.2d 1171).

Judicial Innovation and Legislative innovation.
As indicated in Table 6.10, legislative action preceded judicial action by nearly six years. Although legislators adopted fairly early, the first living will law reflected a number of compromises and was very limited in terms of the scope of its coverage.

The Supreme Court of Illinois adopted a posture of deference to legislative intent, but the justices also demonstrated a willingness to interpret gaps and ambiguities in the statutory law in favor of creating permissive right to die policy. In *Longeway* the court refused to find a constitutional right to die, opting instead to limit its holding to common law principles. This decision reflects a good deal of judicial restraint; not only did the court call upon the Legislature to produce a comprehensive refusal of treatment law, but the justices made clear the fact that subsequent legislation would override the judicially created policy:

> Because we believe the right to refuse artificial sustenance is premised on common law and not necessarily constitutionally based, the legislature is free to streamline, tailor, or overrule the procedures outlined herein. (301)

The court also made clear its willingness to liberally interpret statutes in the absence of legislative clarification. In approving the *Longeway* surrogate policy, the justices held that because it did not explicitly preclude a guardian from refusing nontreatment on a ward's behalf, the state's Probate Act "impliedly" authorized a guardian to make these types of decisions (298). Similarly, noting the conflicting definitions of triggering conditions contained in the two advance directives laws, the court ruled that the (more liberal) DPA definition should guide decision making by surrogates.

Table 6.10
Judicial and Legislative Policy Making in Illinois

Year	Legislative Action	Judicial Action
1983	Living will law adopted. Restrictive provisions: narrow definition of triggering conditions; no discontinuance of artificial sustenance. (Facility Score = 14 points)	
1987	DPA adoption. Permissive: sustenance withdrawal and liberal triggering conditions. (Facility Score = 27 points)	
1988	Living will statute brought into harmony with DPA law, except the former retained stricter triggering conditions. (Facility Score = 25 points)	
1989		Judicial surrogate policy adopted (*Longeway*). Common law, clear and convincing evidence, and judicial approval to end artificial feedings. (Facility score = 5 points)
1990		*Greenspan* decision clarifies requirements. Living will law liberally interpreted. (Facility score = 5 points)
1991	Surrogate law adopted. Highly facilitative: best interests standard; no court approval. (Facility score = 25 points)	
1992		*C.A.* decision applies best interests standard to a number of DNR patients. (Facility score = 8 points)

Judicial and Legislative Interaction

The two Supreme Court opinions attracted a good deal of public attention (as evidenced by the number of friend of the court briefs filed), and lawmakers, taking advantage of the window of opportunity opened by the NCCUSL, responded to the judicial and public calls for action by approving a surrogate policy in 1991. The statute effectively "trumped" many of the most conservative features of the judicial policy. Legislators made clear that prior court approval was not required to discontinue sustenance and that PVS and permanent unconsciousness were appropriate triggering conditions. Also significant is the fact that the statute embraced a "best interest" evidentiary standard. In the following year, the intermediate appellate court in *C.A.* plied the best interests standard and renovated the state's judicial policy in keeping with the evolved legislative standards.

Right to die policy making proved controversial in Illinois, and without judicial policy expansion and the attendant publicity, legislators might have avoided the surrogate decision making issue altogether. Indeed, as no subsequent cases have challenged the legality of the statutes, the issue appears to have faded from the legislative agenda in the Land of Lincoln.

Washington State: Legislative-Judicial Symbiosis

Washington legislators innovated early by adopting a living will law, but they were unwilling to approve a surrogate statute. An activist state judiciary adopted, and then liberally renovated, a judicial surrogate policy. A pattern emerged in which the high court handled surrogate decision-making and the legislature, in turn, liberally renovated advance directives policies. (The chronology of events is summarized in Table 6.11.)

Statutory Law.
The Natural Death Act (Wash. Rev. Code Ann. §§70.122.010 to 70.122.920) was a fairly restrictive living will law. The legislation was not amended until 1992, when PVS was recognized and the removal of feeding tubes was sanctioned; in that same session, lawmakers also approved a proxy policy with similar features (Washington Durable

Power of Attorney Act, Wash. Rev. Code Ann. §§70.122.010 to 70.122.920).

Judicial Innovation/Case Law.
In 1983 the Washington Supreme Court became the first state court west of the Mississippi River to hear a refusal of treatment case. *Matter of Welfare of Colyer* (660 P.2d 738) created a surrogate policy that allowed guardians of incompetent patients to apply a substituted judgment standard, with court approval required prior to the removal of life support systems. In the following year, the Washington Supreme Court modified (and further liberalized) its holding in *Colyer*. In *Matter of Guardianship of Hamlin* (689 P.2d 1372, 1984) the court engaged in judicial deregulation by limiting judicial involvement to cases involving conflict and by endorsing the use of a best interests standard.

In 1987 the Supreme Court further buttressed the permissive character of its evolving right-to-die policy. The court's holding in *In Re Guardianship of Grant* (747 P.2d 445) clarified diagnostic requirements and rejected any distinction between artificial sustenance and other types of treatment. While the ruling in *Grant* essentially constituted a "clear sweep" for right to die advocates, cautious policy proponents were careful to note the growing division on the Supreme Court. The case was decided by a five to four margin, with two judges "concurring in part and dissenting in part" and two judges (vehemently) "dissenting." In the following year, a seemingly rare event occurred: Justice Durham switched her vote. By joining Justices Andersen and Brachtenbach in the opinion "concurring in part and dissenting in part" (*In Re Guardianship of Grant*, 757 P.2d 534, 1988), Justice Durham left the legality of refusing sustenance open to serious legal debate. There is no longer a clear majority opinion; the opinion Justice Durham joined states that a decision allowing surrogates to decline artificial feeding should come from the legislative branch, not the judicial (the other dissenting opinion would ban surrogate decision-making in its entirety).

Judicial Innovation and Legislative Innovation.
Judicial and legislative policymaking have been intertwined in Washington. Legislators took up the right-to-die issue early by adopting

a living will statute in 1979. A review of the House and Senate calendars reveals that the issue remained on the state's legislative agenda throughout the 1980s and early 1990s. Although the Legislature never passed a surrogate decision-making statute, its endorsement of living wills was seized upon by the Supreme Court in 1983, when the justices articulated guidelines that would form the foundation of the state's surrogate decision making policy. Upon analyzing the preamble to the Natural Death Act, the *Colyer* court concluded that

> Our Legislature has acknowledged both an individual's right to control medical decisions and the right to privacy as grounds for withholding and withdrawing life sustaining treatment. (741)

Moreover, the justices (permissively) interpreted the state's general guardianship statute to enable a legally appointed guardian to withdraw life-sustaining treatment from an incompetent ward. The Supreme Court has repeatedly encouraged legislators to resolve future right-to-die cases by enacting a comprehensive surrogate decision-making policy:

> We invite the Legislature to address this sensitive issue. While the judiciary has the power and authority to decide such issues, our decisions are limited to the facts before us. As these issues necessarily involve society's moral standard as well as legal and medical issues, the Legislature is the body most capable of assessing the views of the people of this state. (*Colyer*, 752)

In subsequent decisions (*Hamlin* and *Grant*) the Supreme Court, as it solidified and liberally expanded surrogate decision-making rights, continued to encourage legislative action. Indeed, the high court appears to have demonstrated a willingness to defer to legislative fiat. For example, in *Dinino* v. *State Ex Rel. Gorton* (684 P.2d 1297, 1984) the Supreme Court declined to consider the constitutionality of the pregnancy restriction contained in the Natural Death Act. Despite the fact that the Superior Court (court of original jurisdiction) declared the pregnancy provision unconstitutional, a majority of Supreme Court justices refused to rule on the substantive, constitutional issue at bar by maintaining that the case presented no justiciable controversy:

Respondent is neither pregnant nor suffering from a terminal condition. As such, respondents' claims present a purely hypothetical and speculative controversy. (1300)

By voiding the ruling of the lower court based upon procedural issues, it seems clear that the Supreme Court's majority wished to avoid a direct confrontation with the Legislature. The two branches of government seemed to settle into a symbiotic relationship, whereby the court innovated only in those extremely controversial areas (e.g., surrogate decision-making) where its legislative counterpart declined (or failed) to take a clear stand.

Further evidence of the high court's reluctance to preempt the Legislature can be gleaned from the *Grant* court's division over the provision of sustenance. At the time the justices were deliberating, a surrogate decision making bill was voted on in a special session of the Legislature. The primary bone of contention appeared to be over provisions of the bill that would have allowed discontinuance of artificial hydration and nutrition: the House supported the provisions and the Senate opposed them. In the end, the bill failed, but it seemed clear that the issue would not immediately fade from the legislative agenda. In his opinion "concurring in part and dissenting in part," Justice Andersen carefully reviewed the legislative history of the surrogate decision-making bill, and he opined that because elected lawmakers had considered and voted against a policy of withdrawing sustenance, the Court should not subvert the will of the Legislature:

> The Legislature enacted the Natural Death Act and if, with the benefit of all its resources, the Legislature can pass a law allowing the withdrawal of food and water while protecting the infirm and helpless, then well and good; if not, then that too should tell us something. (*Grant*, 460)

The NDA itself was silent on whether or not sustenance could be withheld pursuant to the instructions contained in an advance directive. The Legislature once again tackled this issue in 1992. One of the options open to lawmakers was the adoption of a surrogate decision making policy that expressly authorized surrogates to withdraw sustenance. The

Judicial and Legislative Interaction

Legislature did not go quite that far. Instead, the NDA was amended to allow individuals to request cessation of such treatment in their advance directives. The amendments also allowed patients to specify a proxy decision-maker in their directives; proxies were given the authority to decline intubated feeding on behalf of their agents.

From the Legislature's 1992 adoption of the proxy decision making policy and the addition of the NDA sustenance provisions, it is possible to infer two trends. First, the state's Supreme Court had already ruled on the constitutionality of allowing surrogate decision-making; therefore, risk-averse legislators did not need to expend political capital by endorsing a highly controversial policy which already carried the force of law. However, the issue of artificial nutrition and hydration was in a state of legislative and judicial limbo; therefore, legislators helped bring order to this chaos by liberalizing the advance directives statutes to allow for the withdrawal of nutrition and hydration. While this, no doubt, involved a degree of controversy, it was not nearly as contentious as passing a highly facilitative surrogate statute. (Indeed, a majority of states had already adopted proxy/DPA statutes similar to the one before the Washington Legislature.) Bill sponsors and right-to-die proponents, who were familiar with the court's rationale, likely realized that the court had repeatedly held that incompetent patients who had not executed a directive should be accorded the same rights as those who filed such a document pursuant to the NDA. In other words, if the issue were to appear before the courts in the future, it is likely that the Supreme Court, upon noting the amendments to the statute, would rule in favor of allowing surrogates to decline tube feeding. Legislators adopted a fairly "routine" policy (i.e., one which did not carry a lot of "heat"), and in so doing, they potentially freed the Supreme Court (which appeared reluctant to act counter to expressed legislative intent) to liberalize the more volatile surrogate law. (Unfortunately, this issue has not subsequently been before any appellate court.)

In characterizing the role of the Supreme Court and the Legislature in making right-to-die policy a number of generalizations can be made. First, the Legislature did not wait for judicial action before it addressed the issue. Instead, it followed the lead of many of its neighbors and adopted a somewhat controversial Natural Death Act. The Supreme Court extended the rights guaranteed in the act to incompetent patients who had not executed a directive, thereby adopting a much broader policy. The justices repeatedly invited legislative policy reinvention, and when legislators took specific action (i.e., passing or defeating a bill) the justices were reluctant to challenge or preempt the expressed legislative decisions (e.g., the pregnancy and nutrition and hydration provisions). Over time, lawmakers were able to liberalize statutory policy in a manner that both allowed them to portray the issue as noncontroversial, while leaving the more heated issue to a judiciary that was likely to follow suit by extending the policy. These two branches of government have followed a pattern of mutually reinforcing symbiosis.

GENERAL OBSERVATIONS AND CONCLUSIONS

The preceding examples, along with the models estimated in the first part of the chapter, have illustrated a number of points. First, and most importantly, judicial innovation can and does influences legislative innovation, and the reverse holds true as well. Second, judicial and legislative relationships vary across states, with judiciaries taking a more active role in some states, while legislatures were more inclined to policy making in others. These varied patterns of interaction may largely be the function of a number of idiosyncratic forces. For example, several of the innovative court decisions were decided by narrow margins, with the individual characteristics and predispositions of judges exerting influence that is simply difficult to tap in an empirical model or to identify in a case study. Nor did the analysis identify any specific individual policy entrepreneurs who were responsible for issue maintenance on the mass and legislative agendas, but such persons and organizations surely existed. Medical tragedies and family-provider conflicts furnished windows of opportunity for policy making in some states but not in others. The focus on state institutions as the units of analyses may obscure a number of important intrastate dynamics, but is ultimately necessary if nomothetic causal explanations are to be developed. With this in mind, the above case vignettes suggest several variables that should be subjected to greater scrutiny in future research efforts.

Table 6.11
Judicial and Legislative Policy Making in Washington State

Year	Legislative Action	Judicial Action
1979	Washington Natural Death Act (living will law) adopted. Restrictive: narrow triggering conditions; silent on artificial nutrition and hydration. (Facility Score = 19 points)	
1983		Judicial surrogate policy adopted (*Colyer* decision). Constitutional rights, substituted judgment, prior court approval. (Facility Score = 6 points)
1984		Surrogate policy renovated (*Hamlin*). Best interests standard and judicial deregulation. (Facility Score = 9 points) Court declines to review pregnancy restriction in living will law (*Dinino*).
1987	Legislators vote down surrogate statute.	Surrogate policy applied to artificial sustenance (*Grant*).
1988	Surrogate legislation defeated again; sustenance provisions are key source of division.	Justice Durham switches vote in *Grant*. Future of sustenance refusal by surrogates uncertain.
1992	Living will law renovated; triggering conditions and feeding provisions liberalized. (Facility Score = 24) DPA statute adopted. (Facility Score = 20)	

First, judicial posture towards statutory law can influence the willingness of legislatures to take up a policy issue on which the court had previously ruled. When appellate opinions contained language inviting assembly members to revise or streamline judicial guidelines, legislatures usually responded to the challenge. On the other hand, when courts made clear their willingness to find constitutional bases for their decisions, legislatures may have been less likely to innovate, possibly out of fear of judicial review. Another variable with the potential to inform our understanding of the policy process is judicial nondecisionmaking; a number of courts had opportunities to hear cases and declined to do so. Perhaps the number of times *certiorari* is denied is as important as the number of right to die cases heard in a given state. Repeated refusals to hear cases may essentially force a legislature to eventually take up a question it would otherwise hope to avoid. Finally, public salience is a factor that is probably crucial in explaining legislative and judicial policymaking; it is difficult to tell how much sustained attention cases received in various states, and it is also tough to identify the various events and "medialities" that occurred at the intrastate level, yet this type of coverage was undoubtedly taken into consideration by policy makers.

Estimated separately, the judicial and legislative models have yielded results that allow us to form general conclusions about policy diffusion and reinvention. When judicial and legislative policy making are linked, however, the situation becomes more complicated. The concluding chapter attempts to "take stock" of the results from this and the previous two chapters, and an effort is made to identify theoretical and methodological improvements that can lead to greater understanding of the interactions between these two policy making institutions.

CHAPTER 7
Conclusion

TAKING STOCK

In the preceding pages, a theory of permissive policy adoption and reinvention is offered; many empirical models are estimated, with the results indicating that many of the theoretical assumptions are supported, while some receive only modest or no support. In this chapter, I "take stock" of these varied findings. In the first section, I review the findings from the legislative models; upon identifying those influences that were the most and the least important in influencing legislative policy adoption and renovation, I speculate as to why some of the proposed relationships failed to materialize and offer suggestions on how research on legislative policy innovation can be strengthened in future efforts. Next, I review the findings from the judicial models of adoption and renovation. Particular emphasis is placed upon methodological refinements that have the potential to strengthen additional research on the diffusion of judicial innovations and on measuring important concepts such as the roles of attorney generals and other executive actors in encouraging or deterring policy adoption; strategies for assessing the extent of non-decision-making by state appellate courts are also discussed. In the third section of the chapter, I discuss theoretical and methodological improvements that have the potential to inform our understanding of legislative-judicial interaction in the policy making process. The chapter concludes with a discussion of how the theory and models can be extended to new policy areas.

LEGISLATIVE INNOVATION AND REINVENTION

Determinants of Policy Adoption and Renovation

Adoption.
Although policy making varied across the three innovation types, a number of variables emerged as consistently important predictors of the adoption of permissive policies by state assemblies. Horizontal variables clearly exerted disproportionate influence in these models. The creation of model laws by the NCCUSL had a positive and significant impact in all three event history analyses, and changes in regional policy making trends exerted tremendous leverage over the adoption of both types of advance directives policies. This latter finding underscores the importance of examining time-serial changes in policy content across states, not simply looking at dates of adoption. States are clearly influenced by policy trends in their regions and in the nation as a whole; lawmakers would prefer to stay abreast of policy trends, and horizontal developments may be cited by risk averse legislators as justification for the approval of a controversial policy.

Two other variables proved to be major correlates of adoption of living will and surrogate laws. As hypothesized, citizen or part-time legislatures were more likely to innovate than were full time, professionalized assemblies. Representatives of the former bodies are clearly less risk-averse than are their re-election oriented counterparts in other states. This constitutes a major finding, perhaps unique to permissive policies, that runs counter to the corpus of findings in the extant innovation literature. Also consistent with theoretical expectations is the finding that lawmakers were far more likely to approve controversial innovations in "off years;" electoral threat, to some extent, weighs on the calculus of all legislators, and it is understandable that legislators prefer to act on controversial issues when re-election looms farthest on the horizon. To a lesser extent, organized interest groups also exerted influence over the adoption process, with the Catholic Church being more successful at blocking innovations than were organized medicine and geriatric lobbies at promoting it; this finding suggests that, consistent with prior research, organized opposition to a policy contributes more to its defeat than organized support for the policy contributes to its prospects for adoption.

Adoption and diffusion patterns varied across the three policy types. Living will laws, the core innovation, were influenced by the largest number of independent variables, reflecting the theoretical assumption that political and institutional factors should be most important in influencing policy adoption of a first type of innovation. Health care proxy laws, the first type of tangential innovation, diffused at a remarkably accelerated rate when compared to the core innovation. As predicted, policy makers were able to portray DPA and proxy appointment statutes as noncontroversial outgrowths of existing policy. Indeed, the only major factors influencing adoption of proxy laws were the regional facility scores and the 1989 NCCUSL model law adoption; other types of political and institutional variable were not terribly influential. This was, however, not the case with surrogate decision making statutes; contrary to expectations, these policies proved to be far more controversial than either type of advance directives laws, and few legislative bodies (Arkansas and North Carolina being the clear exceptions) were able to market surrogate proposals as being routine and nonconflictual in nature.

The failure of the tangential surrogate innovations to diffuse quickly (or in any clear order) may be indicative of a consideration that is largely ignored in the theory: the extent of policy controversy. Indeed, I assumed that all types of permissive policies were controversial in nature, but that tangential innovations would always invite less opposition and attention than core innovations. This assumption may be unwarranted; in fact, it is possible that the presence of a policy option, like health care surrogate proposals, on a state's legislative agenda may increase the likelihood of a state adopting (or renovating) a core or tangential policy with less widespread opposition; it was clear that in some laggard states (e.g., New York and New Jersey) advance directives laws were only given serious consideration when they were portrayed as "lesser evils" than, and as substitutes for, the far more permissive surrogate policies.

Also surprising was the failure of earlier policy making patterns to account for the adoption of later types of policies. The presence or absence of a permissive core innovation had no appreciable impact on the adoption of either type of tangential innovation. This was explained in part, in Chapter 4, by the unanticipated pattern of dual or joint adoptions of policy types, with a number of state's turning "hat tricks" (the adoption of all three types of policies at once). However, the failure of past adoptions to influence later policy patterns may also be indicative of another trend for which it is a bit more difficult to account: as time progresses, a plethora of influences emerge and policy cues come from many different sources (e.g., courts, copycat legislatures, the NCCUSL, interest groups, the media, etc.). It is undoubtedly much simpler to account for the diffusion of a core policy in its "early days" than it is to pinpoint the sources of policy influence once states are bombarded with policy proposals and alternatives stemming from a multitude of sources.

Renovation.
As hypothesized, for all three legislative policy types, renovation was most likely when a substantial amount of time had progressed, resulting in a state's existing policy falling below regional and national standards. The results from the living will model also suggest that interest groups can be particularly effective in blocking subsequent policy renovation and liberalization. Recall that the state Catholic conferences, which began lobbying for weak and limited living will policies in the mid-1980s, were able to preclude the adoption of subsequent amendments to first policies. Other variables that were important in the adoption of a given policy (e.g., electoral threat and legislative professionalism) proved to have little effect on the willingness of lawmakers to amend these policies. Renovation may have proved less contentious than policy adoption, and it also appears that many states approved amendments to one type of policy at the same time as they passed a related innovation; the passage of time and the concomitant increase in policy cues confound the analysis of policy renovation in much the same way they do the estimation of policy adoption models.

Potential Improvements to Legislative Innovation Models

Research on legislative innovation and reinvention stands to benefit from the operationalization of several different concepts.

One crucial variable is policy salience. The amount of a coverage a particular issue or policy proposal receives on a state's mass agenda constrains the range of options to which legislators may avail themselves. To obtain state-level measures, it would be necessary to consult major periodicals and newspapers in the state; while this task is prohibitive given the fact that most of these sources do not have indexes that extend back in time, it is worth noting that, in recent years, many major newspapers have created electronic data bases (replete with search engines) that would allow for a policy specific search of articles and editorials. For "new" policies that have begun to diffuse in recent history, this might prove a viable (albeit laborious) research endeavor.

Also related to salience is the level of public support that exists for a given policy at the intrastate level. General measures of ideology (e.g., the mean ADA score of a state's congressional delegation) may mask important nuances in public opinion. Unfortunately, policy-specific measures are also difficult to find; for example, Gallup has conducted a number of national surveys on the right to die, but the samples are generally limited to about one thousand respondents, meaning that, even if the data set were obtained with a listing of each respondent's state of residence, the sample size for each state would prove too small to make meaningful inferences to state-level population parameters. However, on a number of issues, state newspapers and research organizations often conduct statewide polls, and, if the figures from these surveys were obtained and archived, it could prove possible to use interpolation techniques to create rough time-series for each of the fifty states. Increasingly, many national interest groups are making efforts to collect and disseminate these types of survey results to their members.

More precise measures of past policy making would also benefit research on policy adoption. In many states policy entrepreneurs drafted right to die proposals and introduced them in their general assemblies on an annual basis (Glick 1992), realizing that placing an issue squarely on the legislative agenda often requires numerous attempts. It would be helpful to track the introduction and relative successes of policy proposals in each state in each year; while obtaining legislative calendars may prove prohibitive, particularly in studies that extend back in time, many interest groups have initiated programs that record the success and failure of all policy proposals before state legislatures; Choice in Dying, for example, has a list of all drafted bills and their outcomes that extends from 1988 to the present day (Choice in Dying 1999).

The above measures would make fine additions to the models estimated in the previous chapters, and, when applied to new types of legislative policies, could yield interesting and useful results. Similar improvements can be made to the judicial models, as discussed in the next section.

JUDICIAL INNOVATION AND REINVENTION

Determinants of Adoption and Renovation

Adoption.
The theory did reasonably well in accounting for variation in the diffusion of judicial surrogate policies. Institutional variables were the strongest correlates of appellate adoption. States in which attorney generals were elected were more than twenty percent less likely to approve judicial surrogate policies than were states with appointed attorney generals. Judicial reputation was also positively related to adoption, with lesser reputed judiciaries adopting well after some of the most prestigious tribunals had created policies. Finally, the amount of prior case activity on the right to die in a state had a pronounced impact on the decision to approve a judicial surrogate policy, implying that efforts at agenda maintenance are a crucial ingredient in the *certiorari* process.

Interest groups were also active in the judicial process, but their impact was exactly the opposite of that which characterized legislative adoption. Opposition by the Catholic Church was a major obstacle to legislative adoption, but the size of groups supporting the right to die in a given state was positively related to the likelihood of approval of judicial policies. This suggests that opposition groups are most effective in the legislative arena, while policy advocates enjoy greater success in seeking judicial resolution of policy questions.

The most surprising finding was that horizontal variables did not appear to exert a major influence over judicial policy adoption. In fact, these variables behaved counter to expectations. Adoption was less likely in the wake of the *Cruzan* decision, and the propensity of judiciaries to innovate actually decreased as regional trends moved in the direction of greater policy facility. This was in marked contrast to the pattern that dominated the adoption and reinvention of legislative policies.

Renovation.
The model of judicial renovation failed to predict a single alteration of judicial policies. Upon approving an innovation, most courts either never had an opportunity to hear subsequent cases, or denied review, or were otherwise unwilling to depart from their original logic. Only a handful of courts made substantive alterations to their previously approved policies, and these decisions owed a good deal to chance factors such as the emergence of a unique court case or statutory adoption or renovation by a state assembly.

Potential Improvements to Judicial Innovation Models

The research points to the importance of attorney generals in influencing the judicial policy making process. This is an area which has received little substantive attention in the academic literature, and these executive officials may be one of the crucial links in integrating research on interinstitutional relations, as attorney generals have the power to issue directives apprising practitioners and others about the types of conduct that will or will not be subject to challenge by state law enforcement officers. (In the case of the right to die, attorney generals in several states issued advisory opinions indicating that, despite statutory guidelines to the contrary, when all parties to a nontreatment decision were in agreement, no effort would be made to prosecute or block implementation of the withdrawal of life supports.) For a given policy area, a data set of all advisory opinions issued in a state could be compiled, and these directives could be content analyzed and included in future judicial (and legislative) innovation models. Future efforts would benefit from a greater exploration of all of the formal policy powers exercised by attorney generals.

Other executive actors also play important roles in the policy process. Regulations governing standard operating procedures in hospitals and nursing homes are usually developed by a state's office of health and human services; several jurisdictions now charge their secretaries of state with developing programs monitoring the filing and drafting of advance directives; and officials such as ombudsman for the elderly and patients' rights advocates also have the ability to influence crucial aspects of right to die polcy implementation. For any given policy, a variety of different executive officials have the ability to issue regulations and spearhead programs that may make, break or otherwise shape the success of new policy programs. The extent and nature of formal rulemaking could be tracked in future research.

Perhaps the most important consideration bearing upon the prospects for judicial policy adoption is the role of state courts of last resort in granting review of appeals. In addition to counts of the number of prior intrastate cases in a state, it would also be useful to tabulate the number of those cases that were appealed but ignored by high courts. In fact, the adoption process could be estimated by way of a two-stage procedure; first, all of the variables that condition the likelihood of *certiorari* could be included in a simple binary response model, and, in the second phase, policies could be scored for content, with these outcomes being regressed on those variables hypothesized to affect the level of policy permissiveness or facility. It is this type of methodological improvement that has the potential to help further "sort out" the temporal development of policy making by state courts. Similar techniques can be utilized in integrated models of policy adoption and reinvention. Indeed, as discussed in the next section, when multiple policies and actors are considered, the process of explanation becomes increasingly complex, and new tools are needed if we are to eventually see the forest and the trees.

JUDICIAL-LEGISLATIVE INTERACTION IN THE POLICY PROCESS

Difficulty in Identifying Patterns

The empirical models estimated in Chapter 6 failed to yield clear results. Judiciaries dominated the process in some states; legislatures took the lead in others, and the two branches complemented one another in a handful of other jurisdictions. The six case studies simply reinforced the observation that different processes are operative in different states. These varied and inconclusive observations are perhaps a function of the fact that, when several different types of policies and more than one institution are considered, the situation becomes more complicated.

Predicting the adoption of core innovations is considerably less challenging than explaining the approval of later types of policies. It is worth noting that there were no states that emerged as clear, systematic policy leaders. After initial innovations, "copycats" and "reinventers" emerge in unexpected ways -- witness the 1977 core adoptions by North Carolina and Arkansas. Moreover, once the diffusion process is under way, a plethora of policy forms, ideas and entrepreneurs emerge, and multiple institutions are invited to broker conflict and tackle difficult questions. The explosion in policy making means that any permutation of relationships can be found in a given state in a given time. With so many actors and ideas attempting to influence the process, it would be tempting to conclude that, with the passage of time, the production of policy becomes more random than systematic. However, as discussed below, there are many promising avenues for future research that may help researchers to bring conceptual and theoretical order to a multifaceted and intertwined set of complex interactions.

Strategies to Strengthen Theory and Method

The theory of legislative-judicial interaction presented in the previous pages is very simple, and could benefit tremendously from further development. There are two ways to proceed in this theory-building effort. First, because there are so few studies of the relationship between courts and legislatures in the diffusion process, there is a good deal to be gained from inductive case studies of different policy areas. As more results become available, it may be possible to identify common patterns and trends, which will, in turn, contribute to the construction of comprehensive, deductive theories.

A second fruitful approach might be to utilize advanced econometric and time-series techniques for identifying temporal causal patterns. Recall from Chapter 6 that the integrated models, due to the inclusion of lagged variables, were, on several occasions, unable to detect patterns of interaction that occurred within the same year; similarly, as the case studies showed, actors in one branch of government often exhibited delayed responses to actions undertaken by another level of government. Granger testing and similar techniques might help to isolate causal trends and determine which, if either, branch of government is most reactive and which institution of state government is most likely to set in motion the wheels of the diffusion process. Similarly, the construction and estimation of nonrecursive causal models would also allow for reciprocal influences in the policy process, and it would be possible to discern the relative impact, both direct and indirect, that adoptions in one branch of state government have on adoption and renovation in another branch.

Finally, future research needs to continue to apply theories of legislative and judicial innovation to new policy areas. Certainly, additional types of permissive policies, such as gay rights and sodomy laws, hate crime laws, and abortion reforms need to be the subject of future investigations. Research in other policy areas (i.e., distributive and redistributive) is also important, as the results from these studies may allow for a greater understanding of how innovation and reinvention vary across different policy types. The study of judicial and legislative policy adoption and renovation is relatively nascent, and there is a seemingly unlimited array of options ripe for further research.

APPENDIX A
Listing of Right-to-Die Statutes

This appendix contains a state-by-state listing of all right to die statutes that were used to calculate the living will, health care proxy, and surrogate decision-making facility scores. The year(s) within brackets following the name of each act indicate the year of enactment and any subsequent amendments.

ALABAMA
Alabama Natural Death Act [1981], Ala. Code §§22-8A-1 to 22-8A-10 (1990).

ALASKA
Alaska Rights of Terminally Ill Act [1986, 1994], Alaska Stat. §§18.12.010 to 18.12.100 (1994).

ARIZONA
Arizona Living Wills and Health Care Directives Act [1985, 1991, 1992, 1994], Ariz. Rev. Stat. Ann. §§36-3201 to 36-3262 (1993 & Supp. 1995).

ARKANSAS
Arkansas Rights of the Tenninally Ill or Permanently Unconscious Act [1977, 1987], Ark. Code Ann. §§20-17-201 to 20-17-217 (Michie 1991).

CALIFORNIA
California Natural Death Act [1976,1991, 1994], Cal. Health & Safety Code §§7185 to 7194.5 (West Supp. 1996).
California Durable Power of Attorney for Health Care Act [1984, 1985, 1988, 1990, 1991, 1992, 1993, 1994, 1995], Cal. Prob. Code §§4600 to 4779 (West Supp. 1996).

COLORADO
Colorado Medical Treatment Decision Act [1985, 1989, 1991], Colo. Rev. Stat.§§15-18-101 to 15-18-113 (1987 & Supp. 1995).
Colorado Patient Autonomy Act [1992, 1994], Colo. Rev. Stat. §§15-14-501 to 15-14-509 (1987 & Supp. 1995).

CONNECTICUT
Connecticut Removal of Life Support Systems Act [1985, 1991, 1993, 1994], Conn. Gen. Stat. §§19a-570 to 19a-580c (Supp. 1995).
Connecticut Statutory Short Form Durable Power of Attorney Act [1990, 1991], Conn. Gen. Stat. §§1-43 to 1-54a (1988 & Supp. 1995).

DELAWARE
Delaware Health-Care Decisions Act [1982, 1983, 1994, 1996], Del. Code Ann. tit. 16, §§2501 to 2517.

FLORIDA
Florida Health Care Advance Directives Act [1984, 1985, 1990,1992, 1994], Fla. Stat. Ann. §§765.101 to 765.401 (Supp. 1996).

GEORGIA
Georgia Living Wills Act [1984, 1986,1987, 1989, 1992, 19931, Ga. Code Ann. §§31-32-1 to 31-32-12 (Michie 1991 & Supp. 1995).
Georgia Durable Power of Attorney for Health Care Act [1990], Ga. Code §§31-36-1 to 31-36-13 (Michie 1991).

HAWAII
Hawaii Medical Treatment Decisions Act [1986], Hawaii Rev. Stat. §§327D-1 to 327D-27 (1993).
Hawaii Durable Power of Attorney for Health Care Decisions Act [1992], Hawaii Rev. Stat. §§551D-1 to 551D-7 (Supp. 1993).

IDAHO
Idaho Natural Death Act [1977, 1986, 1988], Idaho Code §§39-4501 to 39-4509 (1993).

ILLINOIS
Illinois Living Will Act [1984,1988], Ill. Comp. Stat. Ann. ch. 755, §§35/1 to 35/10 (West 1993).

Illinois Powers of Attorney for Health Care Act [1987, 1988], Ill. Comp. Stat. Ann. ch. 755, §§45/4-1 to 45/4-12 (West 1993).

INDIANA
Indiana Living Wills and Life-Prolonging Procedures Act [1985, 1993, 1994], Ind. Code Ann. §§16-36-4-1 to 16-36-4-21 (Burns 1993 & Supp. 1995).

Indiana Powers of Attorney Act [1991], Ind. Code Ann. §§30-5-1-1 to 30-5-10-4 (Burns 1995).

IOWA
Iowa Life-sustaining Procedures Act [1985, 1987, 1992], Iowa Code Ann. §§144A.1 to 144A.12 (1989 & Supp. 1995).

Iowa Durable Power of Attorney for Health Care Act [1991], Iowa Code Ann. §§144B.1 to 144B.12 (Supp. 1995).

KANSAS
Kansas Natural Death Act [1979], Kan. Stat. Ann. §§65-28,101 to 65-28,109 (1992).

Kansas Durable Power of Attorney for Health Care Decisions Act [1989, 1994], Kan. Stat. Ann. §§58-625 to 58-632 (1994).

KENTUCKY
Kentucky Living Will Directives Act [1990,1994], Ky. Rev. Stat. Ann. §§311.621 to 311.644 (Michie 1995).

LOUISIANA
Louisiana Natural Death Act [1984, 1985, 1990, 1991], La. Rev. Stat. Ann. §§40:1299.58.1 to 40:1299.58.10 (West 1992).

Louisiana Power of Attorney Act [1981, 1990], La. Civ. Code Ann. art. 2997 (West 1994).

MAINE
Maine Uniform Health-Care Decisions Act [1985, 1990, 1991, 1995], Me. Rev. Stat. Ann. tit. 18-A, §§5-801 to 5-817 (West Supp. 1995).
Maine Powers of Attorney Act [1986, 1991], Me. Rev. Stat. Ann. tit. 18-A, §§5-501 to 5-506 (West 1981 & Supp. 1995).

MARYLAND
Maryland Health Care Decisions Act [1985, 1986, 1987, 1993, 1994, 1996], Md. Health-Gen. Code Ann. §§5-601 to 5-618 (1994 & Supp. 1995).

MASSACHUSETTS
Massachusetts Health Care Proxies by Individuals Act [1990], Mass. Gen. L. Ch. 201D (Law Co-op. 1994).

MICHIGAN
Michigan Power of Attorney for Health Care Act [1990], Mich. Comp. Laws, §§700.496 (West 1995).

MINNESOTA
Minnesota Living Will Act [1989, 1992, 1993, 1995], Minn. Stat. §§145B.01 to 145B.17 (West Supp. 1996).
Minnesota Durable Power of Attorney for Health Care Act [1993], Minn. Stat. §§145C.01 to 145C.15 (West Supp. 1996).

MISSISSIPPI
Mississippi Withdrawal of Life-Saving Mechanisms Act [1984], Miss. Code Ann. §§41-41-101 to 41-41-121 (Law Co-op. 1993).
Mississippi Durable Power of Attorney for Health Care Act [1990, 1993], Miss. Code Ann. §§41-41-151 to 41-41-183 (Law Co-op. 1993).

MISSOURI
Missouri Life Support Declarations Act [1985], Mo. Ann. Stat. §§459.010 to 459.055 (Vernon 1992).
Missouri Durable Power of Attorney for Health Care Act [1991, 1992], Mo. Ann. Stat. §§404.800 to 404.872 (Vernon Supp. 1996).

Listing of Right-to-Die Statutes 253

MONTANA
Montana Rights of the Terminally Ill Act [1985, 1989,1991], Mont. Code Ann. §§50-9-101 to 50-9-111, 50-9-201 to 50-9-206 (1995).

Montana Durable Power of Attorney Act [1974, 1985], Mont. Code Ann. §§72-5-501 to 75-5-502 (1995).

NEBRASKA
Nebraska Rights of the Terminally Ill Act [1992, 1993], Neb. Rev. Stat. §§20-401 to 20-416 (Supp. 1994).

Nebraska Power of Attorney for Health Care Act [1992, 1993], Neb. Rev. Stat. §§30-3401 to 30-3432 (Supp. 1994).

NEVADA
Nevada Uniform Act on the Rights of the Terminally Ill [1977, 1985, 1987, 1991, 1993, 1995], Nev. Rev. Stat. §§449.535 to 449.690 (1991 & Supp. 1995).

Nevada Durable Power of Attorney for Health Care Act [1987, 1991, 1993], Nev. Rev. Stat. Ann. §§449.800 to 449.860 (1991 & Supp. 1995).

NEW HAMPSHIRE
New Hampshire Living Wills Act [1985, 1991, 1992], N.H. Rev. Stat. Ann. §§137-H:1 to 137-H:16 (1990 & Supp. 1995).

New Hampshire Durable Power of Attorney for Health Care [1991, 1992], N.H. Rev. Stat. Ann. §§137-J:1 to 137-J:16 (Supp. 1995).

NEW JERSEY
New Jersey Advance Directives for Health Care Act [1991], N.J. Stat. Ann. §§26:2H-53 to 26:2H-78 (West Supp. 1995).

NEW MEXICO
New Mexico Uniform Health-Care Decisions Act [1995] N.M. Stat. Ann. §§24-7A-1 to 24-7A-18 (Supp. 1995).

New Mexico Right to Die Act [1977,1984], N.M. Stat. Ann.§§24-7-1 to 24-7-11 (Michie 1994).

New Mexico Durable Power of Attorney Act [1989], N.M. Stat. Ann. §§45-5-501 to 45-5-502 (Michie 1993).

NEW YORK
New York Health Care Proxy Act [1990,1994], N.Y. Pub. Health Law §§2980 to 2994 (McKinney 1994 & Supp. 1996).

NORTH CAROLINA
North Carolina Right to Natural Death Act [1977, 1979, 1981, 1983, 1991], N.C. Gen. Stat. §§90-320 to 90-322 (1993).

North Carolina Health Care Powers of Attorney Act [1991, 1993], N.C. Gen. Stat. §§32A-15 to 32A-26 (1995).

NORTH DAKOTA
North Dakota Uniform Rights of the Terminally Ill Act [1989, 1991, 1993], N.D. Cent. Code §§23-06.4-01 to 23-06.4-14 (Michie 1991 & Supp. 1995).

North Dakota Durable Powers of Attorney for Health Care Act [1991, 1993], N.D. Cent. Code §§23-06.5-01 to 23-06.5-18 (Michie 1991 & Supp. 1995).

OHIO
Ohio Modified Uniform Rights of the Terminally Ill Act [1991], Ohio Rev. Code Ann. §§2133.01 to 2133.15 (Anderson 1994 & Supp. 1995).

Ohio Power of Attorney for Health Care Act [1989,1991], Ohio Rev. Code Ann. §§1337.11 to 1337.17 (Anderson 1993 & Supp. 1995).

OKLAHOMA
Oklahoma Rights of the Terminally Ill or Persistently Unconscious Act [1985, 1987, 1990, 1992], Okla. Stat. Ann. tit. 63, §§3101.1 to 3101.16 (West Supp. 1996).

Oklahoma Hydration & Nutrition for Incompetent Patients Act [1987, 1990, 1992], Okla. Stat. Ann. tit. 63, §§3080.1 to 3080.5 (West Supp. 1996).

OREGON
Oregon Health Care Decisions Act [1977, 1983, 1987, 1993], Or. Rev. Stat. §§127.505 to 127.640 (Supp. 1994).

PENNSYLVANIA
Pennsylvania Advance Directive for Health Care Act [1992, 1994], Pa. Stat. Ann. tit. 20, §§5401 to 5416 (West Supp. 1995).
Pennsylvania Durable Powers of Attorney Act [1982], Pa. Stat. Ann. tit. 20, §§5601 to 5607 (West Supp. 1995).

RHODE ISLAND
Rhode Island Rights of the Terminally Ill Act [1991, 1992], R.I. Gen. Laws §§23-4.11-1 to 23-4.11-14 (West Supp. 1995).
Rhode Island Health Care Power of Attorney Act [1986, 1989, 1992, 1993, 1994], R.I. Gen. Laws §§23-4.10-1 to 23-4.10-12 (West 1989 & Supp. 1995).

SOUTH CAROLINA
South Carolina Death with Dignity Act [1986, 1988, 1991], S.C. Code Ann. §§44-77-10 to 44-77-160 (Law Co-op Supp. 1994).
South Carolina Powers of Attorney Act [1986, 1990, 1992], S.C. Code Ann. §§62-5-501 to 62-5-505 (Law Co-op Supp. 1995).

SOUTH DAKOTA
South Dakota Living Will Act [1991, 1994], S.D. Codified Laws Ann. §§34-12D-1 to 34-12D-22 (Michie Supp. 1994).
South Dakota Durable Powers of Attorney Act [1977, 1979, 1990, 1992], S. D. Codified Laws Ann. §§59-7-2.1 to 59-7-2.8, 59-7-8 (Michie 1993).

TENNESSEE
Tennessee Right to Natural Death Act [1985, 1991, 1992], Tenn. Code Ann. §§32-11-101 to 32-11-112 (Michie Supp. 1994).
Tennessee Durable Power of Attorney for Health Care Act [1990], Tenn. Code Ann. §§34-6-201 to 34-6-214 (Michie 1991).

TEXAS
Texas Natural Death Act [1977, 1979, 1983, 1985, 1989, 1993], Tex. Health & Safety Code Ann. §§672.001 to 672.021 (Vernon 1992 & Supp. 1996).
Texas Durable Power of Attorney for Health Care Act [1989, 1991], Tex. Civil Practice & Remedies Code Ann. §§135.001 to 135.018 (Vernon Supp. 1996).

UTAH
Utah Personal Choice and Living Will Act [1985, 1988, 1993], Utah Code Ann. §§75-2-1101 to 75-2-1119 (Michie 1993 & Supp. 1995).

VERMONT
Vermont Terminal Care Document Act [1982], Vt. Stat. Ann. tit. 18, §§5251 to 5262 (1987) and tit. 13, §§1801 (1987).

Vermont Durable Powers of Attorney for Health Care Act [1987], Vt. Stat. Ann. tit. 14, §§3451 to 3467 (1989 & Supp. 1995).

VIRGINIA
Virginia Health Care Decisions Act [1983, 1988, 1989, 1991, 1992, 1994], Va. Code §§54.12981 to 54.12993 (Michie 1994).

WASHINGTON
Washington Natural Death Act [1979, 1992], Wash. Rev. Code Ann. §§70.122.010 to 70.122.920 (West Supp. 1996).

Washington Durable Power of Attorney Act [1989], Wash. Rev. Code Ann. 11.94.010 (West Supp. 1996).

WEST VIRGINIA
West Virginia Natural Death Act [1984, 1991], W. Va. Code §§16-30-2 to 16-30-13 (Michie 1995).

West Virginia Medical Power of Attorney Act [1990], W. Va. Code §§16-30A-1 to 16-30A-20 (Michie 1995).

WISCONSIN
Wisconsin Declaration to Physicians and Do-Not-Resuscitate Orders Act [1984, 1986, 1988, 1991, 1992, 1996], Wisc. Stat. Ann. §§154.01 to 154.29 (West 1989 & Supp. 1995).

Wisconsin Power of Attorney for Health Care Act [1990, 1992, 1993], Wisc. Stat. Ann. §§155.01 to 155.80 (West Supp. 1995).

WYOMING
Wyoming Living Will Act [1984, 1985, 1987, 1991, 1992, 1993], Wyo. Stat. §§35-22-101 to 35-22-109 (Michie 1994).

Wyoming Durable Power of Attorney for Health Care Act [1991, 1992, 1993], Wyo. Stat. §§3-5-201 to 3-5-213 (Michie Supp. 1995).

APPENDIX B
Measurement Operations and Data Sources

This appendix presents the measurement operations described in Chapter 3 in summary form. Table B.1 displays the variable names, descriptions and data sources for all of the variables used in the legislative empirical models in Chapter 4. Table B.2 reports the measures used in the judicial models estimated in Chapter 5; note that variables which are common to the legislative and judicial models are not re-listed in Table B.2.

Table B.1
Measures for Legislative Models

Variable	Measure	Source
Living Will Adoption	Dummy variable coded 1 if a state adopts a living will law in a given year, 0 if it does not.	citations: Choice in Dying, 1997 and *Lexus-Nexus*.
Health Care Proxy Adoption	Dummy variable coded 1 if a state adopts a durable power of attorney or health care proxy law in a given year, 0 if it does not.	citations: Choice in Dying, 1997 and *Lexus-Nexus*.
Surrogate Statute Adoption	Dummy variable coded 1 if a state adopts a surrogate decision-making law in a given year, 0 if it does not.	citations: Choice in Dying, 1997 and *Lexus-Nexus*.

Table B.1 (continued)
Measures for Legislative Models

Variable	Measure	Source
% Catholic	Percentage of a state's population having membership in the Catholic Church.	*Official Catholic Directory*, annual editions.
Piecewise 1983 Catholic Interaction Term	A measure of the Catholic Church's influence after 1983, calculated annually using the formula: (Current %Cath. - 1983 %Cath.) * (0 if 1983 or prior, 1 if after).	Calculated by author.
Senior Citizens	percentage of a state's citizens over the age of 65.	U.S. Bureau of the Census, annual.
Physicians	Number of medical doctors per 100,00 population	U.S. Bureau of the Census, annual.
Legislative Salary	Measure of legislative professionalism operationalized as mean salary + per diem expenses. In constant 1982 dollars.	Council of State Governments, *Book of the States*, annual (for salary figures). CPI operations by Laura Langer.
Interparty Competition	Ranney party control index, folded. Annual scores computed from the three period scores (1989-94, 1981-88 and 1975-80) using a 5-year moving average.	Folded-Ranney scores: Bibby, et. al., *Politics in the American States*, editions 6, 5, and 4.
Electoral Threat Index	Mooney and Lee's (1995) state legislative election index. Index increasing from 0 by the fraction of each of the following actors up for election in a given year: state House of Representatives, state Senate, and incumbent governor.	Council of State Governments, *Book of the States*, annual.
Post-1985 NCCUSL Draft	Impact of 1985 NCCUSL Uniform Living Will Act. Dummy variable coded 0 for all pre-1985 cases, 1 for 1985 and after.	Calculated by author.

Measurement Operations and Data Sources 259

Table B.1 (continued)
Measures for Legislative Models

Variable	Measure	Source
Post-1989 NCCUSL Draft	Impact of 1989 NCCUSL Uniform Advance Directives Act. Dummy variable coded 0 for all pre-1989 cases, 1 for 1989 and after.	Calculated by author.
Post-1991 NCCUSL Draft	Impact of 1991 NCCUSL model law. Dummy variable coded 0 for all pre-1991 cases, 1 for 1991 and after.	Calculated by author.
Divided Government	Dummy variable indicating the existence of divided government; coded 0 for years when both of a state's legislative chambers and the gubernatorial office are controlled by a single party, 1 otherwise.	Council of State Governments, *Book of the States*, various years.
Adoption Date	Date of adoption of a state's first living will, proxy and surrogate laws, calculated for each policy by subtracting 100 from the last two digits of the year of adoption.	Calculated by author.
Facility Score	Statutory permissiveness; for a given policy type, the facility score was calculated by scoring the provisions of a state's relevant statutes in a given year.	Calculated by author. See Appendix C.
Mean Regional Facility Score	Mean facility score of states in the previous year (excluding the state in question) in the one of the 9 U.S. Census Bureaus in which a exists.	Calculated by author.
Piecewise 1985 Regional Facility Interaction Term	A measure of regional policy influence after the NCCUSL's 1985 adoption, calculated annually using the following formula: (Lagged regional living will facility score - lagged 1985 score) * (0 if 1985 or before, 1 if after).	Calculated by author.

Table B.1 (continued)
Measures for Legislative Models

Variable	Measure	Source
Piecewise 1989 Regional Facility Interaction Term	A measure of regional policy influence after the NCCUSL's 1989 adoption, calculated annually using the following formula: (Lagged regional proxy facility score - lagged 1989 score) * (0 if 1989 or before, 1 if after).	Calculated by author.
Piecewise 1991 Regional Facility Interaction Score	A measure of regional policy influence after the NCCUSL's 1991 adoption, calculated annually using the following formula: (Lagged regional surrogate facility score - lagged 1991 score) * (0 if 1991 or before, 1 if after).	Calculated by author.
Distance From Region Score	A measure calculated annually for each of the three policies using the following formula: (State's lagged facility score - lagged regional facility score).	Calculated by author.
Years Since First Adoption	The number of years elapsed since a state adopted its first policy; calculated annually for living will, proxy, and surrogate policies.	Calculated by author.

Table B.2
Measures for Judicial Models

Variable	Measure	Source
Elected Attorney General	Dummy variable denoting wheter or not a state's Attoney General is selected by popular election; coded if if appointed, coded 1 if elected.	Council of State Governments, *Book of the States*, annual.
Cumulative Intrastate Cases	Lagged count of all published right to die cases previously issued by appellate courts in a given state.	Calculated by author. A list of these cases appears in Appendix D.
Facility Score	Policy Permissiveness; for each surrogate decision making poicy, the facility score was calculated by scoring the provisions of a state's relevant opinions in a given year.	Calculated by author. See Appendix C.
Mean Regional Facility Score	Mean facility score of states in the previous year (exluding the state in question) in the one of the 9 U.S. Census Bureaus in which a state was found.	Calculated by author.
Piecewise 1990 Regional Facility Interaction Term	A measure of regional influences after the U.S. Supreme Court's ruling in *Cruzan*. Calculated using the following formula: (Lagged regional judicial facility score - lagged 1990 score) * 0 if 1990 or before, 1 if after.	Calculated by author.
Post-1990 *Cruzan*	Impact of 1990 *Cruzan* decision; dummy variable coded 1 if 1990 or before, 0 otherwise.	Calculated by author.
Intermediate Appellate Court	Dummy variable coded 1 if state has an intermediate appellate court, 0 if a two-tiered system.	Council of State Governments, *Book of the States*, annual.

Table B.2 (continued)
Measures for Judicial Models

Variable	Measure	Source
Elected Justices	Dummy variable coded 1 if a state's court of last resort justices are elected, 0 if otherwise.	Council of State Governments, *Book of the States*, annual.
Judicial Reputation	Measure of a state's judicial prestige; the number of times opinions issued by a state's court of last resort were cited by tribunals in other jurisdictions in the 1980's.	Caldeira (1988).
Population	Number of state residents (in real numbers).	Council of State Governments, *Book of the States*, various years.
Distance From Region Score	A measure calculated annually using the following formula: (State's lagged facility score - lagged regional facility score).	Calculated by author.
Years Since First Adoption	The number of years elapsed since a state adopted its first judicial surrogate policy; calculated annually.	Calculated by author.

APPENDIX C
Facility Score Construction

This appendix presents the coding schemes for the policy facility scores discussed in Chapter 3 and used in the empirical models in Chapters 4-6. Tables C.1, C.2, and C.3 show how scores were calculated for living will, health care proxy, and surrogate decision-making policies, respectively. Table C.4 displays the coding scheme used for judicial policies. The first column in each table denotes the type of provision under consideration, and the second column shows the numerical values assigned to the various policy options. The reader will recall that higher numerical values indicate greater levels of policy facility, while lower values are indicative of more restrictive provisions. For each given policy type (i.e., for each table), the points from each of the provisions are summed in order to calculate a given state's facility score in a given year.

Table C.1
Living Will Facility Scores

Provision	Policy Options and Corresponding Facility Points
Drafting and Execution: Execution	When a valid living will can be drafted. 0 Declaration may be drafted at any time, but must be (re)executed after patient is certified as "qualified" (e.g., terminally ill or in PVS). 1 A valid living will may be executed at any time; no re-execution requirements.

Table C.1 (continued)
Living Will Facility Scores

Provision	Policy Options and Corresponding Facility Points
Drafting and Execution: Expiration	Time limitations on living will validity. 0 Living will becomes invalid after a specified time period and must be re-executed. 1 No renewal requirements.
Drafting and Execution: Filing	Placement of living will in medical records and state-maintained data base. 0 No requirement that living will be placed in patient's permanent medical records. 1 Living will must be placed in permanent medical records or filed with a state agency. 2 Living will must be placed in permanent medical records and filed with a state agency.
Drafting and Execution: Format	Format of living will declaration. 0 Form contained in statute must be used; no additions or deletions. 1 Living will must be substantially in statutory format; no mention of personalized instructions. 2 Personalized instructions allowed (may/must substantially use statutory format or no form appears in statute).
Drafting and Execution: Revocation	Procedures governing revocation by declarant. 0 No provisions for revocation. 1 Such provisions exist.
Implementation: Waiting Period	Length of time patient must remain in triggering condition(s) before directive can be honored. 0 Waiting period of 12 months. 1 Waiting period of 1-7 days. 2 Waiting period of under 24 hours. 3 No waiting period.
Implementation: Blocking Procedures	Provisions for temporarily blocking implementation of living will by requesting appointment of guardian by court. 0 Such a provision exists. 1 No such provision.

Table C.1 (continued)
Living Will Facility Scores

Provision	Policy Options and Corresponding Facility Points

Drafting and Execution:
 	
Witnessing Procedures
	Witnessing requirements which must be satisfied for a directive to be valid.
	0 Any one <u>or more</u> of the following are <u>required</u>: [regardless of additional requirements listed below in 2 or 3]
	  Θ must use the same legal formalities required for the execution of a standard will;
	  Θ living will must be notarized;
	  Θ must be certified before a court official;
	  Θ if patient resides in skilled nursing home or long-term health care facility, living will must be witnessed by any one <u>or more</u> of the following: state-employed patient advocate, state-employed ombudsman for health care, or medical director of the care facility.
	1 Any one <u>or more</u> of the following are <u>forbidden</u> from serving as witnesses: [regardless of additional requirements listed below in code 2]
	  Θ declarant's physician or anyone employed by declarant's physician;
	  Θ employee of the health care facility in which declarant is currently a patient;
	  Θ fellow patient in a health care facility;
	  Θ employee of a life or health insurance provider.
	2 Statute has any one <u>or more</u> of the following witnessing *requirements*: [may <u>not</u> contain any requirements listed above in codes 0 or 1)
	  Θ adult witness;
	  Θ witness unrelated by blood, marriage or adoption;
	  Θ witness <u>not</u> responsible for patient's health care costs;
	  Θ witness with <u>no</u> claim on declarant's estate.
	3 No witnessing requirements if will is handwritten by declarant.

Table C.1 (continued)
Living Will Facility Scores

Provision	Policy Options and Corresponding Facility Points
Implementation: Triggering Conditions	Circumstances under which treatment may be withdrawn or withheld. 0 Patient is suffering from a "terminal" illness or injury and death is "imminent" or estimated to occur within a specified time period. 3 Patient is suffering from a "terminal" illness or injury from which death is imminent <u>or</u> an "irreversible coma," "permanent unconsciousness," "PVS," or "permanent loss of ability to communicate concerning medical treatment decisions." 5 Declarant is allowed to specify own triggering conditions (i.e., include non-terminal/non-comatose provisions).

Implementation: Artificial Nutrition and Hydration	Circumstances under which nasogastric and/or implanted feeding tubes may be refused or withdrawn.
	0 Nutrition and hydration may not be terminated under any circumstances <u>or</u> are not included in statutory definition of "life-sustaining procedure."
	1 Nutrition and hydration may not be withdrawn if necessary to provide "comfort care" <u>and</u> statute is ambiguous regarding situations in which food and hydration are *not* necessary to provide comfort care.
	3 No specific mention of nutrition or hydration.
	5 Statute expressly permits withdrawal of nutrition and hydration through one of the following mechanisms:
	   Θ statute states that nutrition and hydration may be forgone;
	   Θ nutrition and hydration included in definition of "life-sustaining procedure;"
	   Θ nutrition and hydration included in living will form checklist of treatments to be forgone;
	   Θ statute allows declarant to specifically request that nutrition and hydration not be administered.

Table C.1 (continued)
Living Will Facility Scores

Provision	Policy Options and Corresponding Facility Points
Implementation: Pregnancy	Status of pregnant woman's directive. 0 Invalid if patient is pregnant. 1 Invalid <u>only if</u> fetus is "viable" or able to develop to viability with the application of life-sustaining procedures to the mother. 2 No pregnancy restrictions <u>or</u> statute permits declarant to specify wishes in the case of pregnancy.
Implementation: Portability	Status of declaration executed in another state. 0 Living wills executed in another state are invalid or not recognized. 1 Out-of-State declarations are recognized.
Enforcement: Comply or Transfer	Provision requiring attending physician/health care facility to comply with directive or transfer patient to another facility/physician. 0 No such provision. 1 Such a provision exists.
Enforcement: Noncompliance Penalties	Penalties prescribed for failure to comply with a directive or to arrange a suitable transfer. 0 No penalties. 1 Failure to transfer is "unprofessional conduct." 2 Civil penalties. 3 Criminal penalties.
Enforcement: Additional Penalties	Penalties for Alteration, Concealment or Forgery of a directive (penalties applicable to health care professionals and private citizens). 0 No penalties. 1 Civil penalties. 2 Criminal penalties.

Table C.1 (continued)
Living Will Facility Scores

Provision	Policy Options and Corresponding Facility Points
Enforcement: Life Insurance Protection	Provision stating that execution or implementation of a living will cannot affect the purchase or terms of a life insurance policy. 0 No protection. 1 Provision stating that forgoing treatment pursuant to a living will does not constitute suicide and/or that living wills may not adversely affect the sale or conditions of a policy.
Enforcement: Provider Immunity	Immunity from legal liability for health care professionals. 0 No immunity provisions. 1 Qualified immunity for professionals having acted in "good faith" and/or pursuant to "reasonable medical standards." 2 Wholesale immunity for professionals having acted in "good faith" and/or pursuant to "reasonable medical standards."

Table C.2
Health Care Proxy Facility Scores

Provision	Policy Options and Corresponding Facility Points
Drafting and Enforcement: Accessibility	Extent to which right to designate a proxy is made explicit by statute. 0 Designation recognized in living will's "special instructions," but there is no mention of a surrogate in the sample living will form. 1 Separate DPA/health care proxy statute or living will form allows for appointment or combined form/statute.
Drafting and Enforcement: Expiration	Time limitations on declaration validity. 0 Declaration becomes invalid after a specified time period and must be re-executed. 1 No renewal requirements.
Drafting and Enforcement: Filing	Placement of declaraton in medical records and state-maintained data base. 0 No requirement that declaration be placed in patient's permanent medical records. 1 Declaration must be placed in permanent medical records or filed with a state agency. 2 Declaration must be placed in permanent medical records and filed with a state agency.
Drafting and Enforcement: Instructions	Format of durable power of attorney for health care/proxy appointment. 0 Form contained in statute must be used; no additions or deletions; no choices or instructions to proxy. 1 Declaration must be substantially in statutory format; no mention of personalized instructions to proxy. 2 Personalized instructions allowed (no form appears in statute or mandatory form includes checklist and/or comment lines).
Drafting and Enforcement: Revocation	Procedures governing revocation, suspension or nullification by declarant. 0 No provisions for revocation. 1 Such provisions exist.

Table C.2 (continued)
Health Care Proxy Facility Scores

Provision	Policy Options and Corresponding Facility Points

Drafting and Execution:
 	
 Witnessing Procedures
	Witnessing requirements which must be satisfied for a directive to be valid.
	 0 Any one <u>or more</u> of the following are <u>required</u>: [regardless of additional requirements listed below in 2 or 3]
	      ⊖ must use the same legal formalities required for the execution of a standard will/DPA;
	      ⊖ declaration must be notarized;
	      ⊖ must be certified before a court official;
	      ⊖ if patient resides in skilled nursing home or long-term health care facility, document must be witnessed by any one <u>or more</u> of the following: state-employed patient advocate, state-employed ombudsman for health care, or medical director of the care facility.
	 1 Any one <u>or more</u> of the following are <u>forbidden</u> from serving as witnesses: [regardless of additional requirements listed below in code 2]
	      ⊖ declarant's physician or anyone employed by declarant's physician;
	      ⊖ employee of the health care facility in which declarant is currently a patient;
	      ⊖ fellow patient in a health care facility;
	      ⊖ employee of a life or health insurance provider.
	 2 Statute has any one <u>or more</u> of the following witnessing *requirements*: [may <u>not</u> contain any requirements listed above in codes 0 or 1)
	      ⊖ adult witness;
	      ⊖ witness unrelated by blood, marriage or adoption;
	      ⊖ witness <u>not</u> responsible for patient's health care costs;
	      ⊖ witness with <u>no</u> claim on declarant's estate.
	 3 No witnessing requirements if will is handwritten by declarant.

Table C.2 (continued)
Health Care Proxy Facility Scores

Provision	Policy Options and Corresponding Facility Points
Drafting and Enforcement: Alternate	Provisions allowing for designation of an alternate or concurrent proxy. 0 No such provision. 1 Such a provision exists.
Implementation: Triggering Conditions	Circumstances under which treatment may be withdrawn or withheld. 0 Patient is suffering from a "terminal" illness or injury or PVS and death is "imminent" or estimated to occur within a specified time period. 3 Declarant is allowed to specify own triggering conditions (i.e., include non-terminal/non-comatose provisions).

Implementation:
 	
Artificial Nutrition and Hydration
	Circumstances under which nasogastric and/or implanted feeding tubes may be refused or withdrawn.
	0 Nutrition and hydration may not be terminated under any circumstances _or_ are not included in statutory definition of "life-sustaining procedure."
	1 Nutrition and hydration may not be withdrawn if necessary to provide "comfort care" _and_ statute is ambiguous regarding situations in which food and hydration are _not_ necessary to provide comfort care.
	3 No specific mention of nutrition or hydration.
	5 Statute expressly permits withdrawal of nutrition and hydration through one of the following mechanisms:
	   Θ statute states that nutrition and hydration may be forgone;
	   Θ nutrition and hydration included in definition of "life-sustaining procedure;"
	   Θ nutrition and hydration included in proxy form checklist of treatments to be forgone;
	   Θ statute allows declarant to specifically request that nutrition and hydration not be administered.

Table C.2 (continued)
Health Care Proxy Facility Scores

Provision	Policy Options and Corresponding Facility Points
Implementation: Waiting Period	Length of time patient must remain in triggering condition(s) before treatment can be withdrawn. 0 Waiting period of 12 months. 1 Waiting period of 1-7 days. 2 Waiting period of under 24 hours. 3 No waiting period.
Implementation: Pregnancy	Authority of proxy to withdraw treatment from a pregnant woman. 0 No authority if patient is pregnant; 1 No authority <u>only if</u> fetus is "viable" or able to develop to viability with the application of life-sustaining procedures to the mother. 2 No pregnancy restrictions <u>or</u> statute permits declarant to specify wishes in the case of pregnancy.
Implementation: Blocking Procedures	Provisions for temporarily blocking decision of proxy by requesting appointment of guardian by a court. 0 Such a provision exists. 1 No such provision exists.
Implementation: Portability	Status of declaration executed in another state. 0 Declarations executed in another state are invalid or not recognized. 1 Out-of-State declarations are recognized.
Enforcement: Comply or Transfer	Provision requiring attending physician/health care facility to comply with proxy or transfer patient to another facility/physician. 0 No such provision. 1 Such a provision exists.
Enforcement: Noncompliance Penalties	Penalties prescribed for failure to comply with a directive or to arrange a suitable transfer. 0 No penalties. 1 Failure to transfer is "unprofessional conduct." 2 Civil penalties. 3 Criminal penalties.

Table C.2 (continued)
Health Care Proxy Facility Scores

Provision	Policy Options and Corresponding Facility Points
Enforcement: Additional Penalties	Penalties for Alteration, Concealment or Forgery of a directive (penalties applicable to health care professionals and private citizens). 0 No penalties. 1 Civil penalties. 2 Criminal penalties.
Enforcement: Provider Immunity	Immunity from legal liability for health care professionals. 0 No immunity provisions. 1 Qualified immunity for professionals having acted in "good faith" and/or pursuant to "reasonable medical standards." 2 Wholesale immunity for professionals having acted in "good faith" and/or pursuant to "reasonable medical standards."
Enforcement: Life Insurance Protection	Provision stating that execution or implementation of a health care proxy cannot affect the purchase or terms of a life insurance policy. 0 No protection. 1 Provision stating that forgoing treatment pursuant to a proxy directive does not constitute suicide and/or that directives may not adversely affect the sale or conditions of a policy.

Table C.3
Surrogate Decision Making Facility Scores

Provision	Policy Options and Corresponding Facility Points
Surrogate Assignment: Priority	Ordinal ranking of persons qualified to make decisions. 0 "Entire Family" or "All Relatives" lumped in one priority class. 1 "Immediate Family," "Relatives of First Order," or "Next of Kin" lumped in one priority class. 2 Hierarchical ranking, with surrogates in highest class having absolute authority.
Surrogate Assignment: Others	Inclusion of domestic partners and close friends on list of potential surrogates. 0 No mention of non-familial relations. 1 Close friends and/or domestic partners eligible, but the latter are not given "spousal status." 2 Domestic partners accorded full spousal status.
Surrogate Assignment: Resolution	Procedures for resolving disputes among surrogates of equal status. 0 No procedures OR unanimous decision required or referred to probate court. 1 Majority rule within a given priority group. 2 Disputants required to attempt resolution through sessions facilitated by institutional representative(s) (e.g., ethics committee, counselor, social worker) or attending physician or health care provider allowed to break tie.
Surrogate Assignment: Evidence	Requirements for proving that principal would have approved of surrogate's decision to withhold treatment (if subjective or substitute judgement standard is operative). 0 Written, specifically attested and/or "clear and convincing" evidence standard. 1 "Good faith" requirement or "best interest" standard.
Implementation: Blocking Procedure	Provisions for temporarily barring surrogate's decision by requesting a court-appointed guardian. 0 Such a provision exists. 1 No such provision exists.

Table C.3 (continued)
Surrogate Decision Making Facility Scores

Provision	Policy Options and Corresponding Facility Points
Implementation: Triggering Conditions	Circumstances under which treatment may be withdrawn or withheld. 0 Patient is suffering from a "terminal" illness or injury and death is "imminent" or estimated to occur within a specified time period. 3 Patient is suffering from a "terminal" illness or injury from which death is imminent <u>or</u> an "irreversible coma," "permanent unconsciousness," "PVS," or "permanent loss of ability to. communicate concerning medical treatment decisions."

Implementation:
 	
Artificial Nutrition and Hydration
	Circumstances under which nasogastric and/or implanted feeding tubes may be refused or withdrawn.
	0 Nutrition and hydration may not be terminated under any circumstances <u>or</u> are not included in statutory definition of "life-sustaining procedure."
	1 Nutrition and hydration may not be withdrawn if necessary to provide "comfort care" <u>and</u> statute is ambiguous regarding situations in which food and hydration are *not* necessary to provide comfort care.
	3 No specific mention of nutrition or hydration.
	5 Statute expressly permits withdrawal of nutrition and hydration through one of the following mechanisms:
	   Θ statute states that nutrition and hydration may be forgone;
	   Θ nutrition and hydration included in definition of "life-sustaining procedure;"
	   Θ statute allows surrogate to make any decisions the patient could have made if (s)he had executed a living will, <u>and</u> statute permits declarants to refuse artificial sustenance.

Table C.3 (continued)
Surrogate Decision Making Facility Scores

Provision	Policy Options and Corresponding Facility Points
Implementation: Waiting Period	Length of time patient must remain in triggering condition(s) before treatment can be withdrawn or withheld. 0 Waiting period of 1 to 12 months. 1 Waiting period of 1 to 30 days. 2 Waiting period of under 24 hours. 3 No waiting period.
Implementation: Pregnancy	Status of surrogate's decision in the event principal is pregnant. 0 Life-sustaining treatment must be applied if patient is pregnant. 1 Life-sustaining treatment must be applied <u>only if</u> fetus is "viable" or able to develop to viability with the application of treatment to the mother. 2 No pregnancy restrictions.
Enforcement: Comply or Transfer	Provision requiring attending physician/health care facility to comply with surrogate's decision or transfer patient to another facility/physician. 0 No such provision. 1 Such a provision exists.
Enforcement: Noncompliance Penalties	Penalties prescribed for failure to comply with a surrogate's decision or to arrange a suitable transfer. 0 No penalties. 1 Failure to transfer is "unprofessional conduct." 2 Civil penalties. 3 Criminal penalties.
Enforcement: Provider Immunity	Immunity from legal liability for health care professionals. 0 No immunity provisions. 1 Qualified immunity for professionals having acted in "good faith" and/or pursuant to "reasonable medical standards." 2 Wholesale immunity for professionals having acted in "good faith" and/or pursuant to "reasonable medical standards."

Table C.4
Judicial Surrogate Facility Scores

Provision	Policy Options and Corresponding Facility Points
Legal Basis	Legal basis of incompetent's right to decline unwanted life-sustaining treatment. 0 No legal basis. 1 Statutory only. 2 Common law rights (i.e., the right to be free from nonconsensual bodily invasions or the right to self-determination in medical affairs); may also include statutory rights. 3 Constitutional rights (i.e., the right to privacy or equal protection); may also include statutory and/or common law rights.
Evidentiary Standard	Standard to be utilized by a surrogate decision maker. 1 Strict "clear and convincing" standard (must be written evidence or corroboration of an explicit prior oral directive). 2 Relaxed "clear and convincing" standard (allows reliable "character" testimony or informal and/or inspecific prior oral directives). 3 Substituted judgment standard (allows family member to reach decision that she or he believes the patient would most likely have made). 4 "Best interests" standard (allows family member to make decision she or he believes is best for the patient).
Judicial Approval	Provision requiring a probate judge or other magistrate to approve of a nontreatment decision before treatment can be withheld. 0 Approval must be granted by a probate or other trial court judge before a nontreatment decision can be implemented. 2 No judicial proceedings required except to resolve disputes among parties to the treatment decision.

APPENDIX D
Listing of Right-to-Die Cases

This appendix contains a state-by-state listing of all right to die appellate decisions that were used to calculate the judicial surrogate policy facility scores. Entries are only included for states whose courts produced refusal of treatment cases.

ARIZONA
  Rasmussen v. Fleming, 741 P.2d 674, 1987.

CALIFORNIA
  Barber v. Superior Court, 195 Cal. App. 3d 484, 1983.
  Bartling v. Glendale Adventist Medical Center, 228 Cal. App. 3d 97, 1986.
  Bartling v. Superior Court, 163 Cal. App. 3d 186, 1984.
  Bouvia v. Superior Court, 179 Cal. App. 3d 1127, 1986.
  In Re Conservatorship of Drabick, 200 Cal. App. 3d 185, 1988.
  Thor v. Superior Court, 855 P.2d 375, 1993.
  Westhart v. Mule, 213 Cal. App. 3d 542, 1989.

CONNECTICUT
  Foody v. Manchester Memorial Hospital, 482 A.2d 713, 1984.
  McConnell v. Beverly Enterprises, 553 A.2d 596, 1989.

DELAWARE
In Re Gordy, 658 A.2d 613, 1994.
In Re Severns, 425 A.2d 156, 1980.
Severns v. *Wilmington Medical Center*, 421 A.2d 1334, 1980.
In Re Tavel, 661 A.2d 1061, 1994.

FLORIDA
In Re Guardianship of Barry, 445 So.2d 365, 1984.
In Re Guardianship of Browning, 568 So.2d 4, 1990.
Corbett v. *D'Allasandro*, 487 So.2d 368, 1986.
John F. Kennedy Memorial Hospital v. *Bludworth*, 452 So.2d 921, 1984.
Satz v. *Perlmutter*, 379 So.2d 359, 1980.

GEORGIA
In Re Jane Doe, 418 S.E.2d 3, 1992.
Kirby v. *Spivey*, 307 S.E.2d 538, 1983.
In Re L.H.R., 321 S.E.2d 716, 1984.
In Re McAfee, 385 S.E.2d 651, 1989.

ILLINOIS
In Re C.A., 603 N.E.2d 1171, 1993.
In Re Greenspan, 558 N.E.2d 1194, 1990.
In Re Estate of Longeway, 549 N.E.2d 292, 1989.

INDIANA
In Re Lawrance, 579 N.E.2d 32, 1991.

IOWA
Morgan v. *Olds*, 417 N.W.2d 232, 1987.

KENTUCKY
DeGrella v. *Elston*, 858 S.W.2d 698, 1993.

LOUSIANA
In Re P.V.W., 424 So.2d 1015, 1982.

MAINE
In Re Gardner, 534 A.2d 947, 1987.
In Re Swan, 569 A.3d 1202, 1990.

MARYLAND
Mack v. Mack, 618 A.2d 744, 1993.
In Re Riddlemoser, 564 A.2d 812, 1989.

MASSACHUSETTS
In Re Care and Protection of Beth, 587 N.E.2d 1377, 1992.
Brophy v. New England Sinai Hospital, Inc., 497 N.E.2d 626, 1986.
In Re Dinnerstein, 380 N.E.2d 134, 1978.
In Re Guardianship of Jane Doe, 583 N.E.2d 1363, 1992.
In Re Hier, 464 N.E.2d 959, 1984.
In Re R.H., 622 N.E.2d 1071, 1993.
In Re Spring, 405 N.E.2d 115, 1980.
Superintendent of Belchertown State School v. Saikewicz, 370 N.E.2d 417, 1977.

MICHIGAN
In Re Rosebush, 491 N.W.2d 633, 1992.

MINNESOTA
In Re Torres, 357 N.W.2d 332, 1984.

MISSOURI
Cruzan v. Harmon, 760 S.W.2d 408, 1988.

NEW JERSEY
In Re Conroy, 486 A.2d 1209, 1985.
In Re Farrell, 529 A.2d 404, 1987.
In Re Jobes, 529 A.2d 434, 1987.
In Re Moorhouse, 593 A.2d 1256, 1991.
In Re Peter, 529 A.2d 419, 1987.
In Re Quackenbush, 383 A.2d 785, 1978.
In Re Quinlan, 355 A.2d 647, 1976.
In Re Requena, 517 A.2d 869, 1986.
In Re Schiller, 372 A.2d 360, 1977.
In Re Visbek, 510 A.2d 125, 1986.

NEW YORK
In Re Beth Israel Medical Center, 519 N.Y.S.2d 511, 1987.
Delio v. Westchester County Medical Center, 516 N.Y.S.2d 677, 1987.
In Re Eichner, 420 N.E.2d 64, 1981.
In Re Storar, 420 N.E.2d 64, 1981.
In Re Westchester County Medical Center, 531 N.E.2d 607, 1988.

OHIO
Couture v. Couture, 549 N.E.2d 571, 1989.
In Re Guardianship of Crum, 580 N.E.2d 876, 1991.
Leach v. Shapiro, 469 N.E.2d 1047, 1984.
In Re Milton, 505 N.E.2d 255, 1987.

TENNESSEE
Dockery v. Dockery, 559 S.W.2d 952, 1977.

WASHINGTON
In Re Colyer, 660 P.2d 738, 1983.
Dinino v. State ex. rel. Gorton, 684 P.2d 1297, 1984.
In Re Guardianship of Grant, 747 P.2d 445, 1987.
In Re Guardianship of Grant, 757 P.2d 534, 1988.
In Re Guardianship of Hamlin, 689 P.2d 1372, 1984.
In Re Guardianship of Ingram, 689 P.2d 1363, 1984.

WEST VIRGINIA
Belcher v. Charleston Area Medical Center, 422 S.E.2d 827, 1992.

WISCONSIN
In Re Guardianship of L.W., 482 N.W.2d 60, 1992.

Notes

CHAPTER 1

1. The facts from these two cases, unless otherwise indicated, are taken from two opinions published by the Supreme Judicial Court of Maine: In Re Gardner (534 A.2d 947, 1987) and In Re Swan (569 A.2d 1202, 1990). These cases and the legal reasoning employed therein are described in much greater detail in the Maine case study presented in Chapter Five.

2. This vignette is taken from Eisendrath and Jonsen (1983), and page numbers are cited in parentheses in the text in this section. The name "Mrs. T" is obviously used to protect the identity of the patient. The California Natural Death Act, the landmark statute that enabled individuals to execute living wills in California, is discussed in detail in Chapter Four.

3. The facts from this vignette are taken from a decision published by the Court of Appeals of Maryland (Mack v. Mack, 618 A.2d 744, 1993). The Florida and Maryland statutes and court decisions are discussed in greater detail in Chapter Six.

4. Numerous written accounts of the right to die movement in the U.S. and in other nations can be found in the extant literature. My intent in this opening section is simply to provide a brief overview of developments in order to lay out the various types of refusal of treatment policies that exist in the U.S. to date. For a comprehensive history of American right-to-die policy making on passive euthanasia, see Glick (1992). An informative chronology of the push for assisted suicide in the U.S. can be found in Urofsky (2000), and a number of law review articles on this topic also warrant careful attention (Hardaway, Peterson and Mann 1999; Martyn and Bourguignon 1997; Sunstein 1997). A general overview of the philosophical and cultural foundations of both assisted suicide and passive euthanasia (as well as other topics pertinent to the right-to-die) appears in Filene (1998).

5. Interstate variation across these various policy dimensions is explored in much greater detail in Chapters 4 and 5. These terms are introduced here in order to introduce the reader to the policy "jargon" and to equip her or him with a basic understanding of the right to die terms that form the bases of the facility scores discussed in Chapter Three.

CHAPTER 2

1. This typology could also be applied to judicial policies; however, in this study I examine three different types of legislative policies (living will laws, DPA policies, and surrogate statutes), but there is only one major type of judicial right to die policy (surrogate laws). Legislatures always have the option of availing themselves to core and tangential policy innovations, whereas courts, at least in the case of refusal of treatment policy, can only approve one (broad) type of law. The concept of tangential judicial innovations is beyond the scope of the present analysis.

2. Glick (1994) argues that policies are permissive in two ways. Policies are permissive in the sense that they create a new class of rights for individuals. But policies are also permissive when they afford individual states (or governmental units) a good deal of latitude in guaranteeing and limiting these rights. For example, when the U.S. Supreme Court declares an issue to be the responsibility of state governments, some states will adopt policies that grant greater rights than others.

3. In discussing the various concepts related to the adoption of permissive policies, I only provide "right-to-die-specific" hypotheses when variables unique to this narrow policy area need to be identified. In the present example, it is appropriate to identify right-to-die supporters and opponents, as different groups lobby for different types of permissive policies. The discussion of legislative professionalism contained in the next section, however, does not require policy-specific elaboration, as legislative professionalism is a constant variable and is hypothesized to affect all permissive policies in the same manner.

4. For ease of exposition, the terms "reinvention through renovation" and "renovation" are used interchangeably throughout the manuscript.

5. Some readers might argue that only decisions of state courts of last resort should qualify as innovations, as the decisions of intermediate appellate courts (in states with more than one such body) are only binding authority in a given circuit. However, when courts of last resort refuse to review these decisions, the policy of a lower court is, at least tacitly, endorsed by the higher judicial authority. Excluding cases decided by intermediate appellate courts would limit a number of potentially important decisions that have state-wide policy implications.

6. This proposition is likely to be controversial, as some would argue that only the creation of rights (not the refusal to identify such rights) constitutes an innovation. For purposes of the right to die empirical models in this manuscript, this objection is of little consequence; indeed, only one state court produced a "negative" decision, and dropping this case from the event history analysis in Chapter 5 does not appreciably alter the results. My crucial point is this: no legislature has ever approved laws banning advance directives or surrogate decision-making; instead, when insufficient support for a policy existed, these bodies engaged in conflict avoidance and created "nondecisions;" courts that rule on the substantive policy issue at bar, regardless of the outcome of the decision, create innovations.

7. If a legislature offers an amendment to its existing surrogate decision making statute to extend policy coverage to dialysis patients, this would constitute a legislative renovation. Because legislatures, in formulating policy guidelines, always have the option of anticipating different contingencies and approving a host of different requirements, the absence of any type of prevision from a statute is evidence of a deliberate or conscious attempt to exclude this type of provision or deny a certain type of coverage. Courts, although they may do so in dicta, simply do not have this option of articulating comprehensive and exhaustive sets of policy guidelines.

8. For exceptions see Glick (1992) and Glick and Hays (1995).

CHAPTER 3

1. Some additional justification is in order regarding the inclusion of the senior citizens variable in these models. AARP and other groups representing aging populations have not played very active roles in lobbying for right to die laws, and previous research (e.g., Glick 1992) suggests that seniors groups have taken very neutral (if any) stands on refusal of treatment proposals. I include this variable because, all things being equal, states with the largest geriatric populations should be host to the most cases or incidences involving conflict over treatment at the end-of-life (most patients who are incompetent and suffering debilitating illnesses reside in nursing homes and other long-term treatment facilities). Even if seniors groups do not actively respond to these medical crises, individual citizens are likely to petition their legislators for action, and health care providers may be inclined to actively seek regulation in order to reduce the threat of liability. In addition, legislators may be inclined to respond to the size of a state's elderly population, even in the absence of direct pressure from leaders representing this segment of the population.

2. This variable is included only in the living will model. It is omitted from the proxy model because the first of such statutes was not adopted until 1982, and after 1983, Catholic conferences in many states were actively promoting their own durable power of attorney laws. The Catholic Church has always opposed surrogate decision-making laws, thereby eliminating the need to test the interaction hypothesis in the third model.

3. These data were calculated by, and are available from, Laura Langer, University of Arizona.

4. Nebraska, due to its nonpartisan legislature, is excluded from the EHA analyses. This exclusion has no major implications, as I estimated all three models with Nebraska included and the divided government variable excluded, and the results were not appreciably altered.

5. Annual scores calculated by Laura Langer, University of Arizona.

6. In addition to testing substantive hypotheses, these interaction terms serve another important purpose. The event history method assumes that all observations (adoptions) are independent of one another; however, recent research suggests that this assumption is often unwarranted. The presence of temporal dependence can result in underestimation of variability and the inflation of t-scores, causing an analyst to make overly-optimistic inferences. Beck, Katz and Tucker (1998) recommend the inclusion of annual time dummies in these models to test for temporal dependence; however, this approach can sharply reduce the number of degrees of freedom and invite multicollinearity. To avoid these problems, Beck, Katz and Tucker suggest substituting a natural or cubic spline term for these year dummies. I generated such spline terms using a routine in the STATA econometrics package, and when I included it in the models, the spline terms were highly correlated with those of the piecewise interaction terms. Therefore, I include only the latter variables; the piecewise interaction terms not only convey information about substantive hypotheses, but their structure is determined by a theoretical assumption about temporal events (model laws) and how they affect the underlying hazard rates.

7. These scores represent the number of courts of last resort in other states that cited a major opinion of a given state's court in the previous year (Caldeira 1988). For example, the Supreme Judicial Court of Massachusetts, with a score of 49, was cited by courts in all of the other states.

CHAPTER 4

1. Glick and Hays (1996) perform an event history analysis on living will adoptions from 1976 through 1989. My model builds on their work through extension of the diffusion period by five years and the inclusion of six new independent variables.

2. Recall that the estimated effect of a post-1985 regional facility score is simply the sum of the facility score and interaction coefficients. Although the latter is not statistically significant, it should be noted that it is in the hypothesized direction and is significant at conventional levels if a one-tailed test is utilized. Therefore a brief interpretation of the interaction term coefficient is warranted. The negative coefficient indicates that in the period following the NCCUSL adoption, the impact of regional patterns is diminished by nearly 13%; a one standard deviation increase in percentage of Catholics results in a 13.64% increase in likelihood of adoption, as opposed to a 26.45% increase in the earlier period. A test of the linear constraint hypothesis that there is no effect of regionalism after 1985 (i.e., that the two coefficients sum to 0) can be squarely rejected at better than 99% confidence.

3. As explained in Chapter 2, the durable power of attorney is a specific policy type that is subsumed under the broader rubric of "health care proxy." Although some states adopted DPA laws while others opted for the Delaware approach, both policy types provide a mechanism designed to confer the same powers and engender the same policy ends. In the following section, the terms "durable power of attorney" (DPA) and "proxy" will be used interchangeably to refer to any innovation that allows individuals to designate a health care agent to make decisions at the end of life.

4. The EHA model correctly predicts five of the forty-eight adoptions (a proportional reduction in error of over 10%), whereas the living will model predicts three of forty-seven innovations (a PRE of 6.4%). While these results may not appear to be impressive when compared to PRE measures from conventional OLS models, given the high skew in the EHA models, the level of improved prediction is quite reasonable. Moreover, when the cutpoint probability for predicting an adoption is lowered from the standard threshold of >.5 to >.25, the PRE improves to 21.3% for living wills and 29.2% for proxy laws.

5. The EHA model fails to correctly predict a single surrogate adoption. Lowering the cutpoint probability for predicting an adoption from the conventional threshold of >.5 to >.25 does little to improve the situation; in fact, this only results in the ability to successfully predict three adoptions, and numerous "false positive" predictons result.

6. When the proxy and surrogate EHA models were re-estimated with nonlagged prior policy adoption variables, the coefficients for these variables were positive, robust and statistically significant. Obviously, there are problems with this type of specification, particularly in terms of satisfying the causal criterion of temporal precedence.

CHAPTER 5

1. Cases were only counted once (i.e., a decision which worked its way through three levels of a court system was only scored in the year in which the ultimate judgment was rendered), and unpublished opinions were excluded from analysis. Trial court opinions were included only if two conditions were satisfied: the opinion had to be published, and an appellate court had to deny review or *certiorari*. These trial court opinions are significant because, in many cases, the opinion was published at the request of a trial court judge who requested that the ruling be certified by a higher court. The fact that these cases were appealed or otherwise presented to a higher court and were dismissed in summary fashion (i.e., without written explanation and without the consideration of arguments) by an appellate court denotes judicial nondecision-making. While these trial court opinions merit consideration in the present discussion of the rise of right-to-die litigation, they are not used in any of the empirical/regression models in this chapter, nor was any trial court opinion ever scored as an innovation.

2. Given the high skew in the dependent variable (i.e., there is only a scant probability of a state adopting a judicial innovation in a given year), it is not surprising that the model only correctly predicts one judicial adoption. However, when the cutpoint probability is lowered to >.25, the model correctly predicts six innovations.

3. It could be argued that some measure of the liberalism of a state's electorate could serve as a proxy for the support for the right-to-die in a given state. However, when the mean ADA score of a state's congressional delegation was included in the model, the result was severe multicollinearity.

4. Several alternate specifications were utilized. For example, I replaced the cumulative count of all cases in a state with a count of all "positive" right to die cases, and I used a measure of all "negative" decisions previously issued by a state's courts. In addition to using cumulative counts, I also tried simply recording the number of cases heard in the previous year. None of the results from the various regressions differed appreciably, but the "cumulative total cases" measure outperformed the others, and, as discussed in Chapter 3, this is the most theoretically justified measure.

5. One possible concern that could be raised regarding this finding is that the relationship might be spurious, due to a conservative southern political climate. However, the attorney general selection variable and a dummy variable distinguishing between southern and non-southern states do not appear to be strongly correlated ($r = .0816$). Moreover, when the southern dummy variable is added to the full EHA model, the resulting coefficient is negative and statistically insignificant, with none of the substantive results being appreciably altered.

Notes

6. As in the preceding chapter, I ran two sets of regressions. I began by comparing "first" policies (i.e., the core and subsequent tangential innovations), and the substantive coefficient was minuscule and statistically insignificant. Next, I examined "last" (i.e., 1994) scores and reached an identical conclusion regarding the impact of time on the content of judicial policies. (It should be noted that Tennessee, with its score of 0, was dropped from this analysis.)

7. Only one published opinion by an appellate court considering the surrogate decision making issue has altogether rejected the right to die. In an early decision, *Dockery v. Dockery* (559 S.W.2d 952, 1977), the Eastern Section of the Court of Appeals of Tennessee overturned a permissive lower court ruling that would have legalized decision making by family members of incapacitated patients. The intermediate appellate court threw out much of the decision on grounds of mootness, but the justices also ruled that, in order for surrogates to be permitted to make such decisions, explicit legislative authorization was required.

8. In subsequent decisions, the Supreme Judicial Court affirmed the DNR ruling in *Dinnerstein*, but noted that judicial approval of DNR orders is required in instances in which an individual is a ward of the state. [The SJC approved no-code orders for a terminally ill, abandoned infant (*Custody of a Minor*, 434 N.E.2d 601, 1982) and for an irreversibly comatose child in the custody of the Massachusetts Department of Social Services (*Care and Protection of Beth*, 587 N.E.2d 1377, 1992).]

9. In *Custody of a Minor* (379 N.E.2d 1053, 1978), the Supreme Judicial Court ruled against withdrawing chemotherapy from a small child, and, in a subsequent decision involving the same parties, held that the child's parents be required to end an experimental "metabolic therapy" that undermined the chemotherapy treatment (393 N.E.2d 836, 1979). In 1984, an appeals court allowed refusal of life-saving gastrostomy surgery on behalf of an incompetent patient in a state psychiatric hospital (*Matter of Hier*, 464 N.E.2d 959). In *Guardianship of Doe* (583 N.E.2d 1263, 1992), the SJC, while providing no guidelines regarding when judicial approval is required, offered some guidance to trial courts by requiring them to consider five factors in exercising substituted judgement: patient's expressed preferences; patient's religious convictions; impact on patient's family; probability of adverse side effects; and the prognosis with and without treatment (1268). While the first of these factors is difficult to assess in the case of never-competent patients, the SJC in *Matter of R.H.* (622 N.E.2d 1071, 1992) ruled that the "level of incompetence" of a patient is a factor in making a substituted judgement, and that any "expressed preferences" must be considered.

10. This decision had an almost immediate impact on decision making by trial courts. Only nine days after this ruling was handed down, a trial court, citing *Delio* as precedent, refused to order intubated feeding for a competent nursing home patient who refused to eat (*In Re Application of Brooks*, N.Y. Supreme Court, Albany County, June 10, 1987 -- discussed in Choice in Dying 1997).

CHAPTER 6

1. All of the "full" models were also estimated (i.e., the predicted probability variables were dropped and replaced with all of the "original" variables). The results were not appreciably altered, nor did any of the coefficients of the substantive "new" variables change in direction or statistical significance. Four of the "full" models did suffer from multicollinearity, with high pairwise correlations among the piecewise interaction terms and a few other variables.

2. I also tried running each of these three independent variables as "change scores," whereby I first-order differenced each of the time series. In addition, I also included a dummy variable denoting the simple presence or absence of a judicial policy. Next, I speculated that perhaps judicial reputation would influence the likelihood of legislative adoption; this variable had no effect, and I also allowed it to interact with each of the variables mentioned above, with similar null results. Finally, I utilized an admittedly atheoretical "fishing expedition" approach; I took all of the substantive variables and allowed them to interact with all of the other substantive variables and ran a stepwise regression model. None of these attempts altered the fundamental results of the analysis: judicial policymaking variables did not affect legislative outcomes.

3. Once again, I first-order differenced the six legislative variables, and I also included simple dummies denoting the presence or absence of a given legislative policy type. When neither of these approaches yielded significant results, I also tried including the legislative professionalism variable and allowed it to interact with the legislative regressors. As this yielded no significant results, I utilized another "garbage can" stepwise model, with the result being null findings.

References

Allison, Paul D. 1978. "Measures of Inequality." *American Sociological Review* 43:865-80.

Allison, Paul D. 1984. *Event History Analysis*. Beverly Hills, CA: Sage.

Arnold, R. Douglas. 1990. *The Logic of Congressional Action*. New Haven, CT: Yale University Press.

Bachrach, Peter and Morton S. Baratz. 1962. "The Two Faces of Power." *American Political Science Review* 56:947-52.

Bachrach, Peter and Morton S. Baratz. 1963. "Decisions and Nondecisions: An Analytical Framework." *American Political Science Review* 57:632-42.

Baum, Lawrance A. and Bradley C. Canon. 1982. "State Supreme Courts as Activists: New Doctrines in the Law of Torts." In M.C. Porter and G.A. Tarr (eds.), *State Supreme Courts: Policymaking in the Federal System*. Westport, CT: Greenwood.

Beebe, Kristen L. 1992. "The Right to Die: Who Really Makes the Decision?" *Dickinson Law Review* 96:649-72.

Beck, Nathaniel and Jonathan N. Katz. 1997. "The Analysis of Binary Time-Series-Cross-Section Data and/or The Democratic Peace." Paper presented at the Annual Meeting of the Political Methodology Group, Columbus, Ohio, July 1997.

Beck, Nathaniel, Jonathan N. Katz, and Richard Tucker. 1998. "Taking Time Seriously: Time-Series-Cross-Section Analysis with a Binary Dependent Variable." *American Journal of Political Science* 42:1260-88.

Berry, Frances Stokes and William D. Berry. 1990. "State Lottery Adoptions as Policy Innovation: An Event History Analysis." *American Political Science Review* 84:395-415.

Berry, Frances Stokes and William D. Berry. 1992. "Tax Innovation in the States: Capitalizing on Political Opportunity." *American Journal of Political Science* 36:715-42.

Bingham, Richard D. 1976. *The Adoption of Innovation by Local Government.* Lexington, MA: Lexington Books.

Bose, A. B. and P.C. Saxena. 1965. "The Diffusion of Innovations in a Village in Western Rajasthan." *The Eastern Anthropologist* 18:138-51.

Bosso, Christopher J. 1987. *Pesticides and Politics.* Pittsburgh: University of Pittsburgh Press.

Bowman, Ann O. and Richard C. Kearney. 1988. "Dimensions of State Government Capability." *Western Political Quarterly* 41:341-62.

Brace, Paul and Melinda Gann Hall. 1994. "Studying Courts Comparatively: The View from the American States." *Political Research Quarterly* 48:5-29.

Brittain, James E. 1974. "The International Diffusion of Electrical Power Technology, 1870-1920." *Journal of Economic History* 34:108-21.

Busby-Mott, Susan. 1993. "The Trend Toward Enlightenment: Health Care Decisionmaking in *Lawrance* and *Doe.*" *Connecticut Law Review* 25:1159-1225.

Caldeira, Gregory A. 1983. "On the Reputation of State Supreme Courts." *Political Behavior* 5:83-108.

Caldeira, Gregory A. 1985. "The Transmission of Legal Precedent: A Study of State Supreme Courts." *American Political Science Review* 79:178-93.

Caldeira, Gregory A. 1988. "Legal Precedent: Structures of Communications Between State Supreme Courts." *Social Networks* 10:29-55.

Caldeira, Gregory A. and John R. Wright. 1988. "Organized Interests and Agenda Setting in the U.S. Supreme Court." *American Political Science Review* 82:1109-27.

Canon, Bradley C. and Lawrence Baum. 1981. "Patterns of Tort Law Innovations: An Application of Innovation Theory to Judicial Doctrines." *American Political Science Review* 75:975-87.

Cantor, Norman L. 1987. *Legal Frontiers of Death and Dying*. Bloomington, IN: University of Indiana Press.

Carmines, Edward G. 1974. "The Mediating Influence of State Legislatures on the Linkage Between Interparty Competition and Welfare Policies." *American Political Science Review* 68:1118-23.

Choice in Dying, Inc. 1997. *Right to Die Law Digest: Refusal of Treatment Legislation*. New York: Choice in Dying, Inc.

Clark, Jill. 1985. "Policy Diffusion and Program Scope: Research Directions." *Publius* 15:61-70.

Clark, Jill and Lawrence French. 1984. "Innovation and Program Content in State Tax Policies." *State and Local Government Review* 16:11-16.

Clark, Terry N. 1968. "Community Structure, Decision-making, Budget Expenditures, and Urban Renewal in 51 American Communities." *American Sociological Review* 23:576-93.

Council of State Governments. Various years. *The Book of the States*. Lexington, KY: Council of State Governments.

Downs, George W. 1976. *Bureaucracy, Innovation, and Public Policy*. Lexington, MA: Lexington Books, D.C. Heath.

Downs, George W. and Lawrence B. Mohr. 1976. "Toward a Theory of Innovation." In John A. Agnew (ed.), *Innovation Research and Public Policy*. Department of Geography: Syracuse University Monograph.

Edelman, Murray. 1964. *The Symbolic Uses of Politics*. Urbana, IL: University of Illinois Press.

Eisendrath, Stuart J. and Albert R. Jonsen. 1983. "The Living Will: Help or Hindrance?" *Journal of the American Medical Association* 249:2054-58.

Epstein, Lee. 1994. "Exploring the Participation of Organized Interests in State Court Litigation." *Political Research Quarterly* 47:335-51.

Eyestone, Robert. 1977. "Confusion, Diffusion and Innovation." *American Political Science Review* 71:441-47.

Feder, Gershon. 1982. "Adoption of Interrelated Agricultural Innovations: Complementarity and the Impact of Risk, Scale and Credit." *American Journal of Agricultural Economics* 64:94-101.

Filene, Peter G. 1998. *In the Arms of Others: A Cultural History of the Right-to-Die in America*. Chicago: Ivan R. Dee.

Foster, John L. 1978. "Regionalism and Innovation in American States." *Journal of Politics* 40:179-87.

Freeman, Patricia K. 1985. "Interstate Communication Among State Legislators Regarding Energy Policy Innovation." *Publius* 15:99-111.

Froman, L.A., Jr. 1968. "The Categorization of Policy Contents." In Austin Ranney, ed., *Political Science and Public Policy*. Chicago: Markham.

Glick, Henry R. 1981. "Innovation in State Judicial Administration: Effects on Court Management and Organization." *American Politics Quarterly* 9:49-69.

Glick, Henry R. 1992. *The Right to Die: Policy Innovation and Its Consequences*. New York: Columbia University Press.

Glick, Henry R. 1994. "The Impact of Permissive Policies: The U.S. Supreme Court and the Right to Die." *Political Research Quarterly* 47(1):207-22.

Glick, Henry R. and Craig F. Emmert. 1987. "Selection Systems and Judicial Characteristics." *Judicature* 70:228-35.

Glick, Henry R. and Scott P. Hayes. 1991. "Innovation and Reinvention in State Policymaking: Theory and the Evolution of Living Will Laws." *Journal of Politics* 53:835-50.

Glick, Henry R. and Scott P. Hays. 1995. "Agenda Setting to Innovation: A Demonstration of Linkage Through Event History Analysis." Paper presented at the Annual Meeting of the Midwest Political Science Association: Chicago, IL.

Glick, Henry R., Marie E. Cowart, and J. Donald Smith. 1995. "Advance Medical Directives in U.S. Hospitals and Nursing Homes: The Implementation and Impact of the Patient Self-Determination Act." *Politics and the Life Sciences* 14:47-59.

Gormley, William T. 1989. "Custody Battles in State Administration." In Carl E. VanHorn (ed.), *The State of the States*. Washington, DC: Congressional Quarterly.

Gray, Virginia. 1973. "Innovation in the States: A Diffusion Study." *American Political Science Review* 67:1174-85.

Gray, Virginia and Bruce Williams. 1973. *The Organizational Politics of Criminal Justice*. Lexington, MA: Lexington Books.

Grether, Ewald T. 1937. *Price Control Under Fair Trade Legislation*. New York: Columbia University Press.

Griliches, Zvi. 1957. "Hybrid Corn: An Exploration in the Economics of Technological Change." *Econometrica* 25:501.

Grupp, Fred W., Jr. and Alan R. Richards. 1975. "Variations in Elite Perceptions of American States as Referents for Public Policy Making." *American Political Science Review* 69:850-58.

Haider-Markel, Donald P. 2001. "Policy Diffusion as a Geographical Expansion of the Scope of Political Conflict: Same-Sex Marriage Bans in the 1990's." *State Politics and Policy Quarterly* 1:5-26.

Hamann, Ardath R. 1993. "Family Surrogate Laws: A Necessary Supplement to Living Wills and Durable Powers of Attorney." *Villanova Law Review* 38:103-77.

Hardaway, Robert M., Miranda K. Peterson, and Cassandra Mann. 1999. "The Right to Die and the Ninth Amendment: Compassion and Dying After *Glucksberg* and *Vacco*." *George Mason Law Review* 7:313-59.

Harris, Peter. 1979. "Some Predictors of the Interstate Diffusion of State Common Law." Presented at the Annual Meeting of the Law and Society Association, San Francisco, CA.

Harris, Peter. 1980. "Problematic Cases and the Judicial Search for Authority." Presented at the Annual Meeting of the Law and Society Association, Madison, WI.

Harris, Peter. 1982. "Structural Change in the Communication of Precedent Among State Supreme Courts." *Social Networks* 4:201-12.

Hastings Center. 1987. *Guidelines on the Termination of Life-Sustaining Treatment and the Care of the Dying 7*. Hastings-on-Hudson, NY: Hastings Center.

Hayes, M. T. 1981. *Lobbyists and Legislators: A Theory of Political Markets*. New Brunswick, NJ: Rutgers University Press.

Hays, Scott P. 1996. "Influences on Reinvention During the Diffusion of Innovations." *Political Research Quarterly* 49:631-50.

Hays, Scott P. and Henry R. Glick. 1997. "The Role of Agenda Setting In Policy Innovation: An Event History Analysis of Living Will Laws." *American Politics Quarterly* 25:497-516.

Holbrook, Thomas M. and Emily Van Dunk. 1993. "Electoral Competition in the American States." *American Political Science Review* 87:955-62.

Jacob, Herbert. 1988. *Silent Revolution: The Transformation of Divorce Law in the United States*. Chicago: University of Chicago Press.

Jacob, Herbert. 1996. "Courts: The Least Dangerous Branch?" In Virginia Gray and Herbert Jacob (eds.), *Politics in the American States: A Comparative Analysis*. 6th ed. Washington, D.C.: Congressional Quarterly.

References

Johnson, Charles A. and Bradley C. Canon. 1984. *Judicial Politics: Implementation and Impact*. Washington, DC: Congressional Quarterly.

Kenwood, A.G. and A.L. Lougheed. 1982. *Technological Diffusion and Industrialization Before 1914*. New York: St. Martins Press.

Kincaid, John. 1994. "Developments in Federal-State Relations, 1992-93." In *The Book of the States*, 1994-95. Lexington, KY: Council of State Governments.

Kingdon, John W. 1984. *Agendas, Alternatives, and Public Policies*. Boston: Little, Brown.

Kronmiller, W. 1988. "A Necessary Compromise: The Right to Forego Artificial Nutrition and Hydration Under Maryland's Life-Sustaining Procedures Act." *Maryland Law Review* 47:1188-1207.

Kuklinski, James H. And John E. Stanga. 1979. "Political Participation and Government Responsiveness: The Behavior of the California Superior Courts." *American Political Science Review* 73:1090-99.

Lauer, Robert H. 1971. "The Scientific Legitimation of Fallacy: Neutralizing Social Change Theory." *American Sociological Review* 36:881-89.

Lieberson, Alan D. 1992. *Advance Medical Directives*. Deerfield, IL: Clark, Boardman, Callaghan.

Light, Alfred R. 1978. "Intergovernmental Sources of Innovation in State Administration." *American Politics Quarterly* 6:147-65.

Lowi, Theodore J. 1964. "American Business, Public Policy, Case-Studies, and Political Theory." *World Politics* 16:677-715.

Lutz, James M. 1986. "The Spatial and Temporal Diffusion of Selected Licensing Laws in the United States." *Political Geography Quarterly* 5:141-59.

Lynn, J. and J. Childress. 1983. "Must Patients Always be Given Food and Water?" *The Hastings Center Report* October, 1983: 17-27.

March, James and Herbert Simon. 1958. *Organizations*. New York: Wiley.

Martyn, Susan R. and Henry J. Bourguignon. 1997. "Physician-Assisted Suicide: The Lethal Flaws of the Ninth and Second Circuit Decisions." *California Law Review* 85:371-426.

Meier, Kenneth J. 1994. *The Politics of Sin: Drugs, Alcohol, and Public Policy*. Armonk, NY: M.E. Sharp.

Meisel, Alan. 1992. "A Retrospective on *Cruzan*." *Law Medicine and Health Care*. 20:340-53.

Menzel, Donald C. and Irwin Feller. 1977. "Leadership and Interaction Patterns in the Diffusion of Innovations Among the American States." *Western Political Quarterly* 30:528-36.

Mintrom, Michael. 1997. "Policy Entrepreneurs and the Diffusion of Innovation." *American Journal of Political Science* 41:738-70.

Mintrom, Michael and Sandra Vergari. 1998. "Policy Networks and Innovation Diffusion: The Case of State Education Reforms." *Journal of Politics* 60:126-48.

Moen, Matthew C. 1984. "School Prayer and the Politics of Life-Style Concern." *Social Science Quarterly* 65:1070-81.

Mohr, Lawrence. 1969. "Determinants of Innovation in Organizations." *American Political Science Review* 63:111-26.

Mooney, Christopher Z. 2001. "Modeling Regional Effects on State Policy Diffusion." *Political Research Quarterly* 54:103-24.

Mooney, Christopher Z. and Mei-Hsien Lee. 1995. "Legislating Morality in the American States: The Case of Pre-Roe Abortion Regulation Reform." *American Journal of Political Science* 39:599-627.

Musmann, Klaus and William H. Kennedy. 1989. *Diffusion of Innovations: A Select Bibliography*. New York: Greenwood.

Nice, David. 1984. "Teacher Competency Testing as Innovation." *Policy Studies Journal*. 13:45-54.

Nice, David. 1986. "State Support for Constitutional Balanced Budget Requirements." *Journal of Politics* 48:134-42.

Nice, David. 1994. *Policy Innovation in State Government*. Ames, IO: Iowa State University Press.

O'Connor, Karen and Lee Epstein. 1982. "*Amicus Curiae* Participation in U.S. Supreme Court Litigation." *Law and Society Review* 16:311-19.

Pankhurst, J.G. 1982. "Factors in Post-Stalin Emergence of Soviet Sociology." *Sociological Inquiry* 52:165-83.

Peters, David A. 1987. "Advance Medical Directives: The Case for the Durable Power of Attorney for Health Care." *Journal of Legal Medicine* 8:437-464.

Regens, James L. 1980. "State Policy Responses to the Energy Issue." *Social Science Quarterly* 61:44-57.

Ripley, Randall B. and Grace A. Franklin. 1987. *Congress, the Bureaucracy, and Public Policy*. 4th ed. Chicago: Dorsey Press.

Roach, Cathaleen A. 1991. "Paradox and Pandora's Box: The Tragedy of Current Right-to-Die Jurisprudence." *University of Michigan Journal of Law Reform* 25:133-90.

Rogers, Everett M. 1962. *Diffusion of Innovations*. New York: Free Press.

Rogers, Everett M. 1966. *Bibliography on the Diffusion of Innovations*. East Lansing, MI: Michigan State University Press.

Rogers, Everett M. 1983. *Diffusion of Innovations*. 3rd ed. New York: Free Press.

Sabatino, Charles P. 1992. "Death in the Legislature: Inventing Legal Tools for Autonomy." *New York University Review of Law and Social Change* 19:309-39.

Salisbury, R.H. 1968. "The Analysis of Public Policy: A Search for Theories and Roles." In *Political Science and Public Policy* (ed.), Austin Ranney. Chicago: Markham.

Savage, Robert L. 1981. "The Diffusion of Information Approach." In *Handbook of Political Communication* (ed.), Dan D. Nimmo and Keith R. Sanders. Beverly Hills: Sage.

Savage, Robert L. 1985. "Diffusion Research Traditions and the Spread of Policy Innovations in the American Federal System." *Publius* 15:1-27.

Saxonhouse, Gary R. 1974. "A Tale of Japanese Technological Diffusion in the Meiji Period." *Journal of Economic History* 34:149-65.

Scott-Stevens, Susan R. 1987. *Foreign Consultants and Counterparts: Problems in Technology Transfer*. Boulder, CO: Westview Press.

Sigelman, Lee, Phillip W. Roeder, and Carol Sigelman. 1981. "Social Service Innovation in the American States." *Social Science Quarterly* 62:503-15.

Smith, J. Donald. 1998. "Decisions to Adopt and Reinvent Right-to-Die Statutes in the American States: Three Event History Analyses." Paper Presented at the Annual Meeting of the Midwest Political Science Association. April, Chicago.

Smith, J. Donald and Henry R. Glick. 1995. "The Right to Die: A Cross-National Analysis of Agenda Setting and Innovation." *Environment and Planning C: Government and Policy* 13:479-501.

Smith, R.A. 1979. "Decision-Making and Non-Decision-Making in American Cities: Some Implications for Community Structural Research." *American Sociological Review* 44:147-61.

Solomon, M.Z., L. O'Donnell, B. Jennings, V. Guifoy, S.M. Wolf, K. Nolan, R. Jackson, D. Koch-Weiser, and S. Donnelley. 1993. "Decisions Near the End of Life: Professional Views on Life-Sustaining Treatments." *American Journal of Public Health* 83:14-22.

Songer, Donald R. 1979. "Concern for Policy Outputs as a Cue for Supreme Court Decisions on *Certiorari*." *Journal of Politics* 41:1185-94.

Sunstein, Cass R. 1997. "The Right to Die." *Yale Law Journal* 106:1123-63.

Tanenhaus, J., M. Schick, M. Muraskin, and D. Rosen. 1981. "The Supreme Court's *Certiorari* Jurisdiction: Cue Theory." In S. Sidney Ulmer (ed.), *Courts, Law and Judicial Processes*. New York: Free Press.

Teger, S. H. and D. Kosinski. 1980. "The Cue Theory of Supreme Court *Certiorari* Jurisdiction: A Reconsideration." *Journal of Politics* 42:834-46.

Tillman, Beth. 1992. "Exercising the Right to Die: North Carolina's Amended Natural Death Act and the 1991 Health Care Power of Attorney Act." *North Carolina Law Review* 70:2108-24.

Truman, David. 1951. *The Governmental Process: Political Interests and Public Opinion*. New York: Knopf.

Ulmer, S. Sidney. 1980. "Conflict With Supreme Court Precedents and the Granting of Plenary Review." *Journal of Politics* 45:474-78.

Urofsky, Melvin I. 2000. *Lethal Judgments: Assisted Suicide and American Law*. Lawrence, KS: University Press of Kansas.

Vose, Clement E. 1958. "Litigation as a Form of Pressure Group Activity." *The Annals of the Academy of Political and Social Sciences*. 319:20-31.

Walker, Jack L. 1969. "The Diffusion of Innovations in the American States." *American Political Science Review* 63:880-99.

Weir, Robert F. 1989. *Abating Treatment With Critically Ill Patients*. New York: Oxford University Press.

Winder, David W., James T. LaPlatt, and Larry E. Carter. 1999. "State Lawsuits Against Big Tobacco: A Test of Diffusion Theory." Presented at the Annual Meeting of the Southwestern Political Science Association, San Antonio, TX, April 1-3.

Yecaris, Constantine A. 1970. "Political Conflict and the Diffusion of Innovations." *Rural Sociology* 35:488-99.

Index

Advance directives for health care, 8, 15, 77, 117, 121, 125, 129, 172, 186, 234-235, 240, 285. *See also* Living will laws; Durable power of attorney laws; and Surrogate decision-making policies, statutory
Advisory opinions, *see* Attorney generals, role in judicial policy-making
Agudah Israel of America, 143
Americans United for Life, 143
American Academy of Neurology, 143
American Association of Retired Persons, 36, 83, 145, 285
American Civil Liberties Union, 143
American College of Physicians, 143
American Geriatrics Society, 143
American Hospital Association, 143
American Medical Association, 143
Amicus curiae participation, 46, 134, 141, 143-146, 190, 209, 216, 231
Artificial Feeding, *see* Artificial nutrition and hydration

Artificial nutrition and hydration, 17, 95-97. *See also* Living will laws; Durable power of attorney laws; and Surrogate decision-making policies, statutory and judicial
   in California statutes, 7-10, 70
   in *Conroy, In re*, 165
   in *Couture* v. *Couture*, 217
   in *Cruzan* v. *Harmon*, 148, 223-225
   defined, 17
   in *Eichner, In re*, 171
   in Florida statutes, 204-205
   in *Gardner, In Re*, 2-3, 176-177
   in *Grant, In re*, 232
   in Indiana statutes, 213-214
   in *Lawrance, In re*, 214-216
   in *Leach* v. *Shapiro*, 217
   in *Longeway, In re Estate of*, 229
   in *Mack* v. *Mack*, 10-11, 209-210
   in Maryland statutes, 208-209
   in Missouri statutes, 223
   in New York State trial courts, 172

in Ohio statutes, 218, 220
in *Swan, In re*, 4, 176-178
in Washington State statutes, 234-236
Application of Brooks, In re, 289
Application of Lydia E. Hall Hospital, 171
Arkansas Rights of the Terminally Ill Act, 114-115
Arkansas Rights of the Terminally Ill and Permanently Unconscious Act, 115
Assisted suicide, 283
Attorney generals, 48, 65
in Missouri, 148-149
in New Jersey, 134
role in judicial policy-making, 48, 147-148, 244-245
selection method, 65, 244, 288
Association for Retarded Citizens, 143

Barber v. *Superior Court*, 135, 151
Barry, In re Guardianship of, 146, 151, 204-205
Bartling v. *Superior Court*, 152
Belcher v. *Charleston Area Medical Center*, 153
Best interests evidentiary standard, 12, 18, 162, 171, 175, 177, 209-211, 214, 228-229, 231-232
Beth Israel Medical Center, Matter of, 171
Blood transfusions, 133
Bouvia v. *Superior Court*, 152
Brother Fox, 170. See also *Eichner, In re*
Brophy v. *New England Sinai Medical Center, Inc.*, 152, 168-169

Browning, In re Guardianship of, 153
Busalacchi, In re, 148, 225

C.A., In re, 153, 229, 231
Caldeira's judicial reputation score, 7, 65, 68, 146, 192, 286
California, 6-10, 76-77
legislative innovation, 6, 8-9, 33, 76-77, 283
judicial innovation, 9-10
judicial-legislative interaction, 9-10
"Mrs. T.", case of, 6-8
California Catholic Conference, 76
California Fair Trade Law, 30
California Natural Death Act, 6, 8-9, 33, 76-77, 283
Care and Protection of Beth, 289
Catholic Church, 35-36, 59, 75, 240, 244, 286. See also National Conference of Catholic Bishops
in California, 76
in Florida, 205
papal declaration, 75
state Catholic conferences, 35-36, 82, 104, 143-144, 189, 286
state populations, 35, 58, 82, 85, 104, 145, 190, 287
Catholic Lawyers' Guild, 143
Choice in Dying, 143-144
Clear and convincing evidentiary standard, 3, 11, 17-18, 148, 161-162, 170-174, 177-179, 210, 225, 228
Colyer, In re, 151, 232-233, 237
Compassion in Dying v. *State of Washington*, 141
Concern for Dying, 143-144

Index

Concerned Taxpayers of America, 143
Connecticut, 179-182
  judicial innovation, 179-180, 182
  legislative innovation, 180, 182
  statutory law, 179
Conroy, In re, 135, 152, 165-166, 168-169
Corbett v. D'Allesandro, 152
Core innovations, 30, 32, 91, 136, 150, 179, 241, 247, 284
  defined, 30-32
  diffusion of permissive policies, 34-39
  policy content, 39-40
  reinvention through renovation, 40-41
core tangential innovations, 32-33, 100, 114, 116, 164, 166, 189
Couture v. Couture, 153, 217-222
Cruel and unusual punishment, 134
Cruzan, Nancy, 14, 148, 223-225
Cruzan v. Harmon, 14, 50, 148, 152, 193, 223-227, 245
Custody of a Minor, 289
Cue theory of certiorari, 46

DeGrella v. Elston, 154
Delaware Health Care Decisions Act, 100-101
Delio v. Westchester County Medical Center, 152, 172, 174, 289
Deukmejian, George, 77
Developmental Disabilities Law Center, 143
Dinino v. State ex. rel. Gorton, 233-234
Dinnerstein, In re, 151, 167-168, 289

Do-not-resuscitate Orders, 150, 167, 289
Dockery v. Dockery, 151, 289
Doe, In re Guardianship of, 153, 289
Drabick, Conservatorship of, 152
Durable power of attorney for health care laws, 9, 11, 77, 99-100, 172, 284
  alternate proxy provisions, 112
  artificial nutrition and hydration provisions, 100, 112-113
  defined, 9, 15, 120, 287
  in Delaware, 33, 100-101
  diffusion of, 42, 101-106, 128-140, 188-194, 196-197, 241-242
  drafting and execution provisions, 111-112
  enforcement provisions, 112
  in Illinois, 228
  in Indiana, 213-214
  in Maryland, 209
  in Missouri, 223
  in Ohio, 218-219, 221-222
  problems with, 15
  reinvention through renovation, 43, 106-113, 198
  triggering conditions, 100, 112
  in Washington State, 231-232
  witnessing requirements, 100-111

Eichner, In re, 151, 170-171
Euthanasia Education Council, 75
Event History Analysis, 27, 57-58, 286-287
  judicial adoption model, 64, 70
  judicial renovation model, 67
  legislative adoption model, 58
  legislative renovation model, 63

overview of technique, 57-58
in previous diffusion studies, 27
results from DPA regressions, 104-106, 108-109
results from living will regressions, 81-86, 88-89
results from integrated judicial-legislative regressions, 195-200
results from statutory surrogate regressions, 119-121, 123
results from surrogate judicial regressions, 140-142, 144-150, 157-158
summary of regression results, 189-194
temporal dependence in, 286
Evidentiary standards, *see* Best interests evidentiary standard; Clear and convincing evidentiary standard; and Substituted judgment evidentiary standard

Facility scores, 61-63, 66, 263-267
calculation of, 61-63, 263-267
DPA reinvention, 106-113
intercoder reliability, 63
living will reinvention, 85-99
in previous innovation research, 62
statutory surrogate reinvention, 122-128
surrogate judicial reinvention, 150-164
Farrell, In re, 152, 166
Florida, 12, 146-147, 204-206
judicial innovation, 146-147
judicial-legislative interaction, 204-206
legislative innovation, 12

Florida Catholic Conference, 205
Florida Life-Prolonging Procedures Act, 205

Gardner, Joseph V., 2-4, 15
Gardner, In re, 2-4, 5, 152, 176-179, 283
General-trait theory of policy adoption, 26
Grant, In re Guardianship of, 152, 232-234, 237
Greenspan, In re Estate of, 153, 228-230
Guardian *ad litem*, 3, 148, 153

Hamlin, Matter of Guardianship of, 151, 232-233, 237
Harvard Medical School, 75
Hastings Center, 75
Health care agent law, *see* Durable power of attorney for health care laws
Health care proxy law, *see* Durable power of attorney for health care laws
Hier, Matter of, 289
Hospital associations, state-level, 143-144

Illinois, 208, 228-231
judicial innovation, 228-229
judicial-legislative interaction, 208, 228-231
legislative innovation, 228
Illinois Health Care Surrogate Act, 228
Illinois Living Will Act, 228
Illinois Powers of Attorney for Health Care Act, 228
Indiana, 208, 213-216
judicial innovation, 214

Index

judicial-legislative interaction, 208, 215-216
legislative innovation, 213-214
Indiana Health Care Consent Act, 213-216
Indiana Living Wills and Life-Prolonging Procedures Act, 213-215
Informed consent, common law doctrine of, 3, 15, 176, 209, 219
Innovation research, 23-33
  conceptual definitions, 24-25
  extent of innovation literature, 27-28
  history of, 23-24
  policy reinvention studies, 28-30
  timing of adoption of innovations, 30-33
  typology of innovations, 30-33
Internal determinants model of policy diffusion, 26
Issue-specific model of policy diffusion, 26

Jane Doe, In re Guardianship of, 154
Jehova's Witnesses, 133
Jobes, In re, 152, 166, 168-169, 210
John F. Kennedy Hospital v. *Bludworth,* 147, 151, 205
Judicial federalism, 50, 193
Judicial-legislative interaction, 52-53, 183-238
  difficulties in identifying patterns, 246-247
  in Florida, 204-206
  in Illinois, 228-231
  improvements to interaction models, 247-248
  judicial influence over legislatures, 53-54, 184-186, 196-198
  legislative influence over judiciaries, 54-55, 186-188, 199-200
  in Maryland, 204, 210-212
  in Missouri, 222, 225-227
  in Ohio, 218-222
  timing of surrogate policy adoptions, 201-207
  in Washington State, 231-237
Judicial surrogate decision-making policies, *see* Surrogate decision-making policies, judicial

Kennedy Institute on Ethics, 75
Kirby v. *Spivey,* 151

L.H.R., In re, 151
L.W., In re Guardianship of, 153
Lawrance, In re, 153, 214-216
Leach v. *Shapiro,* 151, 217, 219
Legislative-Judicial Interaction, *see* Judicial-legislative interaction
Living will laws, 6, 14, 106, 109, 111, 120, 165, 172, 284
  artificial nutrition and hydration provisions, 95-97
  in California, 6-9, 14, 33, 76-77
  defined, 6, 14
  diffusion of, 42, 72, 78-85, 128-139, 140, 188-194, 195-197, 241-242
  drafting and execution requirements, 91-94
  enforcement provisions, 98-99
  in Illinois, 228
  implementation rules, 94-98

in Indiana, 213-214
in Maryland, 208-209, 210-212
model law, 39, 60, 76, 78, 84, 97, 193, 210, 213, 222, 287
in Missouri, 222-223
in Ohio, 218
in previous diffusion research, 27, 29, 40, 34, 72-73, 286
problems with, 14-15, 113
reinvention through renovation, 43, 85-99, 194-195, 198
triggering conditions, 94-95
in Washington State, 231-232
witnessing requirements, 93
Lobotomies, 133
Longeway, In re Estate of, 153, 228-230

Mack, Ronald W., 10-11, 13, 15
Mack v. Mack, 10-13, 154, 209-211, 283
Maine, 2-5, 176-179
  District Attorney, 170
  judicial innovation, 2-5, 176-179
  judicial-legislative interaction, 5
  legislative innovation, 5
Maine Uniform Health Care Decisions Act, 5
Maryland, 10-13, 95-96, 204, 208-212
  judicial innovation, 10-13, 209-210
  judicial-legislative interaction, 12-13, 204, 208, 210-212
  legislative innovation, 12-13, 95-96, 208-209
Maryland Health Care Decisions Act, 208-209, 211

Massachusetts, judicial innovation and reinvention, 164-169, 174
McAfee, In re, 153
McConnell v. Beverly Enterprises, 153
Medical Associations, state-level, 143-144. *See also* American Medical Association
Medical ethics committees, 7-8, 176
Metabolic therapy, 289
Milton, In re, 152
Minnesota, judicial innovation, 174-176, 182
Minnesota Patients' Bill of Rights, 175
Missouri, 94, 148-149, 222-227
  Attorney General, 148-149
  judicial innovation, 148-149, 223-225
  judicial-legislative interaction, 208, 222, 225-227
  legislative innovation, 94, 222-223
Missouri Durable Power of Attorney for Health Care Act, 223
Missouri Rights of the Terminally Ill Act, 223
Moorhouse, In re, 153
Mooney and Lee's electoral threat index, 59
Morgan v. Olds, 152

National Association for Persons with Severe Handicaps, 143
National Association of Pro-life Nurses, 143
National Conference Commission on Uniform State Laws, 38, 77, 128, 193, 240, 242

Index

model living will law, 39, 60, 76, 78, 84, 97, 193, 210, 213, 222, 287
model DPA law, 42, 60, 101, 104, 193, 216, 241
model surrogate law, 42, 60, 116, 120, 124, 127, 193, 216, 241
National Conference of Catholic Bishops, 35, 58, 82, 85
National Conference of State Legislatures, 38
National Governors' Association, 38
Natural death laws, 14. *See also* Living will laws; Durable power of attorney laws; and Surrogate decision-making policies, statutory
New Jersey, judicial innovation and reinvention, 164-166, 134-135, 169
New Jersey Catholic Conference, 134
New York, judicial innovation and reinvention, 170-174, 181
Nixon, Jay, 149
North Carolina Right to a Natural Death Act, 114-115, 241, 247
Nursing Home Action Group, 143

O'Brien, Matter of, 171, 178
O'Connor, on Behalf of, 152, 172-174
Ohio, 208, 217-222
  judicial innovation, 217-218
  judicial-legislative interaction, 208, 212-222
  legislative innovation, 218
Ohio Power of Attorney for Health Care Act, 218

Ohio Modified Rights of the Terminally Ill Act, 218

P.V.W., In re, 151
Parens patriae, 171
Patients' bill of rights, 1, 175
Permissive policies, 19, 34-55, 284
  defined, 34, 284
Permissive policies, judicial, 44-52
  adoption of innovations, 45-50
  agenda-setting, 44
  conceptualization, 45
  content of innovations, 52
  improvements to judicial innovation models, 245-246
  reinvention through renovation, 50-52
Permissive policies, judicial-legislative interaction, 52-53, 184-185
  improvements to interaction models, 247-248
  judicial influences on legislatures, 53-54, 184-186
  legislative influences on judiciaries, 54-55, 186-188
Permissive policies, legislative, 34-44
  adoption of innovations, 34-39, 41-42
  content of adoptions, 39-40, 43
  improvements to legislative in-innovation models, 242-244
  reinvention through renovation, 40-41, 43-44
Persistent vegetative states, 2, 16-17, 95
  in *Barry, In re Guardianship of*, 204
  in *Brophy* v. *New England*

Sinai Medical Center, Inc., 168-169
   in California's core innovation, 76
   in *Cruzan v. Harmon*, 148-149, 222-223
   defined, 2, 16-17
   in *Eichner, In re*, 170
   in Florida statutes, 205
   in *Gardner, In re*, 3, 176-177
   in Illinois statutes, 231
   in Indiana statutes, 213
   in *John F. Kennedy Hospital v. Bludworth*, 205
   in *Lawrance, In re*, 214
   in living will statutes, 95
   in *Longeway, In re Estate of*, 229
   in *Mack v. Mack*, 10-12, 209-210
   in Maryland statutes, 208
   in Missouri statutes, 223
   in Ohio statutes, 218
   in *Quinlan, In re*, 135
   in *Swan, In re*, 4
Peter, In re, 152, 166
Policy innovation, *see* Innovation research
Proxy laws for health care, *see* Durable power of attorney for health care laws

Quinlan, Karen Ann, 14
Quinlan, In re, 14, 134-135, 136, 150, 159, 164-166, 167, 170

R.H., Matter of, 289
Ranney party control index, 159
Rasmussen v. Fleming, 152
Regional diffusion model of innovation, 27

Religious freedom, 133-134
Renovated reinventions, 9, 31-33, 284
Riddlemoser, In re, 153, 209, 211
Right-to-life committees, state-level, 143
Rosebush, In re, 153

Satz v. Perlmutter, 146, 151, 205
Self-determination, common law doctrine of, 15
Severns, In re, 151
Social learning theory of policy innovation, 38, 78, 188
Society for the Right to Die, 143, 144, 209
Spring, In re, 151, 168-169
Sterilization practices, 133
Storar, In re, 151, 170-172, 174, 178
Subsequent innovations, 30-33
Substituted judgment evidentiary standard, 17, 162, 166-168, 170-171, 173-175, 177, 210, 217, 224, 232
Superintendent of Belcher State School v. Saikewicz, 151, 166-167, 169
Sustenance, delivery of, *see* Artificial nutrition and hydration
Surrogate decision-making policies, judicial, 12, 15-16, 44-45, 137-164, 199-200, 284-285
   in California, 155
   in Connecticut, 164, 179-180
   defined, 12, 15-16, 44-45, 201
   diffusion of, 137-150, 189-194, 199-200, 207, 244-245
   evidentiary standards, 17-18, 161-162
   in Florida, 146-147

Index

in Illinois, 228-229
in Indiana, 214-216
interaction with statutory law, 201-207
in Maine, 3-5, 164, 176-179
in Maryland, 11-13, 209-210
in Massachusetts, 164, 166-169
in Minnesota, 164, 174-176
in Missouri, 148-149, 223-225
in New Jersey, 134-135, 164-166
in New York State, 164, 170-174
in Ohio, 217-218
reinvention through renovation, 150-164, 199-200, 245
in Washington State, 232
Surrogate decision-making policies, statutory, 12, 15, 33, 42, 78, 116-121, 128-131, 189-194, 196-197, 207, 284
in Arkansas, 114-116, 241, 247
artificial nutrition and hydration provisions, 114-115, 125
conflict resolution provisions, 125-127
defined, 12, 15, 33, 113, 201
diffusion of, 42, 116-121, 128-131, 189-194, 196-197, 207, 241-242
domestic partner recognition, 127-128
drafting and execution provisions, 114-115
eligibility requirements, 125-126
enforcement provisions, 114
in Illinois, 228
implementation provisions, 114-115
in Indiana, 213-214
interaction with judicial case law, 201-207
in Maryland, 12, 209
in Missouri, 223
in North Carolina, 114-116, 241, 247
in Ohio, 218
reinvention through renovation, 43, 116-128, 198, 242
triggering conditions, 114-115, 125
in Washington State, 231-232
Swan, Chad Eric, 4, 15
Swan, In re, 4-5, 153, 177-179, 283

Tangential innovations, 32, 72, 77-78, 99, 104, 106, 109, 189, 194, 242
adoption of, 41-42
content of adoptions, 43
reinvention through renovation, 43-44
Terminal condition, 94. *See also* Triggering conditions
Thor v. *Superior Court*, 154
Torres, In re, 151
Torres, Matter of Conservatorship of, 175-176
Triggering conditions, 16-17, 94-95, 100, 112. *See also* Persistent vegetative states
defined, 16-17
in durable power of attorney laws, 100, 112
in living will laws, 94-95

U.S. Senate Committee on Aging, 75
United Handicapped Federation, 143

Vogel v. *Forman*, 172

Washington State, 208, 231-237
    judicial innovation, 232
    judicial-legislative interaction, 231-237
    legislative innovation, 231-232
Washington Durable Power of Attorney for Health Care Act, 231-232
Washington Natural Death Act, 231-235
Webster, William L., 148
Westhart v. *Mule*, 153
Workmen's Circle Home v. *Fink*, 172
Wicker v. *Spellman*, 173